THE OPERAGOER'S GUIDE

The Operagoer's Guide

ONE HUNDRED STORIES AND COMMENTARIES

❧

M. Owen Lee

AMADEUS PRESS
Portland, Oregon

For permission to reprint from the following works, grateful acknowledgment is hereby made to

Oxford University Press, Inc., for material adapted from *First Intermissions* by M. Owen Lee (copyright 1996 by Oxford University Press);

The University of Toronto Press, for material adapted from *A Season of Opera: From Orpheus to Ariadne* by M. Owen Lee (copyright 1998 by the University of Toronto Press);

The Gale Group, for material adapted from the author's entries on *Aida, Lohengrin, Tannhäuser, Il Trovatore,* and *Les Troyens* in *The St. James Opera Encyclopedia,* edited by John Guinn and Les Stone (copyright 1996 by Visible Ink Press).

Cover image: Tosca, 1985 Metropolitan Opera production. Photograph by Winnie Klotz, Metropolitan Opera.

Frontispiece: Wagner, overwhelmed by opera.

Published in 2001 by
Amadeus Press (an imprint of Timber Press, Inc.)
The Haseltine Building
133 S.W. Second Avenue, Suite 450
Portland, Oregon 97204, USA

Printed in Hong Kong

Library of Congress Cataloging-in-Publication Data

Lee, M. Owen, 1930–
    The operagoer's guide : one hundred stories and commentaries / M. Owen Lee.
        p.   cm.
    ISBN 1-57467-065-4 (pbk.)
    1. Operas—Stories, plots, etc.

MT95 .L515 2001
782.1′0269—dc21

                                                        2001016119

for

John Cook

John St James

John Stookey

James and Diana Holman

with gratitude

CONTENTS

Contents

Contents

PREFACE

The first book of opera plots I ever saw—and purchased for fifty cents at a Sears store in 1942—was called *The Story of a Hundred Operas*. It measured three-and-a-half by five inches, and took pride in the fact that it fit "handily in milady's handbag" and caused "scarcely a bulge in mimaster's coat pocket." It also presumed that on a night at the opera milady and mimaster might be seeing Victor Herbert's *Natoma* or Paderewski's *Manru*.

For the past several years Henry W. Simon's *One Hundred Great Operas* has been the best-selling small volume of opera plots. Four times the size of its predecessor, but nonetheless capable of insertion in a largish pocket or purse, it contains a wealth of offbeat information and takes a good-humored approach to what it calls the "magnificent absurdities" of the standard opera plot. But, first published in 1957, it overlooks Mozart's *Idomeneo* and *Tito*, much of Britten and all of Janáček, and observes that *Cenerentola, Don Carlo, Fidelio, Hansel and Gretel*, and the whole operatic output of Handel are "seldom given" or have trouble finding audiences.

Clearly tastes in opera continue to change, and there may be room, in what is now a crowded field, for another small volume of stories of a hundred operas. But which operas? How will the present volume look in another decade or two, as a hundred new works find their way each year to the boards of our opera houses and university work shops? Opera today is reaching wider audiences than ever before, and ways of composing, staging, and appreciating it are changing, as they always have in the past. It is easy to pick sixty repertory favorites for inclusion, and relatively easy to pick thirty more on the basis of past importance, present popularity, and future prospects. It's the last ten that pose a problem. Among the operas clamoring for inclusion here and not making the final cut are such twentieth-century pieces as *Lady Macbeth of Mtsensk, Mahagonny*, and *The Medium*, such past favorites as *La Sonnambula, Louise, Lakmé*, and *Thaïs* (any one of which may make an unexpected comeback if the right star appears), and such important Russian classics as *Khovantschina* and *Prince Igor*. I would like to have included some Haydn, more Janáček, more early Verdi, more Gluck, and much more by the still-underappreciated George Frideric Handel. I can only hope that I have chosen wisely.

This book is intended for the twenty-first-century operagoer—someone who, when he or she gets to the opera house, will be reading the text translated—accurately, I hope—via surtitles, supertitles, or Met titles. I decided that that operagoer might need, in advance of a performance, less plot and more comment—a brisk plot summary that concerned itself not so much with comings and goings as with motivations, and a commentary that would provide some background information on the evening's opera as well as some idea of the directions taken by recent criticism, where interesting opinions are put forward and debated with a passion unknown to past generations (and not just in the vexed matter of Wagner).

I have suggested a recording for each of the operas discussed. These are personal choices that do not favor a new performance in state-of-the-art sound over an older performance that is clearly better from every other point of view. At the time of this writing, all of the recommendations are available via online CD distributors.

I have been careful to locate the operas in Wetzlar or Windsor or wherever they are supposed to take place, as one cannot depend on today's aberrantly deconstructionist directors not to transfer the action of any opera to a World War II battleship. (Let's hope that such produceritis will soon go the way of the dodo.) I have also apportioned the acts according to current performance practice. (Most opera houses now play *Faust* in three rather than five acts.) I have for the most part described each scene in a separate paragraph. And I have used square brackets in the plot summaries to indicate which scenes are usually omitted in standard performances. I make no apology for the uneven length of the entries; *Die Meistersinger* both requires and deserves more attention than does *La Gioconda*.

Finally, some remarks about languages. Few operagoers speak fluent Italian, German, or French, but most of them use the original Italian, German, and French titles when speaking of their favorite operas and arias. I have accordingly used the original titles for both the operas and their famous arias, save where current usage dictates otherwise. With less familiar languages I have resorted to English. Few opera fans, or critics for that matter, refer to *The Bartered Bride* as *Prodaná Nevěsta*—though I rather think the day will come when they will.

I should like to thank Oxford University Press, the University of Toronto Press, and the editors of the *International Dictionary of Opera* (reissued as the *St. James Opera Encyclopedia*) for permission to repeat here, in altered and often expanded form, comments I first published with them. I also owe a debt of thanks to Eve S. Goodman of Amadeus Press for faithfully seeing this book into print and to Franni Bertolino Farrell, an editor as quick-witted and vivacious as ever could be, for helping me to speak clearly to the opera-goer en route to the opera house.

Aida

Music by Giuseppe Verdi
Text by Camille du Locle, Antonio Ghislanzoni,
and Auguste Mariette
First performance: Cairo, 24 December 1871

ACT I

A brief prelude strikingly contrasts the gently coiling theme of Aida, a captive Ethiopian slave at the royal palace at Memphis, and the stern theme of Ramfis and his priestly caste, the real power in the land of the pharaohs.

Aida is actually the daughter of King Amonasro of Ethiopia, but in captivity she has kept her royal status secret and quietly served Amneris, the Pharaoh's daughter. Both the slave and the princess have fallen in love with the handsome Radamès, who ardently returns the love of the captive slave ("Celeste Aida") and keeps the princess at a respectful distance. It is Radamès who is, ironically, chosen by the goddess Isis to lead the Egyptian forces in a second war against Aida's people. Aida, torn between her love for Radamès ("Ritorna vincitor") and her allegiance to her father and brothers, finally asks the gods simply to let her die ("Numi, pieta").

In the temple of the fire god, Ramfis and his priests ceremoniously invest Radamès with the armor and weapons of victory.

ACT II

In her private chambers, Amneris cruelly tricks Aida into revealing her love for Radamès, telling her, falsely, that he has been killed in battle and then watching her reaction when she announces, truthfully, that Radamès has been victorious. Aida, defenseless, asks her gods again to let her die.

At the triumphal arch of the city of Thebes, Radamès enters with his armies and the spoils of victory ("The Grand March") and asks for mercy for his captives, not knowing that among them is Aida's father. Amonasro whispers to his daughter not to reveal his royal status, and cunningly tells the Egyptians how he saw the Ethiopian king die of his many wounds. Despite stern warnings from Ramfis, the Pharaoh pardons the captives. He then announces that Radamès will have as his victor's reward the hand of Amneris in marriage.

ACT III

On the eve of her wedding, Amneris sails up the Nile with Ramfis to pray in a small temple on the river bank. Aida, in despair, arrives at the same spot to meet Radamès, vowing she will throw herself into the Nile if this is to be their last time together. She is filled with longing for her native land ("O patria mia"). Amonasro finds her there, tells her that Ethiopia is preparing a third advance, conjures up a frightening vision of what might happen to her people if they go down in defeat again ("Pensa che un populo vinto"), and prevails upon her to persuade Radamès to desert his country and flee with them. Amonasro hides as Radamès arrives for his secret meeting with Aida. He too knows that another war with Ethiopia is imminent: he is to lead the Egyptian forces once again. Aida says that their only hope for happiness now is a precipitous flight to her beautiful forests ("Là tra foreste vergini"). Though he sees that future as one of endless deserts, Radamès eventually succumbs to her pleading and even, when questioned about the safest escape route, mentions that the Egyptians will be marshaling in the gorges of Napata. That is all the information the concealed Amonasro needs to hear. But Ramfis and Amneris, emerging from the temple, have also heard. They send their soldiers after Amonasro. Aida flees. Radamès, to save his honor, surrenders his sword.

ACT IV

Amneris repents of her vindictiveness and pleads with the imprisoned Radamès to let her save him from execution. He adamantly refuses her, happy only to hear that, while Amonasro has been caught and killed, Aida has escaped. Amneris, left alone, is almost driven mad when she hears, from a subterranean crypt, the voices of Egypt's priests, led by the implacable Ramfis, condemning Radamès to be buried alive.

Sealed in his tomb beneath the altar where he was first invested, Radamès finds to his astonishment that Aida has already found her way there to die with him. The final action plays on two stage levels: Amneris prays for Radamès' soul in the temple above, and Aida and Radamès in the tomb below sing rapturously ("O terra, addio") that their souls are flying upward to the rays of an eternal day.

♣

Verdi had to be persuaded to write *Aida*. He had twenty-three operas behind him, regarded the old battles as won, and wanted to retire to his beloved farm. But one of his Paris librettists, Camille du Locle, showed him a four-page synopsis for an opera for Cairo, to be set in ancient Egypt, written—so du Locle implied—by the Khedive of Egypt himself, the munificent Ismail Pasha, first of the three viceroys appointed by the Ottoman Empire to rule Egypt during and after the construction of the Suez Canal.

Du Locle probably got the synopsis from Auguste Mariette, a catalogist at the Louvre who had found archaeological fame in the Egyptian sands and was given the title of bey and made inspector general of monuments by the Khedive. Mariette had the beginnings of *Aida*'s story in his own experience: he had actually uncovered a walled-up skeleton when excavating his famous Serapeum.

Verdi, in a canny attempt to discourage the Khedive, asked him for an impossible sum for the premiere, reserving all subsequent rights for himself. The Khedive promptly came through with the 150,000 francs. Du Locle visited Verdi on his Italian farm, and in less than a week the four-page scenario became, between the two of them, the four acts of *Aida*, in French prose. Verdi then had the French translated into Italian verse by the man who had already helped with the revision of *La Forza del Destino*, Antonio Ghislanzoni.

We have thirty-four of the letters that passed between the composer and the librettist, so we can read how Verdi bullied Ghislanzoni till he got, instead of libretto language, the simple, heartfelt dialogue he wanted. Sometimes, tired of waiting for his librettist's verses, Verdi simply wrote his own Italian lines and set them to music. He also suggested some of the best details in the staging, including the split levels in the last act.

The music of *Aida* is of a new richness and complexity, yet accessible even when heard for the first time. Act III, the Nile scene, contains numbers as impassioned and beautifully wrought as anything in opera. The scene is also a master textbook on how to write evocatively for woodwinds: flute and oboe, clarinet and bassoon, wave and undulate in intricate patterns and conjure up the steamy, shimmering night, the ebb and swell of the river, and the noises of its creatures. But Verdi surpasses everything that has gone before in the duet "O terra, addio" in the last act. This grandest of operas ends, as it began, with music that is quiet, luminous, and delicately nuanced. The lovers voice their farewell to earth in a great, spreading arc of melody while the whole orchestra seems to quiver in one vast, cosmic tremolo. In no other music is there anything quite to equal this leaving earth for sky, of quietly walking through space.

Since its Cairo premiere, delayed for almost a year when the Franco-Prussian war broke out and Mariette and all the scenery were closed off in beleaguered Paris, *Aida* has become one of the most popular operas in the world. But Verdi, who had directed that a significant portion of his profits was to be used to relieve the sufferings of "the brave, wounded soldiers" who fought for France in the war, was angered that his new work, while widely admired, reminded some critics of the German Wagner: "If only I had never written *Aida!*" he exclaimed ruefully. "To end up, after more than thirty-five years in the theater, an imitator!"

We, with hindsight, have come to see *Aida* as not Wagnerian at all, but as crafted dramatically along the lines of French grand opera, and musically as the vindication and renewal of Italian vocal art in the face of the onslaughts of German symphonic drama. But Verdi was so saddened about being praised for the wrong reasons that he went into another period of virtual retirement. When he resurfaced sixteen years later, in his late seventies, after Wagner's death, it was to write the two greatest of all Italian works for the musical stage, and the ultimate reconciliation in opera of the vocal and the orchestral—*Otello* and *Falstaff.*

Recording

Perlea / Milanov, Barbieri, Björling, Warren, Christoff (RCA 1955)

Alceste

Music by Christoph Willibald von Gluck
Text by Ranieri de' Calzabigi (after Euripides)
First performance: Vienna, 26 December 1767;
second version, Paris, 23 April 1776

ACT I

A magisterial overture transports the listener to mythic Thessaly at a time of mourning.

Admetus, the young king, is dying, but Apollo's oracle declares that he will live if someone is willing to die in his place. His wife, Alceste, unbeknownst to all but the oracle's high priest, bravely offers herself as the victim ("Divinités du Styx").

ACT II

In the midst of the celebration of his return to health, Admetus hears in horror of Alceste's vow and wants to revoke it, but she tells him it is irrevocable ("Ah, malgré moi").

ACT III

The people of Thessaly are mourning the deaths of Alceste and Admetus, who has followed her to the gates of the underworld, hoping to save her. Meanwhile the hero Hercules, a friend of Admetus, resolves to descend to the world of the dead and bring back both husband and wife.

When Alceste and Admetus arrive in the world below, Death is adamant: only one of the royal couple is called to die. Alceste is about to be taken when Hercules appears and engages Death in a show of strength till Apollo, god of light, intervenes to give the hero, after his many labors, immortality, and to restore both Alceste and Admetus fully to life as emblems of the death-braving love of husband and wife.

♣

The Vienna and Paris versions of *Alceste* are so divergent that they are, in effect, two different operas—the first in Italian, the second in French—sharing much of the same music. The summary given here follows the Paris version, which is the more admired and more often performed of the two, despite its less-than-successful last-act introduction of the figure of Hercules.

The myth of Alcestis, treated tragicomically by Euripides, is here the vehicle for a vast outpouring of serious and high-minded music. Gluck's reform of opera (see the entry on *Orfeo ed Euridice*) continues apace: instead of the baroque excess that characterized the opera of his day, he strives for noble simplicity—and touches greatness.

Gluck and Calzabigi wrote a preface for the initial publication of *Alceste*, stating the principles of their reform. The preface remains among the great manifestos in the history of opera, even though much of its theory had already been demonstrated in Gluck's *Orfeo ed Euridice* (based on another death-braving myth), and other composers, notably Rameau, had for some time been moving in the same direction. In any case, *Alceste* belongs, in the words of David Cairns, to "that handful of special masterpieces" from whose "qualities of hope, compassion and above all honesty of vision . . . [we] can learn to see the truth about ourselves."

Recording

Baudo / Norman, Gedda, Weikl, Krause, Nimsgern (Orfeo 1982)

Andrea Chénier

Music by Umberto Giordano
Text by Luigi Illica
First performance: Milan, 28 March 1896

ACT I

In the ballroom of a chateau outside Paris, the servant Charles Gérard, hopelessly in love with Maddalena, the Countess de Coigny's daughter, is indignant when he sees his father staggering beneath the weight of an elegant sofa, and predicts that the oncoming Revolution will sweep away the powdered decadence of the aristocracy, which he hates. The guests assemble, and Maddalena, initially as frivolous as the others, is moved when the young poet Andrea Chénier extemporizes a lyric denouncing the selfishness of the aristocracy and their callous treatment of the lower classes in France ("Un dì, all'azzuro spazio"). Gérard is sufficiently stirred by the verses to lead a group of peasants into the room, whereupon the Countess dismisses him from her service. Gérard tears off his servant's livery and leads his old father away.

ACT II

Four years later, the Revolution has swept France, and even Chénier is being spied upon. His friend Rouchet urges him to flee the terror. But Maddalena has arranged, through anonymous letters and the fleet work of Bersi, her maid, to meet him at the Café Hottot in Paris, and Chénier stays to defend her against Gérard, who is now an agent of Robespierre and in a position to force himself on her. Chénier wounds Gérard in the ensuing duel, and Gérard, with unexpected grace, allows him to make his escape.

ACT III

A year later, at the Revolutionary Tribunal, Gérard asks for contributions from the assembled crowd, and one old woman offers her fifteen-year-old grandson to the cause. Chénier has been arrested, and Gérard, after some hesitation ("Nemico della patria"), writes out a denunciation of him and submits it to the court. Maddalena comes to plead with Gérard, telling him how terribly her mother died when the revolutionaries burned her chateau ("La mamma morta"), and offering herself to him if he will spare Chénier's life. It is, however, too late: Chénier's impassioned defense before the tribunal ("Sì, fui soldato") seals his fate.

Act IV

In the prison of Saint-Lazare, Chénier awaits his death ("Come un bel dì di maggio"). Gérard, remorseful, brings Maddalena to him. She bribes a jailer to let her take the place of a woman under sentence, and joyfully accompanies Chénier to the guillotine.

♣

Giordano's most popular opera deals with historical characters and draws on some of André Chénier's poems but does not hew to historical fact. The composer effectively applies the new verismo techniques (*Cavalleria Rusticana* was six years into its world-conquering career) to four contrasted genre scenes (*Manon Lescaut*, similarly structured, was three years on *its* successful way). While Giordano's music is never quite first-rate, each of the main characters has an impassioned aria to sing (Chénier has three), and the final "Viva la morte insiem" rings down the curtain in grand style.

Recording
de Fabritiis / Caniglia, Gigli, Becchi (EMI/Angel 1941)

Arabella

Music by Richard Strauss
Text by Hugo von Hofmannsthal
First performance: Dresden, 1 July 1933

Act I

In a slightly run-down Viennese hotel, Count Waldner, an inveterate gambler on the brink of ruin, and his wife, Adelaide, who resorts to fortune tellers in her desperation, have taken the drastic step of passing off their younger daughter Zdenka as a boy, Zdenko, so that their other daughter, the beautiful Arabella, may be presented in society in appropriate style and marry into money. Zdenka has fallen in love with Matteo, a handsome but emotionally unstable army officer who has his heart set on Arabella. Three other suitors are pursuing Arabella, but she, dissatisfied with them all, quietly tells Zdenka that she is waiting for the right man ("Aber der Richtige"). Soon thereafter she sees a sturdy, sad-eyed foreigner standing beneath her window. The stranger calls on her father and introduces himself as Mandryka, a wealthy Croatian landowner; he has fallen in love with the picture of Arabella that her father sent to his rich uncle, and wants to marry her. The father is delighted, especially when Mandryka opens his wallet to him. Meanwhile Arabella prepares to be the queen of the Coachmen's Ball that night.

Act II

Mandryka earnestly proposes to Arabella at the ball, and she, recognizing him as the "right man" of her dreams ("Und du wirst mein Gebieter sein"), accepts him. Quietly she bids all her other suitors farewell and leaves the ballroom. But there is a terrible misunderstanding: Zdenka, desperate to get Matteo into bed, gives him the key to her room, saying that it is the key to Arabella's. Mandryka overhears, thinks Arabella outrageously faithless, and gets hopelessly drunk. In near despair he flirts openly with Milli, the coachmen's yodeling mascot, and grossly insults Arabella's family.

Act III

The misunderstandings continue back at the hotel lobby: Matteo, emerging from what he is thinks has been a passionate encounter with Arabella in the dark of her room, is surprised to see her fully dressed in the lobby, acting as if nothing has happened. Mandryka, seeing Arabella talking with Matteo at this late hour, is sure that she has been intimate with him. Arabella, keeping her dignity, denies everything. It is only when Zdenka appears in her nightgown and confesses her ruse—to the amazement of the two men, who had thought her a boy—that things simmer down. Mandryka, left alone, is utterly humiliated by the ungentlemanly behavior he has shown. Then Arabella graciously descends the stairs bringing him a glass of clear water—the custom in his country for chaste village girls when they accept their lowly suitors. With tears of repentance and joy he takes her in his arms.

♣

Hofmannsthal died before he could put the *ultima manus* to this, his last libretto, but Strauss would allow no touching up by other hands. The opera thus lacks something of the radiance and inventiveness of *Der Rosenkavalier*, another Strauss–Hofmannsthal Viennese comedy-drama, to which it is often unfavorably compared. But *Arabella* is a wonderful, if uneven, creation in its own right. The heroine wisely allows all the other characters their imperfections, quietly restores them to their separate worths as people (Hofmannsthal's doctrine of *das Allomatische*—see the entry on *Die Frau ohne Schatten*), and ends the opera with a gesture that, in a good performance, can bring tears of grateful recognition to anyone who has ever had to ask for or grant forgiveness. The glass-of-water ritual, like the ceremony of the silver rose in *Der Rosenkavalier*, is Hofmannsthal's own invention, and all the more touching for that. Few librettists have bade farewell to the stage with so radiant a scene.

Recording
Solti / della Casa, Gueden, Dermota, London
(Decca/London 1957)

Ariadne auf Naxos

(Ariadne on the Island of Naxos)
Music by Richard Strauss
Text by Hugo von Hofmannsthal
First performance: Stuttgart, 25 October 1912;
second version, Vienna, 4 October 1916

PROLOGUE

Backstage in a little theater in the house of the richest man in eighteenth-century Vienna, we meet the following characters: a snooty Major Domo, who announces that the *opera seria* to be performed that evening will, by order of his master, be followed by a commedia dell'arte farce; the idealistic young Composer of the opera, frantic at the news; his Music Master, trying to soothe his pupil's nerves; the tragic actors—a blustering tenor who isn't satisfied with his wig, and a self-important soprano who doesn't do comedy; and the comedy troop surrounding the vivacious Zerbinetta.

All of them are thrown into confusion when the Major Domo makes a second announcement: as there are to be fireworks at nine, the serious and comic entertainments must, by order of his master, take place simultane-ously. The young Composer, even more frantic at this development, is calmed to a considerable degree when Zerbinetta flirts with him: for the first time, he sees comedy as having depths he has never known. Maybe his music can sound those depths ("Musik ist eine heilige Kunst"). The warning whis-tle sounds for the performance to begin . . .

OPERA

. . . and we watch it from the perspective of the audience. Three mythic nymphs—Naiad, Dryad, and Echo—are unable to console Ariadne, aban-doned on the island of Naxos by her lover Theseus ("Ein schönes war"). Even Harlekin and the other comedians cannot cheer her up ("Lieben, Has-sen, Hoffen, Zagen"). Ariadne longs for the god Hermes to come and take her to the land of the dead ("Es gibt ein Reich"). She refuses to listen to Zer-binetta's coloratura thesis ("Grossmächtige Prinzessin") that any new man who comes along is like a god. The clowns' antics are interrupted when (to the "Love Potion" motif from Wagner's *Tristan*) the three nymphs announce the arrival of Bacchus, a young demigod who has just escaped the clutches of the enchantress Circe. The nymphs sing a lullaby (Trio: "Töne, töne"), and Ariadne, wooed by Bacchus, sinks into a Freudian sleep, undergoes meta-morphosis, and is wafted with her young god to the stars. The clowns stand mystified at this—though Zerbinetta, half-understanding, is sure that it merely supports what she has always said: any new man who comes along is like a god.

♣

Ariadne began its life without its prologue, inserted as the play-within-a play in a Stuttgart performance of Molière's *Le Bourgeois Gentilhomme*. Charm-ingly written for virtuoso singers and a virtuoso (and sometimes marvelously noisy) chamber orchestra, the opera was separated, four years later, from the Molière play, equipped with its prologue, and launched on its own. Several decades passed before it came to be thought the equal of the other Strauss–Hofmannsthal works; many now say it is the finest of them all.

Ariadne is above all about transformations. That is why, when Ariadne and Bacchus finally come together in the last scene, she thinks he is Hermes, the god who takes the soul to a new existence in the world of the dead, and he thinks she is Circe, the island witch who turns men into beasts. They are mistaken: each of them brings about a wonderful transformation in the other: she turns him, not into a beast, but into a god; he takes her, not to death, but to new life among the stars. Transformations are the substance of all of Hofmannsthal's librettos (see the entry on *Die Frau ohne Schatten*), and though Strauss was not always sure what his librettist was up to, and had to be gently informed in the matter of the transformations in *Ariadne*, he too worked subtle transformations in his music for the work: the first song of the three nymphs becomes Ariadne's great cry to be released from her earthly existence ("Du wirst mich befreien"), and the hopeful ditty sung to her by Harlekin becomes the lullaby ("Töne, töne") that accompanies her metamorphosis.

More than that—and perhaps more than either composer or librettist intended—*Ariadne* is about the whole history of opera. In the prologue, a composer (enacted by a soprano, à la Mozart's Cherubino) is called by an unseen "richest man in Vienna," as Mozart was called by God Himself, to combine the serious and the comic on a single stage. The opera we then see performed becomes a collage of genres from opera's history, from its late-Renaissance birth in classic myth, through its French and Italian development as tragic *opera seria* and comic *opera buffa*, to Mozart's eighteenth-century Viennese fusion of the two, to nineteenth-century bel canto coloratura (Zerbinetta's aria), to German Wagner, his atonal *Tristan* chord, his mythic anticipations of Freud, and his transcendent vision. In effect, this amazing Strauss–Hofmannsthal concoction says that, even as transformation is the law of life, opera has survived across the centuries by transforming itself. There is no other opera even remotely like the exhilarating *Ariadne*.

Recording

Kempe / Janowitz, Zylis-Gara, Geszty, King, Prey, Adam
(EMI/Angel 1968)

Un Ballo in Maschera

(A Masked Ball)
Music by Giuseppe Verdi
Text by Antonio Somma, as "Tommaso Anoni"
(after Eugène Scribe)
First performance: Rome, 17 February 1859

ACT I

In his palace, the lighthearted young king Riccardo looks forward to seeing his beloved Amelia at a forthcoming ball ("La rivedrà nell'estasi"), but is told by Renato (his counselor and her husband!) that there is a conspiracy against him. (And in fact the two leading conspirators, Samuel and Tom, are there in the room.) But Riccardo dismisses the thought of conspiracy as rapidly as he dismisses the charge of sorcery brought against a certain Ulrica; in fact, he suggests that, for fun, the whole court, even his page boy Oscar, go in disguise to Ulrica's den to investigate the charge themselves.

In Ulrica's den ("Re dell'abisso"), Riccardo is the first of the royal party to arrive. Dressed as a fisherman, he drops a coin into a sailor's pocket, thus assuring that Ulrica's first prophecy will come true. He then overhears Amelia ask for help in overcoming her guilty love. Ulrica tells her of an herb that must be plucked at midnight at the gallows outside the city, and Riccardo resolves to meet Amelia at that desperate time and place. The disguised courtiers arrive, and Ulrica predicts that Riccardo will be killed by the first man to shake his hand. Characteristically, he laughs (Quintet: "È scherzo od è follia"). Then Renato enters and, knowing nothing of the prophecy, takes the king's hand.

ACT II

At the gallows at midnight, a terrified Amelia searches for the herb ("Ma dall'arido stelo"). Riccardo surprises her and forces her to confess her love for him (Duet: "Oh, qual soave brivido"). Amelia quickly veils her face when her husband arrives to tell the king that the conspirators have him surrounded. Riccardo escapes, wrapped in his counselor's cape. The conspirators laugh Renato to scorn when he finds that the veiled lady he is dutifully protecting is his own wife. Humiliated, Renato invites the ringleaders of the conspiracy, Samuel and Tom, to come to his home the next day.

Act III

As Renato desperately awaits the arrival of the conspirators at his home, he determines to kill his wife. She, protesting that she is innocent, begs to be allowed a few minutes with their son ("Morrò, ma prima in grazia"). Moved by her tears, Renato directs his anger completely against Riccardo ("Eri tu"). The two leading conspirators arrive, and the three men plan the assassination. They draw lots for the honor of killing Riccardo, and Renato wins, just as the page boy Oscar arrives with the very invitation that suits their needs—a "ballo in maschera splendidissima."

In his palace, Riccardo, deciding that for honor's sake he must give up Amelia, appoints her and her husband to a diplomatic post overseas ("Ma se m'è forza perderti").

At the masked ball, Oscar teasingly refuses to tell Renato which masker is the king ("Saper vorresti"). Then, when he is told that the matter is urgent, he reveals his master's disguise. Riccardo is bidding a gracious farewell to Amelia when Renato stabs him in the back. The dying king generously takes the blame for all that has happened, swears that Amelia is sinless, and forgives those who have killed him.

♣

The plot summary above cites no locale for the action. The historical events dramatized in the opera took place at the court of Gustav III of Sweden, but Verdi was forced by the political censors (who feared repercussions if a royal assassination were enacted onstage) to transfer the scene elsewhere. Boston was the site eventually chosen, and at the premiere the names of the characters were as given here, with Riccardo made a governor. Recently, however, the opera has been set in Sweden and the characters given their historical names: Gustavus (Riccardo); Anckarström (Renato), Mlle. Arvidson (Ulrica), and Counts Ribbing and Horn (Samuel and Tom). When the action is set in Sweden, the king is assassinated, as in Stockholm in 1792, by pistol shot.

Riccardo is Verdi's most rewarding role for lyric tenor and was unforgettably sung by the Swedish king of vocalists Jussi Björling (though he often chose to delete his final aria). The whole life of the mercurial king is like a masked ball: he assumes a disguise in each of the three acts and seems to think that there is no problem that cannot be solved by the proper application of wit, daring, and appropriate style. Like certain twentieth-century political leaders, he finds it easier to control dangerous political situations than to control his own amorous instincts. He lives life daringly on the brink, and is brought down by his own recklessness. Verdi consistently invests this light/dark figure with music that reflects his kaleidoscopic life. No opera of Verdi is graced with such an elaborate love duet, or with so many memorable ensembles—trio, quartet, quintet, sextet—as the young king's life colors the others' in light and shadow.

Recording

Panizza / Milanov, Andreva, Castagna, Björling, Sved (Myto 1940)

Il Barbiere di Siviglia

(The Barber of Seville)
Music by Gioachino Rossini
Text by Cesare Sterbini (after Beaumarchais)
First performance: Rome, 20 February 1816

Act I

An overture (borrowed in haste from an earlier opera) sets the bustling tone of the farce to come.

In a street in seventeenth-century Seville, the young Count Almaviva, disguised as a student, serenades the ward of old Dr. Bartolo, the carefully guarded Rosina ("Ecco ridenti in cielo"), and enlists the services of a merry jack-of-all-trades, Figaro ("Largo al factotum"), to help him get into her house. Figaro, who is a personal barber to Dr. Bartolo, suggests that the Count gain entrance to the house as a soldier assigned there for billeting—and the drunker the better.

Inside the house, Rosina wants to marry her "student" ("Una voce poco fa"), and sends him a letter to that effect via Figaro. Meanwhile, her music teacher, the rascally cleric Don Basilio, tells Dr. Bartolo that Count Almaviva is in town, up to no good, and that the best way to deal with the threat is to spread slander about him ("La calunnia"). When the Count enters disguised as a drunken soldier, the situation quickly develops into mass confusion, and the ruse is unsuccessful.

Act II

The Count makes another try, gaining entrance to Dr. Bartolo's house disguised as a clerical music teacher—explaining that his master, Don

Basilio, is ill, and (rather unwisely) presenting Dr. Bartolo with Rosina's letter as proof that he is just as accomplished a meddler as his master. He and Rosina exchange kisses at the piano while Figaro gives Dr. Bartolo a shave. (When Basilio, the real music teacher, shows up, the three schemers bundle him off, convincing him that he has scarlet fever!) The lovers plan an elopement, but Dr. Bartolo overhears them, blows up (to the consternation of the servants), and sends a miraculously recovered Basilio to fetch a notary. He intends to marry Rosina immediately, and he even convinces her she must marry him, producing the letter she sent her "student" as proof that her supposed friends are actually pimping for the notoriously lecherous Count Almaviva.

A storm breaks as Figaro gets the Count inside the house for the elopement. The Count reveals his true identity to Rosina and, to her joy, declares his intentions to be honorable. But their escape (Trio: "Zitti, zitti") is thwarted when they realize that Dr. Bartolo has removed the ladder from the balcony. The Count promptly bribes Basilio, when he arrives with the notary, to marry Rosina to *him*, and not to Dr. Bartolo. (A pistol is part of the persuasion.) The huffing Bartolo is at least relieved to hear that he can keep the dowry.

♣

A fiasco on its opening night, a runaway success ever since, *The Barber* was long favored by coloratura sopranos and subjected to disfiguring cuts, transpositions, and interpolations. Recently it has enjoyed (though it hardly needed) a new lease on life as a host of coloratura mezzos, and even a few bel canto tenors, have learned to sing it as Rossini originally intended. The opera sparkles with wit and musical invention from start to finish. Beethoven may or may not have known Rossini's "serious" operas (among them *Tancredi*, *Moses*, *Semiramide*, and *William Tell*), but he knew where the composer's richest musical vein lay when he told him, "Give us more *Barber*s."

Recording

Humberg / Ganassi, Vargas, Servile, Romero (Naxos 1992)

The Bartered Bride

(Prodaná Nevěsta)
Music by Bedřich Smetana
Text by Karel Sabina
First performance: Prague, 30 May 1866

Act I

A vigorous overture immediately establishes the nationalistic spirit of the opera to follow.

In a Bohemian village, the lively Mařenka loves the newcomer Jeník, but her parents owe money to the landowner Micha, and they arrange, through Kečal the marriage broker, for their daughter to marry—sight unseen—Micha's son, the lavishly praised Vašek.

Act II

Vašek turns out to be something of a stammering simpleton: he has never seen Mařenka, so when he comes shyly looking for her, she, without revealing her identity, is able to persuade him that he ought never to marry his promised one, who, she says, is a capricious creature sure to treat him very badly. Meanwhile, Jeník strikes a disheartening bargain with the marriage broker: for three hundred gulden he will step out of the way of Mařenka's marriage provided she marry no one other than—Micha's son! The villagers are shocked that Jeník has bartered his bride for money.

Act III

Vašek is charmed by the arrival of a circus and is prevailed upon by the tightrope artiste Esmeralda to don a bear suit for the afternoon performance. Meanwhile, Mařenka, hearing about the barter, is convinced that Jeník no longer loves her, until he reveals to one and all that he too is Micha's son—by an earlier marriage, sent from home in his youth by his stepmother. When Vašek appears in his bear suit, his mortified mother (the stepmother who had sent Jeník away) boxes his ears. Micha agrees that his resourceful older son, who has used his gulden to pay off the debt owed by his sweetheart's parents, will be much the better husband for Mařenka.

♣

As Austrian power waned in the latter part of the nineteenth century, national pride in outlying portions of the empire surfaced in new operas drawing on regional folk idioms. None of these was so popular internationally as Bohemia's *The Bartered Bride*. It began life as a rather ordinary operetta, quite uncharacteristic of its serious composer's general output. But interest abroad in the "new" folk music of regions like Bohemia set Smetana to recasting *The Bartered Bride* for Paris as an *opéra comique* and for St. Petersburg as an opera sung from start to finish. Smetana's Czech national opera, for such it soon became, fairly bursts with energetic music, both in the famous dances and in the duets sung by the nicely defined village characters.

Recording

Košler / Beňačková, Dvorský, Kopp, Novák (Supraphon 1980)

Billy Budd

Music by Benjamin Britten
Text by E. M. Forster and Eric Crozier (after Herman Melville)
First performance: London, 1 December 1951

Act I

Prologue: Captain Vere, an old man who has tried to guide others rightly, remembers a decision he was forced to make years before that illustrates the flaw inevitably present in all human goodness.

During the Napoleonic Wars, at a time when the British navy is beset by mutinies, the young and innocent sailor Billy Budd is pressed into service aboard the H.M.S. *Indomitable* and, a natural leader, is stationed in the foretop. He is enthusiastically loyal to Captain Vere ("Star of the morning, I will follow you"). But John Claggart, the master at arms, cruel enough to the others, immediately begins a malicious persecution of Billy ("I have you in my power and I will destroy you"), inventing situations that make it appear that the lad is mutinous.

Act II

The whole ship pulls together to fight the French ("This is our moment"), but a mist allows the enemy to escape. Captain Vere cries, "Oh for the light of clear heaven to separate evil from good"—prophetically, for Claggart then accuses Billy of mutiny, and Billy, whose only flaw is the stammer that prevents him from speaking in his own defense, lashes out at Claggart with his fist and strikes him dead. Though Captain Vere wants to save Billy, he can do nothing to prevent him, after a quickly arranged court martial, from being sentenced to death. (We are not party to the dialogue that the two men have thereafter.)

Billy, in irons, discourages the other sailors from taking up his cause, as mutiny will be the result ("I've sighted a sail in the storm").

On the main deck, Billy is hanged from the yard-arm before officers and crew. His last words are "Starry Vere, God bless you!" The men almost mutiny, but some force seems to hold them back.

Epilogue: Vere concludes, "I could have saved him. But he has saved me. I was lost on the infinite sea, but I've sighted a sail in the storm . . ."

♣

Billy Budd carries still further Britten's personal preoccupation with the misunderstood and victimized (as in *Peter Grimes*), and powerfully anticipates another Britten theme, innocence destroyed (as in *The Turn of the Screw*). It was in fact only after *Billy Budd* was reduced from four acts to a relentlessly turn-of-the-screw two acts that the public began to see deeply into it. Some critics have found in Claggart's destructive obsession with Billy's beauty a homosexual theme, and have traced it further through many, if not all, of the composer's works for the stage. But Britten and his librettists seem mainly interested in exploring, from an almost theological perspective, the nature of good and evil. (Andrew Porter has pointed out the significances of Melville's names: Vere suggests both truth and vacillation; "to clag" is "to adhere as with the touch of pitch or of a spider's web"; Bili and Budd were "appellations of the Celtic Apollo.")

Musically, the struggle between good and evil is stated on the opening page in two conflicting chords, one major and one minor, and continued ingeniously throughout the score. The opera's most effective passage is the succession of thirty-four orchestral chords that depict, with overwhelming sympathy and to a completely empty stage, the words that pass between Captain Vere and Billy after he has been sentenced to death. The scoring for all-male voices only enhances the driven, claustrophobic quality of this uniquely compelling work.

Recording
Britten / Pears, Glossop, Langdon, Tear, Luxon
(Decca/London 1967)

Bluebeard's Castle

Music by Béla Bartók
Text by Béla Balázs (after Charles Perrault)
First performance: Budapest, 24 May 1918

In a circular hall with seven doors, Judith, Bluebeard's new wife, observes that her husband's castle is dank and sunless and resolves to bring it warmth and light. She demands of Bluebeard that the seven doors be opened. They prove, as with growing wonder and horror she unlocks them one by one, to reveal successively her husband's torture chamber, his armory, his treasury, his garden, his kingdom, his lake of tears, and finally his three former wives, crowned and richly garbed in the symbols of morning, noon, and evening. Now, he says, Judith will be his night. He crowns and garbs her appropriately, and she follows the other three wives into the seventh chamber.

♣

And to think that Bartók dedicated this work to his new wife!

Brilliant and unnerving, the one-act *Bluebeard's Castle* (Bartók's only opera) is clearly a symbolic drama, and is usually thought to take place within the male psyche: the seven chambers, which in the Perrault story contain evil revelations, are in the opera a mature man's personal confessions—the successive revelations of his ambitions, cruelties, traumas, and need for understanding. As the spoken prologue to the opera says, "Many of you are thinking of your lives, your problems . . . Here you will find new meanings for those lives, for this story is about you."

Recently *Bluebeard's Castle* has been paired effectively with Schoenberg's *Erwartung* to make a double bill in which Bartók probes, in Freudian terms, the male psyche, and Schoenberg the female. Both composers wrote their works after emerging from personal crises, Bartók after losing his mistress to a violinist, and Schoenberg—shades of *Lulu*!—after losing his wife to a painter who eventually killed himself.

Musically, *Bluebeard's Castle* owes something to the harmonic and orchestral colors of Debussy and Richard Strauss but much more to the composer's own studies in Hungarian folk materials. It seems to have permanently eclipsed the impressionistic treatment of the same story by Paul Dukas, based on Maeterlinck.

Recording

Haitink / von Otter, Tomlinson (EMI/Angel 1997)

La Bohème

Music by Giacomo Puccini
Text by Giuseppe Giacosa and Luigi Illica (after Henri Murger)
First performance: Turin, 1 February 1896

ACT I

On Christmas Eve in an attic in Paris, Rodolfo (a poet), Marcello (a painter), and Colline (a philosopher) are good-naturedly freezing and starving together, ready to warm themselves by burning Marcello's painting "Crossing the Red Sea" (and actually burning one of Rodolfo's literary efforts). But the fourth of the one-room inmates, the musician Schaunard, has had a run of good luck and arrives unexpectedly loaded with provisions. Instead of feasting immediately, the "bohemians" handily outwit Benoit, their landlord, who has come looking for the rent, and set out for their favorite haunt, the Café Momus, leaving Rodolfo behind to finish writing an article for his journal, *The Beaver*. Mimì, a frail grisette who lives in a skylit room still further upstairs, gently knocks at the door and asks for a light for her candle. Rodolfo, reviving her after a momentary faint, touches her hand as together they grope in the darkness for the key she has dropped. He sings of his poet's dreams ("Che gelida manina"), and she tells how, in her little room, she is the first to have the kiss of springtime ("Mi chiamano Mimì"). They fall in love (Duet: "O soave fanciulla") and go off to join Rodolfo's friends.

ACT II

Amid the crowds at the Café Momus, the four penniless bohemians welcome Mimì to their circle. Marcello's former mistress, the brash Musetta, flounces in on the arm of Alcindoro, a sugar daddy. Still in love with Marcello, she taunts both men with a languid, self-congratulatory waltz song ("Quando m'en vo"), kicks her shoe in the air, sends Alcindoro off to get it repaired, and throws herself into Marcello's arms. When the bohemians find that they cannot pay the bill, Musetta leaves it for Alcindoro to pay, and they all escape through the Christmas Eve crowds, swept off in a military parade. (Alcindoro collapses when he returns with the shoe and is presented with the bill, which is enormous.)

Act III

On a wintry dawn at one of the city gates, Mimì comes through the falling snow looking for Marcello, who is living with Musetta in a dingy tavern. (She gives singing lessons and he paints signboard soldiers to adorn the entrance. His picture of the Red Sea is also there, now labeled "At the Port of Marseilles.") Mimì knows that Rodolfo, with whom she has had constant quarrels, is asleep in the tavern, and she hopes that Marcello can help them to part without bitterness. She hides behind a snowy tree when Rodolfo comes outside, and she hears him tell Marcello, "Mimì is terribly ill. Every day she grows worse. The poor little thing is doomed." Then he sees her and desperately embraces her. The two lovers agree that they must part ("Addio, senza rancor"), but only when the spring comes. At the same time, Musetta and Marcello have a shouting match and seem ready to part immediately and forever.

Act IV

Spring has come, and Rodolfo and Marcello are back in the attic, longing for their lost loves (Duet: "O Mimì, tu più non torni") and drowning their sorrows in childish sport with Colline and Schaunard (who has come back this time with nothing much more than a herring for four). In the midst of the merriment, Musetta comes up the stairs with a very ill Mimì. All but Rodolfo hurry off to get money and medicine for her—Colline even goes off to pawn his faithful overcoat ("Vecchia zimarra"). Rodolfo and Mimì, left alone, share a few moments of happiness, reminiscing, but when the others return, and Mimì drops off to sleep, and Rodolfo is preoccupied with drawing a shade to shield her from the sunlight, the room is suddenly still, and Schaunard notices that Mimì is dead. Rodolfo, heartbroken, falls on her body and cries out, "Mimì! Mimì!"

♧

The immensely popular *La Bohème*, however romanticized it may seem, is drawn from life. Rodolfo is a figure for Henri Murger, the headstrong author of the original novel and play *Scènes de la Vie de Bohème*, who shared his room (and even a pair of trousers) with another bohemian and edited a journal called *The Beaver*. Marcello is patterned after several painters Murger knew, in particular one Tabar, who spent years on his "Crossing the Red Sea." (Murger says in his pages that the painting was rejected so often by the Louvre that, if it were put on wheels, it could make the trip from the attic to the committee room and back by itself.) Colline, bearish and bookish, is patterned after a bohemian Murger dubbed "the Green Giant": his overcoat, with its four big pockets named for the four main libraries of Paris, got so old it turned from black to green. And Schaunard, the musician without whose pluck the other three might have starved that Christmas Eve, is based on an Alexandre Schanne who actually called himself Schaunard when he wrote his memoirs—and gave us much of our information on the others. Together they haunted the Café Momus. Puccini himself, in his bohemian days, shared a room in Milan with the future composer of *Cavalleria Rusticana*, Pietro Mascagni, who has vouched for the authenticity of several stories— that he and Puccini not only pooled their pennies to buy the score of *Parsifal* but also ran from their creditors, quartered a herring with two other starving artists, and dined at sidewalk cafés with pretty girls. There is even a story, probably fictitious, of Puccini pawning his overcoat.

Colline's farewell to his overcoat, restated by the orchestra in tragic tones, is the last thing we hear as the curtain falls, and rightly so, for the overcoat quietly symbolizes the opera's real theme: *la vie de Bohème* is an aspiring artist's life spent on the margins of society, in an atmosphere of books, art, thought, and music, but for a true artist it can only be a preliminary stage in his development. He must leave it before it destroys him—not by making him freeze or starve, but by arresting him in a world of dreams and hopes, of promiscuity and rebellion until, never really learning the discipline needed to write his poem or paint his watercolor, he despairs. Marcello sings, "It's a beautiful life of false illusions. You believe, you hope, and everything looks beautiful, but it's all illusions and utopias." Murger called *la vie de Bohème* "a charming life, and a terrible one." Puccini's last act, in which roughhouse antics are the prelude to Mimì's pathetic death, illustrates this perfectly.

Puccini is often thought a practitioner of slice-of-life verismo, but that is not the case in *La Bohème*, where we are given, not brutal realism, but humor, tenderness, and genuine pathos, all in an outpouring of melody that is immediately appealing and beautifully crafted.

Recording

Beecham / de los Angeles, Amara, Björling, Merrill, Tozzi
(RCA 1956)

Boris Godunov

Music and text by Modest Mussorgsky (after Alexander Pushkin)
First performance: St. Petersburg, 8 February 1874

ACT I

Prologue: Outside the monastery where the boyar Boris Godunov is in retreat, the people are bludgeoned by czarist police into pleading with him to ascend to the throne of Russia. Then, in a square in the Kremlin, to the ringing of bells and the acclamation of the crowd, Boris walks in procession to his coronation, vested in the images of imperial might. He prays for God's help, for he knows he is unworthy.

Five years later, Pimen, an aged monk, is nearing the end of his chronicle of Russian history. Grigori, the novice who shares his cell, awakes from a recurrent dream in which he stands on a tower overlooking all Moscow and, mocked by the crowd below, falls headlong. The dream ought to have forewarned him, but when he hears from old Pimen that Dimitri, the child-heir to the throne murdered before Boris' ascendancy, would have been his own age had he lived, Grigori flees the monastery, fired with ambition.

At an inn on the Lithuanian border, the vagrant monk Varlaam, companioned by another renegade, Missail, sings of how Ivan the Terrible took the town of Kazan by exploding mines in the midst of the Tartars. Grigori, on his way to Poland to raise an army, takes the advice of the inn's hostess and leaps out a window to escape the police in search of him.

In his apartments Boris comforts Xenia, his daughter, over the death of her fiancé and encourages Feodor, his young son, in his studies. But he is tormented by the internal troubles of Russia ("I have attained the highest power") and by the memory of the murder of Dimitri, for which he was responsible. His counselor Shuisky tells him that a pretender who calls himself Dimitri is gathering forces against him. Boris, maddened by the ticking of a great clock and a vision of the murdered child smiling at him, collapses, asking God for mercy ("The Clock Scene").

Act II

In a Polish castle, the bored Princess Marina hopes to rise to greatness with the pretender Dimitri, who has fallen in love with her. She is encouraged in her ambition by her Jesuit confessor, Rangoni, who sees this as an opportunity to win all Russia to Catholicism.

In the castle gardens, after a chivalric Polonaise, the seductive Marina brings the false Dimitri to his knees.

Act III

[Before the Cathedral of St. Basil, Boris is publicly accused of murder by a tormented simpleton. He quietly asks the poor man to pray for him.]

At an emergency meeting of the Duma, called over the matter of the pretender Dimitri, Boris shows signs of impending madness. Shuisky, with ambitions of his own, brings in old Pimen to describe a miracle that took place at the tomb of the murdered child. Boris, completely shaken, sends the council away and tells his young son that it is time for him to reign ("Farewell, my son. I am dying"). When the boyars return to watch Boris die, he rises to say "I am still the czar." Then he topples from his throne.

In a clearing in the Kromy forest, the pretender Dimitri, on horseback, is followed by a rabid, torchbearing crowd, which includes clerics both Orthodox and Catholic, to Moscow. The simpleton is left alone to bewail the unending sorrows of Mother Russia.

♣

Mussorgsky was an eccentric genius without experience, and in the face of rejection, censorship, and performance problems (no love interest, no ballet, a cast of ruffians in minor roles) he revised, expanded, and eventually abandoned to others his greatest opera, so that *Boris Godunov* exists in a bewildering variety of versions, three by the composer and perhaps a dozen more by other hands. The glittering revision by Rimsky-Korsakov—who partly recomposed and completely rescored the composer's work—was intended to bring the unwieldy opera to world attention, which it certainly did when the great Feodor Chaliapin took on the title role. Fiercely loyal defenders of Mussorgsky's original versions of 1869 and 1872 now insist that their rough-hewn unevenness is intended realism. But in fact even performances that claim to be "authentic" are touched up to some degree, and the debate over the ordering of the scenes is endless. (The plot summary offered here is based on current performance practice.)

In any form, *Boris* remains a stupendous opera, with a title role that is one of the greatest in the repertory, with flavorsome vocal parts that are, even at their most melodious, extensions of the Russian language, and with choral sections of unprecedented power. The chorus (that is to say, the Russian people) is often said to be the protagonist in *Boris Godunov*, though it should be observed that Mussorgsky's *Khovanshchina*, another panoramic "people's opera," with music of comparable power, has had a much more limited appeal, largely due to its not having a central figure as imposing as Czar Boris.

Historical note: Boris almost certainly did not, as Pushkin and Mussorgsky would have it, order the Czarevitch Dimitri murdered. But he was responsible for virtually creating serfdom in Russia, and he did die unexpectedly as the false Dimitri was marching on Moscow. Dimitri held the throne briefly with his Polish Marina; he executed Boris' son before he was himself assassinated by Shuisky, who became the next czar. The prophetic simpleton in Mussorgsky's opera was thus proved wiser than them all.

Recording

Karajan / Vishnevskaya, Spiess, Ghiaurov, Talvela
(Rimsky-Korsakov version, Decca/London 1970)
Gergiev / Borodina, Lutsuk/Galusin, Putilin/Vaneev, Ohotnikov
(Mussorgsky versions, Philips 1998)

Capriccio

Music by Richard Strauss
Text by Clemens Kraus and Richard Strauss
First performance: Munich, 28 October 1942

In a rococo drawing room adjoining a small theater in a château near Paris, in the latter half of the eighteenth century, we meet the young Countess Madeleine (who loves music and poetry equally), her brother the Count (who thinks opera an absurdity), the composer Flamand (whose string quartet is being played as the curtain rises), the poet Olivier (whose play they have gathered to discuss), the theater director La Roche (who is to produce it), and the actress Clairon (who is to star in it). Olivier reads the sonnet that is to be the play's climax, and Flamand quickly sets it to music: they are rivals for the hand of the Countess, and she is to give her decision the next morning at eleven in the library.

La Roche introduces some of the talent—singers and dancers—in his employ and, as the conversation turns to the relative importance of words and music in opera, he laments the present sorry state of the theater. (Both the text and sentiments here are Strauss' own.) The Countess suggests that Flamand and Olivier collaborate on an opera, and the Count suggests as a topic the very soirée we have been watching. The company disperses, including the prompter, who has fallen asleep in the theater. Moonlight floods the terrace, and the Countess, gazing into her mirror, wonders whether her decision the next day should be in favor of music or poetry. (As she walks offstage, the orchestra, amid various hints, seems to imply that in the end she will favor music.)

♣

A final opera written, like Verdi's *Falstaff*, simply for its aged composer's amusement and, also like *Falstaff*, an opera for connoisseurs, *Capriccio* rewards repeated hearings and viewings as few operas do, for the text is witty and literate and the music always inventive and occasionally as beautiful as the composer's *Four Last Songs*, which would surprise the world five years later. The final scene, with the Countess alone in the moonlit room, introduced by a long meditative French horn solo in Strauss' most autumnal mood, is as touching a valedictory—for the composer and for a Europe that was soon to change inexorably—as anything in music.

Recording

Böhm / Janowitz, Troyanos, Schreier, Prey, Fischer-Dieskau, Ridderbusch (Deutsche Grammophon 1971)

Carmen

Music by Georges Bizet
Text by Henri Meilhac and Ludovic Halévy
(after Prosper Mérimée)
First performance: Paris, 3 March 1875

ACT I

A prelude depicts the excitement of the parade at the *corrida* and ends with a sinister "Fate" motif, which romantics have claimed is the only strain Satan remembered after he was banished from heaven.

In a square in Seville, the village girl Micaëla comes looking for her beloved Don José, a corporal with a troubled past. He arrives when the guard changes. The girls who work in the cigarette factory take a smoking break—last among them the gypsy Carmen, heralded by a flashing statement of the "Fate" motif. She sings a seductive Habanera ("L'amour est un oiseau rebelle"), which José studiously ignores till she impudently throws a cassia flower at him. The effect of the gypsy's flower is not entirely undone when Micaëla, in an intimate scene, gives José a chaste kiss from his mother (Duet: "Parle-moi de ma mère"). Carmen is arrested for starting a brawl in the cigarette factory and placed in José's charge. This time she enchants him with a Seguidilla ("Près des remparts"), and he allows her to escape.

ACT II

A brief prelude depicts José's soldier life.

In a smoky inn popular with gypsies, Carmen and two other gypsy girls, Frasquita and Mercédès, sing an abandoned "Chanson Bohème." The swaggering toreador Escamillo, fresh from a *corrida*, puts in a surprise appearance ("The Toreador Song"). Carmen is eyed both by Escamillo and José's lieutenant, Zuniga, but it is José she is waiting to see: he was demoted to private for allowing her to escape, and has just spent sixty days in the brig. Carmen tells the two gypsy girls and their boyfriends, Remendado and Dancaïre, that she cannot go with them on their next smuggling escapade, and they tease her (Quintet: "Nous avons en tête une affaire") about being in love with her soldier. After the crowd clears, José arrives, still infatuated with Carmen. But a trumpet calls him back to duty, and he protests that he must leave. She is furious, and he, as proof of his love, takes from his doublet the flower she had flung at him: it has kept its perfume and its memories of her

41

(and of the "Fate" motif) intact throughout his days in prison ("La fleur que tu m'avais jetée"). Lieutenant Zuniga reappears, hoping for a night with Carmen, and, furious at finding José there, disdainfully orders him back to his regiment. José draws a sword on his superior officer. The gypsies disarm Zuniga and invite José, now at the end of his military career, to join them for what they vociferously call a life of freedom.

ACT III

A prelude with long-lined flute solo effectively conjures up a non-urban landscape—and perhaps depicts the gentle Micaëla.

In a mountain pass, Carmen, tired of José, tells him it wouldn't be a bad idea if he went back to his mother. In fact, he has begun to show his dangerous side, and Carmen discovers, as the "Fate" motif flickers in the orchestra, that the cards predict her death ("En vain pour éviter"). Micaëla comes in fear to this dangerous place ("Je dis que rien ne m'épouvante"), and José, on sentry, almost kills her with a rifle shot. He also comes near to killing his rival Escamillo in a fight with knives. Micaëla tells José that his mother is dying, and he reluctantly leaves his Carmen, warning her that she will see him again.

ACT IV

A prelude with sinuous English horn solo effectively returns the action to the sultry atmosphere of the city—and perhaps depicts the dangerous Carmen.

Outside the bullring in Seville, Escamillo is hailed by the crowd, offers his love to Carmen, and proceeds to his *corrida* while Carmen, fully aware that her fate is fixed, remains alone outside and faces José. He implores her to start a new life with him. But when she defiantly throws his ring back at him, he fatally stabs her and, as the crowd emerges from the bullring, surrenders to the police, a broken man. The "Fate" motif turns from minor to major.

♣

Carmen has for some time been the most popular opera in the world, though in recent years *La Bohème*, *La Traviata*, and *Le Nozze di Figaro* have been giving it a run for its money. Not entirely successful at its first performances at the family-oriented Opéra-Comique, *Carmen* has won audiences ever since, for it has virtually everything essential to enduring theatrical success: brilliant music, famous solo pieces, orchestral richness such as Paris had never heard from a French composer, a sensational story, comic relief (from the four smugglers), opportunities for dance interludes, and spectacular scenic possibilities, among them one that never fails—parading children and animals onstage.

On the other hand, Micaëla and Escamillo are hardly characters of much dimension, and charismatic and intelligent performances are needed in the leading roles if the show is not to degenerate into an uneven battle between a *femme fatale* and a mama's boy. Though *Carmen* is practically performance-proof, its title role is not. Sopranos of every description have attempted to meet its (not too difficult) vocal and (all too difficult) dramatic challenges, and a significant number of them have come to grief. Similarly, few tenors have been able to suggest, in the first two acts, the violent streak that lies hidden in José.

Carmen's score has been almost universally admired by great composers (Brahms, Richard Strauss, and Stravinsky were particularly lavish in their praise), and Nietzsche, thinking it was high time to "Mediterraneanize" music, used it as a stick to beat Wagner with. But it should be said that Bizet, immensely talented as he was, owes a palpable debt to Gounod in the Micaëla scenes and borrows a tune each from Sebastián Yradier, the composer of "La Paloma" (for the Habanera), and from Manuel García, the father of divas Maria Malibran and Pauline Viardot (for the last-act entr'acte). Pressed by his collaborators at the Comique into last-minute Broadway-style revisions, Bizet wrote the words to the Card Song and the Habanera himself. The Habanera as we have it is the thirteenth number Bizet wrote for Carmen's entrance, and it is not far from the truth to say that it is the only popular aria for which a composer wrote the words but not the music.

For almost a hundred years, a "Paris Opéra version" of *Carmen*, with Gounodesque recitatives supplied by Ernest Guiraud and an interpolated ballet derived from Bizet's incidental music to *L'Arlésienne*, held the stage. But in recent years various "original Opéra-Comique versions," with (often extensive) spoken dialogue and with musical revisions prompted by new scholarship, have been preferred. What was for too long a glamorous "grand opera" became again a vivid piece of pre-verismo realism, in which José Lizzarabengoa reveals himself early on as a dangerous Basque who has left a seminary in Navarre, injured (and possibly killed) a man over a game of *pelota*, and fled to the army before ever meeting Carmen. (In Mérimée's novella he also sinks his knife into a young lieutenant and, with some justification, into the murderous one-eyed desperado who he discovers was, all along, Carmen's gypsy husband.)

Bizet did not, as the legend goes, die of a broken heart after the initial failure of *Carmen*. Despite savage treatment in the press, the opera was at least a middling success for its first run. But the thirty-six-year-old Bizet did die of a heart attack three months after the premiere, and his Carmen, Galli-Marié, collapsed onstage the very hour he lost consciousness. She was obsessed that something terrible was going to happen. Perhaps it was Fate.

Recording

Beecham / de los Angeles, Micheau, Gedda, Blanc
(EMI/Angel 1958)

Cavalleria Rusticana

(Rustic Chivalry)
Music by Pietro Mascagni
Text by Giovanni Targioni-Tozzetti and Guido Menasci
(after Giovanni Verga)
First performance: Rome, 17 May 1890

On Easter morning in a Sicilian village, young Turiddu can be heard serenading Lola, another man's wife ("Siciliana"). The girl he has seduced and left pregnant, Santuzza, is prohibited from attending Easter Mass ("Regina Coeli"), while Lola brazenly comes and goes as she pleases. Santuzza appeals to Mamma Lucia, Turiddu's mother ("Voi lo sapete"), and then to Turiddu himself (Duet: "Tu qui, Santuzza?"). When, impetuously, he throws her to the ground, she hurls an Easter curse at him. Then she tells Lola's husband, Alfio, that Turiddu and Lola are lovers.

The stage is empty while Mass is in progress ("Intermezzo"). Turiddu then leads the villagers in a drinking song outside his mother's wine shop ("Viva il vino spumeggiante"). Alfio confronts him and, biting his ear, challenges him to a duel with knives. Turiddu bids a panicky farewell to his mother ("Mamma, quel vino"), asks her to look after Santuzza, and rushes off to face Alfio. In a moment, a village woman runs in screaming that Turiddu has been butchered.

♣

Mascagni's sensational *Cavalleria Rusticana*, the winner over Puccini's fledgling *Le Villi* in a music publisher's competition, catapulted its unknown twenty-seven-year-old composer to international fame. None of his subsequent works came close to repeating its success, but *Cavalleria* has held the stage for more than a century, kept alive by what can only be called a torrent of crude but hot-blooded melody. Its place in operatic history is assured: it is the first and in many ways the best of the operas that came to be called verismo—realistic slice-of-life depictions of the conflicts of commoners rather than kings. W. H. Auden has made a case for the Easter-morning *Cavalleria*'s being a drama of "the recurrent death and rebirth of nature," with Turiddu the sacrificial victim necessary for the survival of the community. It may at least be of some significance that Turiddu's name, a Sicilian diminutive for Salvatore, means "little savior."

Mascagni's opera was quickly followed by a host of imitations, the most famous of which, Leoncavallo's *Pagliacci*, seems fated to be forever linked with it on opera's most durable double bill.

Recording

Serafin / Callas, di Stefano, Panerai
(EMI/Angel 1953, paired with *Pagliacci*)

La Cenerentola

(Cinderella)
Music by Gioachino Rossini
Text by Giacomo Ferretti (after Charles Perrault)
First performance: Rome, 25 January 1817

ACT I

An ebullient overture, borrowed by the busy young composer from last year's opera, ends in one of the famous slow-building Rossini crescendos.

In Don Magnifico's run-down castle, the stepdaughter Cinderella sits by the cinders in rags while her vulgar stepsisters Clorinda and Tisbe pride themselves on their finery. Cinderella consoles herself amid her many household tasks by singing about a king who married a lowborn but loving girl ("Una volta c'era un re"). Then she shows her own tender heart when she welcomes a beggar to what small hospitality she can extend. A delegation from the palace announces that Prince Ramiro will soon arrive with an invitation to a ball at which he will select his bride. Soon the Prince arrives, dressed as his own valet Dandini, while Dandini skillfully poses as the Prince. Cinderella and the Prince fall in love—she not knowing anything of his royalty and wealth. Don Magnifico and his daughters prepare for the ball; when asked if he hasn't another daughter, he cruelly says that she is dead. Cinderella, left alone amid the ashes, discovers that the beggar she helped is really a kind of guardian angel, Alidoro ("wings of gold"), tutor to the Prince, sent by an all-seeing Providence to help her to the ball.

In the palace, Don Magnifico and his daughters make fools of themselves —he swilling wine, they thinking the Prince the valet and the valet the Prince. They are also struck by the resemblance of an enchanting unknown lady to the lowly Cinderella they torment at home. (Alidoro has clearly stage-managed her appearance at the ball.)

Act II

Taking her leave from the palace, Cinderella refuses the attentions of "the prince" and gives "the valet" a bracelet, saying that he will recognize her thereafter as only she has its twin. The real Prince decides it is time to end the pretence, and the real valet promptly teases Don Magnifico about the deception.

Back at her fireplace, the lowly Cinderella, wearing the other bracelet, is recognized by the Prince (Alidoro has arranged for the royal chariot to break down outside) and is at last made aware of his true identity. He is properly furious when her relatives reject her.

At the wedding banquet, Cinderella generously pardons her malicious father and sisters ("Non più mesta"), showing the same goodness of heart that enabled her to overcome her misfortunes and find happiness.

♣

Written with characteristic speed in little more than three weeks, Rossini's version of the traditional story daringly dispenses with the seemingly indispensable fairy godmother, pumpkin coach, and glass slipper (the last perhaps in deference to Roman censors who would not countenance the emphasis on a feminine ankle). The opera has nonetheless captivated audiences, especially in the last quarter-century, when a bevy of mezzo-sopranos has risen to its coloratura challenges. Modern audiences have also responded to its human qualities: it is goodness, not magic, that propels the action. (The opera's subtitle is "Goodness Triumphant," and the heroine's real name is Angelina—"the angelic one.") Not all the music is absolutely top drawer, but as Rossini said, "All music is good except the boring kind," and *La Cenerentola*, though occasionally overextended, is decidedly not boring.

Recording

Chailly / Bartoli, Matteuzzi, Corbelli, Dara, Pertusi
(Decca/London 1993)

La Clemenza di Tito

(The Clemency of Titus)
Music by Wolfgang Amadeus Mozart
Text by Caterino Mazzolà (after Pietro Metastasio)
First performance: Prague, 6 September 1791

ACT I

A majestic overture, in the key and spirit of the "Jupiter" Symphony, suggests an ancient Rome in eighteenth-century dress.

Vitellia, spurned daughter of an imperial line, induces Sextus, her lover, to lead a conspiracy against the emperor Titus and kill him. Meanwhile, Titus, who has hoped to make Servilia, Sextus' sister, his empress, nobly gives her up when he discovers that she is in love with Sextus' friend Annius. Vitellia then hears that Titus has chosen *her* to be empress. Frantically she tries to call Sextus back from his deadly mission, but it is too late. Soon all Rome is in flames, and it is presumed that Titus has been assassinated.

ACT II

Titus has in fact survived and quelled the attempt against his life. Annius pleads for mercy for Sextus, and Titus, wanting to be remembered for his clemency, tears up the death sentence he has signed. Vitellia confesses that she is the one most guilty. Titus, determined not to resort to vengeance, forgives all the conspirators and devotes himself to the future of Rome.

♣

Mozart wrote the *opera seria La Clemenza di Tito* in his last year, for the coronation ceremonies of Leopold II in Prague. It was a time when monarchies all over Europe were feeling the shock waves of the French Revolution, and when Mozart himself was beset by ill-health, debts, betrayals, and the collapse of his hopes. *Clemenza* is not, as is sometimes said, the last anachronistic gasp of an art form designed to shore up corrupt monarchies, hastily written by a man who had no interest in it but needed the money it would bring in. The facts are that Mozart had chosen the timely subject, and composed several of its greatest pieces, some two years before the commission came from Prague. Mozart found much to respond to in the half-century-old libretto, even though it had already been set to music by many older composers. He saw to it that it was "edited into a true opera" by Mazzolà, a friend of his best librettist, Lorenzo da Ponte. Listening to the music, one can only be struck by how personal the concerns of the title character—loneliness, betrayal, and the need for forgiveness—were to Mozart in his last year.

The numbers range from the heroic *opera seria* arias given Sextus ("Parto, parto" and "Deh, per questo") to Vitellia's superb "Non più di fiori" to Servilia's gentle "S'alto che lagrime" to her luminous little duet with Annius, "Ah perdona" (which provided Beethoven with a tune for improvisations and Shelley with the metrical scheme of "The Indian Serenade"). Though Leopold's empress, perhaps uneasy with the opera's sympathy for assassins, dismissed it at its premiere as "a piece of German piggishness," *Clemenza* was for forty years Mozart's most popular opera, beloved by Goethe, Stendhal, and Mörike. It then lay neglected for a century and a half, due partly to the unavailability of castrati to undertake the roles of Sextus and Annius, partly to its too-lengthy recitatives (by Mozart's pupil Süssmayr, and now cut to a minimum in performance), and mostly to the changes in taste occasioned by the stormy advent of romanticism. Today, thanks to recent scholarship and a number of dedicated performances around the world, we can see *La Clemenza di Tito* in its proper place in the succession of the seven innovative Mozart operas, from *Idomeneo* to *The Magic Flute*, that reach heights to which their genres—*opera seria*, *opera buffa*, and *Singspiel*—had never before aspired.

Recording

Hogwood / Bartoli, D. Jones, Montague, Bonney, Heilmann
(L'Oiseau Lyre 1994)

Les Contes d'Hoffmann

(The Tales of Hoffmann)
Music by Jacques Offenbach
Text by Jules Barbier (after his play with Michel Carré,
based on E. T. A. Hoffmann's tales)
First performance: Paris, 10 February 1881

ACT I

Prologue in Nuremberg: In a tavern run by the put-upon Luther, the poet Hoffmann and his young companion Nicklausse await the arrival of Stella, who is singing in *Don Giovanni* in the opera house next door. Lurking in the shadows is Councilor Lindorf, Hoffmann's nemesis. The students who frequent the tavern ask Hoffmann for one of his famous tales, and he begins to tell of the dwarf Kleinzach—only to drift into reveries about Stella. Primed with drink, he settles down amid the smoking Meerschaums to tell the fantastic stories of three women, each of them a different aspect of his Stella.

Paris: Olympia is a mechanical singing doll, presented in society by the near-crazed inventor Spalanzani. Hoffmann falls in love with her, only to see her smashed to pieces by his nemesis, Coppélius.

ACT II

Munich: Antonia is a frail opera singer, assured by her high-strung father, Crespel, that if she sings she will die. Hoffmann falls in love with her, only to see her destroyed, singing herself to death under the musical direction of his nemesis, Dr. Miracle.

ACT III

Venice: Giulietta is a shadow-stealing courtesan, kept by the shadowless Schlemil. Hoffmann falls in love with her, only to lose his own shadow to her master, Dappertutto. [Alternate version: only to see her destroyed by his nemesis, Dappertutto.]

Epilogue in Nuremberg: Hoffmann, dead drunk when Stella arrives in the tavern, loses her to his nemesis, Councilor Lindorf [but is consoled by Nicklausse, who has accompanied him on his three amorous adventures and is now fully revealed as the Muse who has inspired them].

♣

Offenbach, *maître absolu du Can-Can* and operetta composer *par excellence*, died before he could draw together the scattered parts of his only opera, *The Tales of Hoffmann*. Both the plot summary offered here and the recording listed below follow the "compromise" performing tradition of the opera. In the theater one may also encounter the old "standard" performing edition, in which Giulietta's act precedes Antonia's, or (more confusing still) one may encounter various newer editions that perform all or most of Offenbach's musical sketches for the opera and delete the parts he wrote for other pieces which, over the years, have found their way into *Hoffmann*. Are you still with me, class? Then be forewarned that new-edition performances can last as much as an hour longer than those based on standard or compromise editions.

In any edition, *Hoffmann* is a musical feast and, in the hands of a good director, an engrossing drama as well. Offenbach's librettists have ingeniously drawn on several tales of the historical E. T. A. Hoffmann and made them all refractions of the situation in the tavern (itself taken from the author's spooky tale about *Don Giovanni*). Hoffmann and Nicklausse keep their identities in the three stories, but (as the summary above has been designed to indicate) the three heroines are all aspects of Stella, the three nemeses are all embodiments of Councilor Lindorf, and the three unstable father figures are variations on Luther the tavern keeper. In yet another pattern, each story contains a defective minor figure—the stammering lab assistant Cochenille in Paris, the half-deaf butler Frantz in Munich, and the monosyllabic hunchback Pitichinaccio in Venice—to correspond to the almost inarticulate servant Andrès in the framing situation.

For the record, because they went deliberately unmentioned in the above summary, the best numbers in the score are Hoffmann's "Kleinzach," Olympia's "Doll Song," Antonia's duet with Hoffmann ("C'est un chanson d'amour"), and Giulietta's famous Barcarolle. That's one gem each for Nuremberg, Paris, Munich, and Venice, and there is much besides. The only regret one can have about Offenbach's masterpiece is that the composer had to leave it in as many bits and pieces as Olympia, the smashed mechanical doll.

Recording

Ozawa / Gruberova, Eder, Domingo, Bacquier, Diaz, Morris
(Deutsche Grammophon 1990)

Le Coq d'Or

(The Golden Cockerel)
Music by Nikolai Rimsky-Korsakov
Text by Vladimir Belsky (after Alexander Pushkin)
First performance: Moscow, 7 October 1909

ACT I

Prologue: A mysterious Astrologer informs the audience that the fairy tale they are about to see has an excellent moral.

In the palace of the czars, the Astrologer presents embattled old King Dodon with a Golden Cockerel that will crow at the first sign of an invasion. He also warns that he will return in time to claim his payment. While Dodon sleeps, dreaming of an exotic lady, the Cockerel crows, and Dodon's two sons rush out to do battle. At the second crowing, Dodon himself quixotically dons his armor.

ACT II

Dodon wanders across the battlefield where his two sons have slain each other. The mists clear, and the lady of his dreams, the Queen of Shemakha, emerges from her tent to sing a Hymn to the Sun. She seduces Dodon, makes him dance for her amusement, agrees to be his wife, and starts out with him for his palace.

ACT III

The royal procession reaches the palace and is interrupted by the Astrologer, who, though he is a eunuch, demands the Queen as his payment. Dodon slays him with a blow of his scepter, whereupon the scene grows dark and the Cockerel flies from its perch to peck the King lethally on the head. The Astrologer reappears to lead the Queen away, as if she were under a spell.

Epilogue: The Astrologer steps before the curtain to assure the audience that, in the tale they have seen, only he and the Queen were real.

♣

Le Coq d'Or, the last of Rimsky-Korsakov's operas, has always been the best known in the West, probably due to the once ubiquitous suite of orchestral excerpts from it. But now that *Sadko, Tsar Saltan, The Snow Maiden, May Night, Christmas Eve*, and especially *The Invisible City of Kitezh* (the "Russian *Parsifal*") are becoming better known, *Le Coq d'Or* may yield pride of place to those longer and more varied works. Still, it is hard to resist this compact, colorful fairy-tale concoction that is quite clearly a bitter but brittle early-twentieth-century allegorical satire. But is it about Czar Nicholas' defeat in the Russo-Japanese War (the censor's objection) or about Rasputin and Czarina Alexandra (the suggestion of some recent critics)? *Le Coq d'Or* was perhaps the first opera since the Renaissance "madrigal operas" in which the singers were placed offstage while dancers mimed the parts. Fokine devised this staging for St. Petersburg, and Diaghilev followed suit in Paris, London, and New York. The composer did not live to see his final, and perhaps finest, work in performance, but it has not been without influence: Igor Stravinsky chose a remarkably similar subject for his first opera, *Le Rossignol*, and Diaghilev staged it in similar fashion.

Recording

Svetlanov / Brileva, Gaponova, Biktimirov, Eizen (MCA 1988)

Così Fan Tutte

(Women Are Like That)
Music by Wolfgang Amadeus Mozart
Text by Lorenzo da Ponte
First performance: Vienna, 26 January 1790

Act I

A bustling overture eventually quotes the passage in the opera where the three gentlemen finally agree that "women are like that."

At a café in eighteenth-century Naples, three gentlemen are arguing about women: the young soldiers Ferrando and Guglielmo declare that their teenaged fiancées are models of faithfulness, while the philosopher Don Alfonso counters, "Faithfulness in women is like the phoenix: everyone says it exists, but no one knows where." He bets the boys that if each of them assumes a disguise and makes advances to the other's girl, the girls will succumb within twenty-four hours. The bet is on.

At a seaside villa, the girls, Fiordiligi and Dorabella, sisters in the flesh, are told by Don Alfonso that their fiancés have been ordered off to war. The boys pay a farewell call, and the girls and the old Voltairian watch the ship disappear (Trio: "Soave sia il vento").

The maid Despina, who thinks the sisters' virtuous protestations of fidelity ridiculous, accepts a bribe from Don Alfonso to allow two young Albanian friends of his into the house. The boys appear in elaborate get-ups with massive mustaches, but the girls will have none of them. Fiordiligi all but hymns her constancy ("Come scoglio").

The boys pretend to have taken arsenic out of despair, and Despina, dressed as a physician with glasses and an enormous magnet, revives them via the latest methods of Doctor Mesmer. The girls still refuse to kiss their "new" suitors, but begin to weaken.

Act II

Despina convinces the girls that a little flirtation will do no harm. Dorabella chooses the dark boy (actually Guglielmo, her sister's fiancé), and Fiordiligi chooses the blond one (her sister's own Ferrando).

The rearranged couples shyly begin their experiments. Dorabella succumbs (Duet: "Il core vi dono"), but Fiordiligi holds out ("Per pietà").

Ferrando, crushed that his own fiancée has proved unfaithful, redoubles his efforts to seduce Guglielmo's—and succeeds. Don Alfonso persuades the disillusioned boys to marry their first loves in spite of all, for "così fan tutte."

Despina acts as notary in a trumped-up wedding ceremony. Just as the two sisters sign the contract to marry their "Albanians," they are stunned to hear the sound of soldiers returning from war. They hide the two "Albanians" in the next room, and in a moment the boys reappear sans moustaches and in military garb, feigning indignation at finding a wedding contract and a notary (Despina, despite her complicity in the plan, has not been told the half of it). Explanations follow, the girls are reunited with their original lovers, and all sing the praises of reason as the best guide through the vicissitudes of life.

♣

This most sophisticated of operas did not find worldwide acceptance for a century and a half, and there is still debate about who should be paired off with whom at the close. Eighteenth-century rationalism would have the two couples learn from their experience and return wiser to their original loves; da Ponte always referred to the opera by its subtitle, *The School for Lovers*.

The nineteenth century, with its romantic and then Victorian idealization of love, either ignored the opera or attempted to fit its music to some other text; Beethoven thought it immoral, and Wagner an aberration and a sad waste of genius. Post-Freudian twentieth-century sensibility, supposedly liberated, has insisted that any sexual awakening such as the two girls experience in the second act would alter their outlook completely; most stagings today —in defiance of the subtitle, the musical alignments, the praises of reason at the close, and the plain fact that the boys are just as reprehensible in their actions as the girls—pair the ladies with their new lovers. Yes—but what would Jane Austen, who knew more about these things than Freud did, say to that? Jonathan Miller rightly maintains that present-day directors, too often concerned with their own era ("a sleazy suburb in history"), ought to make some effort to understand works of art in the terms those works set for themselves. *Così* insists that love is a natural impulse that must be cultivated if it is to last. Don Alfonso sees to it that the original lovers come to realize this of their original partners.

The plot of *Così* has an antecedent in the myth of Cephalus and Procris, owes something to Ariosto, and may be based on a court scandal of Mozart's day. Some evidence suggests that Joseph II commissioned it and that Mozart's rival Salieri actually scored two numbers of the libretto before abandoning the project. In any case, we are most fortunate that the project was taken up by Mozart, who in real life loved one sister and married another— and then had to overlook her infidelities. This is his most elegant score, an *opera buffa* in which the two sisters sing *opera seria* arias that mock the older genre while distilling poignancy from it, a drama as formal in its patterns as a game of chess but made touchingly real by music that, in B. H. Haggin's phrase, "pierces the heart as it ravishes the ears." And one can acknowledge the profundity of the opera without losing one's sense of humor about it. When Peter Allen, the host of the Metropolitan Opera broadcasts, was asked what opera he would choose a different ending for, he suggested a *Così* that concluded with the two pairs of lovers throwing Don Alfonso into the Bay of Naples!

Recording

Karajan / Schwarzkopf, Merriman, Otto, Simoneau, Panerai,
Bruscantini (EMI/Angel 1954)

The Cunning Little Vixen

Music and text by Leoš Janáček
First performance: Brno, 6 November 1924

ACT I

A Forester, surrounded by all the animals and insects of the woodland, is awakened from sleep when a tiny frog lands on his nose. He spots a little Vixen, catches her, and takes her home for his two boys to play with.

In the farm enclosure, the boys torment the Vixen, who gets free advice from the dog on how to get along with humans. True to her nature, she attacks and kills the rooster and his subservient hens. Then she breaks her leash and escapes.

ACT II

Back in the forest, the Vixen cunningly evicts the badger from his lair and moves in herself.

In the village inn, three loveless men—the Forester, the Schoolmaster, and the Priest—reminisce about Terynka, the woman they all loved from afar and lost.

Returning home through the forest, the Schoolmaster and the Priest are tripped up by the cunning little Vixen, but the Forester, more sure of his footing, almost succeeds in shooting her.

The Vixen is seduced by a handsome fox and, since the birds have seen her at her lovemaking, is obliged to marry him, amid a forest celebration.

ACT III

At the edge of the forest, Harašta, a lowly poultry dealer, tells the Forester that Terynka is to marry—of all people—him. The Forester, finding a dead hare, guesses that the Vixen is near and sets a trap for her. She easily sees the danger and, with her husband and their happy brood, makes merry over how humans underestimate the intelligence of animals. But she unwarily puts herself in harm's way when she attacks the poultry dealer's stock: he takes aim and shoots her dead.

At the inn, the Forester and the Schoolmaster hear that the Priest has been transferred and is lonely at his new post. They try to ignore Terynka's wedding outside, but notice that she has a new fox-fur muff.

In the woodland, the Forester remembers his own wedding day and, sensing his unity with all nature, contentedly falls asleep amid the same assortment of animals and insects that surrounded him in the first scene—except of course that these are the children, and even the children's children, of those creatures. Waking, he thinks for a moment that he has spotted the Vixen again, but it is her daughter he sees. The tiny frog also seems to be there again, but when questioned it says, "Oh, no! That was my grandpa. He used to tell me about you." The Forester lets his gun slip harmlessly from his hand to the ground.

♣

Though children can enjoy watching, acting in, and even singing in Janáček's fable of animals and humans (drawn originally from a kind of comic strip), it is adults who are likely to be most moved by it—for the composer, with the same honest, unsentimental sympathy that pervades his more veristic works, poignantly depicts the emptiness of human lives against a background of the spontaneous, irrepressible, ever-renewed life of nature's other creatures. In the forest scenes, Janáček's orchestrations seem infallibly to capture the sights and sounds of a quietly omniscient nature. The final scene, where the Forester finally realizes that humans must accept their place, as animals instinctively do, in nature's cycle of birth, death, and renewal, is among the great scenes in twentieth-century opera.

Since Walter Felsenstein effectively staged the *Vixen* at the Komische Oper in East Berlin, producers have found increasingly ingenious ways of presenting it without resorting to the cuteness that would be fatal to its earnest and uniquely lovely seriousness.

Recording
Mackerras / Popp, Randová, Jedlička (Decca/London 1981)

Dialogues of the Carmelites

(Dialogues des Carmélites)
Music by Francis Poulenc
Text by Georges Bernanos
First performance: Milan, 26 January 1957

ACT I

In Paris in the spring of 1789, the carriage of young Blanche de la Force has been attacked by an angry mob, and her father and brother are alarmed when, returning home, she is frightened by a shadow on the wall. She seems to be consumed by a fear of fear itself. Alone with her father, she asks his permission to enter the Carmelite convent at Compiègne.

At the convent, Blanche is told by the ailing but imposing Prioress, Madame de Croissy, that the Carmelite life is not a refuge from the world, and that God means to test not her strength but her weakness. They both know that the Revolution is imminent.

In the convent laundry, Blanche, now a novice, is disturbed by the innocent chatter of her fellow novice, Constance, especially when she suggests that the two of them offer their lives to save the life of the dying Prioress.

The Prioress, on her deathbed, tells Blanche, "To protect you from danger I would gladly have given my life. Now, alas, all I can give you is my death." Then the once superbly calm *religieuse* dies in utter terror.

Blanche, keeping vigil with Constance over the corpse of the Prioress, is overcome with fear but calmed by the stern Mother Marie.

Blanche and Constance are making a cross of flowers for the Prioress' grave, wondering why she died in such terror. Constance says, "It's as if, when He gave her her death, the good Lord made a mistake. It's like a cloakroom attendant giving you someone else's coat. I think her death belonged to someone else. It was a death much too small for her, so small that the sleeves barely reached to her elbows." Blanche asks what that can possibly mean, and Constance answers, "It means that someone else, when the time comes to die, will be surprised to find it so easy."

The newly appointed Prioress addresses the sisters. She is not, as everyone expected, the aristocratic Mother Marie, but a humble peasant woman, Madame Lidoine.

ACT II

Blanche's brother comes to the convent and encourages her to flee from the Revolution with the rest of the family. She refuses, saying that among the Carmelites she has found freedom from her old fear. But when her brother leaves she admits to Mother Marie that what she said was not true.

The nuns' chaplain, who must now go into hiding, takes his last leave of the convent. Mother Marie, with quick-witted answers, faces the mob pursuing him. Blanche, overwhelmed with terror, drops a statue of the Infant Jesus, and its head cracks ominously on the flagstones.

When the new Prioress is called to Paris by the Revolutionary authorities, Mother Marie arranges for the sisters to take a vow of martyrdom. Blanche takes the vow but, overwhelmed by the burden of it, flees the convent.

The sisters, dressed in civilian clothes, are evicted and told, "No more living in community."

Mother Marie, searching for the fugitive Blanche, finds her in what was once her father's house, maltreated by revolutionaries, and encourages her to find a safer haven.

[Near the Bastille, Blanche hears that the Carmelites of Compiègne have been arrested. Fearful as St. Peter when he denied that he ever knew Jesus, Blanche says "I've never been to Compiègne."]

In the Conciergerie, the sisters are told that they have been condemned to death. The new Prioress, who was away when they took the vow of martyrdom, now takes full responsibility for it.

In a street in Paris, Mother Marie, who insisted on the vow but by chance was not with the sisters when they were rounded up, is filled with remorse but told by the chaplain to leave the matter in God's hands.

At the Place de la Révolution, the sisters are marched to the guillotine, and sing a death-braving "Salve Regina" as, one by one, they go to their deaths. Constance, the last to mount the scaffold, catches sight of Blanche in the crowd, exchanges a glance with her, and then proceeds to her execution. Blanche, touched by grace, comes forward and calmly mounts the scaffold to die with her sisters. The crowd disperses in silence.

♣

Dialogues of the Carmelites is based on an actual series of events from the last days of the French Revolution. Like another increasingly popular twentieth-century opera, it is a compelling drama in which each scene is another turn of the screw. But here, as the terror mounts, a theological argument is argued ever more clearly and cogently. Bernanos took a diary by Mother Marie, the only survivor among the sisters, and a German novella by Gertrud von le Fort (who projected herself into the events as Blanche de la Force), and turned them into a statement about the centuries-old Christian doctrine of the Communion of Saints: all believers, living and dead, are bound together in a community, in which one member can win grace for another. Bernanos heightened this to say in effect that one believer could die another's death for him (or her). So in the opera the old Prioress dies Blanche's fearful death for her, while Blanche receives the calm death the old Prioress might have had. Similarly the new Prioress, who did not take the vow of martyrdom, dies the death of Mother Marie, who imposed the vow but was not called to fulfill it. The young novice Constance all but predicts that this will happen: "We die not for ourselves alone, but for one another. Sometimes even in the place of one another." These exchanges of grace are the real "dialogues" of the Carmelites.

Poulenc's score is an eclectic but effective blend of the styles of the composers to whom he dedicated his opera—Verdi, Monteverdi, Mussorgsky, and Debussy. (It is possible also to hear echoes of Ravel, Stravinsky, and even Gershwin.) He underlines each of the text's statements of the doctrine of the Communion of Saints with the same luminous, wide-intervalled motif, which sounds unforgettably for the last time when Constance and Blanche exchange glances at the guillotine, and grace passes from one to the other. Even those who find the theological discussions in the opera of minimal interest are devastated by Poulenc's music for that last scene—music that conveys both mounting terror and shining faith.

Recording

Nagano / Dubose, Fournier, Yakar, Dupuy, Gorr, van Dam
(Virgin Classics 1992)

Dido and Aeneas

Music by Henry Purcell
Text by Nahum Tate (after Virgil)
First performance: London, April 1689

Dido, queen of Carthage, is encouraged by her sister Belinda to yield to her love for Aeneas, a princely survivor from fallen Troy whom she has welcomed to her shores.

A vengeful Sorceress conjures up a storm to disrupt the hunting party of Dido and Aeneas, and sends a spirit disguised as Mercury to tell the Trojan hero that he must depart.

Aeneas' men prepare the fleet for departure as the Sorceress and her witches celebrate their victory. Dido confronts the wavering hero and reproaches him but, as his ship fades from view, hopes he will remember her ("When I am laid in earth"). She dies as angels ("With drooping wings") weep for her.

♣

As this plot summary indicates, England's poet laureate permitted onstage nothing of Virgil that would offend the sensibilities of the young ladies of Josias Priest's boarding school in Chelsea, for whom the work was presumably first written: the storm is sent, not to drive Dido and Aeneas into a cave to consummate their passion, but simply to spoil their afternoon; Aeneas departs not in obedience to his mission but because the Sorceress has tricked him; Dido dies not of her own hand, cursing Aeneas and all his Roman descendants, but from grief, and with a prayer that her death cause "no sorrow."

The hour-long work may have been considerably altered when it was performed later the same year as part of the coronation festivities of William and Mary. The score as we have it, with a baritone hero and bass parts for the chorus, is a century later than the Chelsea premiere, and differs significantly from Tate's published text, which may, according to Tate himself, have been intended as an anti-papist allegory, with the Sorceress representing the Catholic Church.

Dido and Aeneas is Purcell's only opera (*The Fairy Queen*, *King Arthur*, and other fine pieces are plays with incidental music), and it owes something to John Blow's 1683 *Venus and Adonis* (Aeneas' pointed reference to the boar he has killed all but acknowledges the earlier piece). But it is a very accomplished work, one in which the solos, duets, recitatives, choruses, and dance music seem to owe nothing to Italian traditions but to constitute a new and distinctive style for English opera. In this oldest English opera in the standard repertory—in fact the only such for almost three centuries—Purcell anticipated Gluck's reform of baroque opera by some eighty years, and touched greatness with Dido's final aria, an immensely moving if unVirgilian lament floated out over a repeated, sadly resigned, melody in the bass. It might be an elegy for a composer just coming into the fullness of his powers when he died at age thirty-six.

Recording

Davis / Veasey, Donath, Bainbridge, Shirley-Quirk (Philips 1970)

Don Carlo

(Don Carlos)
Music by Giuseppe Verdi
Text by Joseph Méry and Camille du Locle
(after Friedrich Schiller)
First performance: Paris, 11 March 1867

Act I

[During a royal hunt in the snowy forest of Fontainebleau, Princess Elisabeth of Valois has lost her way. Prince Carlo of Spain, to whom she is newly betrothed and who has heretofore seen her only from a distance ("Io la vidi"), finds her, and they fall in love even before she knows who he is. Then news comes that, to secure peace between Spain and France, Elisabeth is to marry Carlo's father, the all-powerful Philip II.]

In Spain, at the monastery of San Yuste, Carlo comes to the tomb of his grandfather, Charles V, to pray for strength to forget Elisabeth. An old friar (who may be Charles V, still living in the monastery in secret) tells him that only in the tomb can the soul find peace. Carlo's idealistic friend Rodrigo, Marquis of Posa, suggests that he sublimate his passion by taking on the cause of Flanders, a Protestant nation cruelly oppressed by his father (Duet: "Dio, che nell' alma infondere"). Philip II and his new Queen also come to pray, and the stepmother and son exchange hurried glances.

In the garden at San Yuste, Princess Eboli, a notorious intriguer, sings to the women of the court a song about veiled intrigue ("The Veil Song"). Rodrigo formally presents Carlo to his stepmother, drawing Eboli, who is also in love with Carlo, aside to allow them privacy. In the tension of the situation Carlo, an epileptic, faints; the shocked Elisabeth reminds him how Oedipal their situation is. King Philip is furious to discover that the Queen has been left unattended, and banishes the Countess of Aremberg, her only compatriot at court. He then asks Rodrigo privately for help in the situation he already perceives has developed between his wife and his son. He also sounds Rodrigo out on the matter of Flanders and warns him, twice, that the Grand Inquisitor is watching him.

ACT II

In the Queen's gardens in Madrid [Eboli, veiled in the Queen's regalia, sends Carlo an unsigned note urging him to come to the spot, and] Carlo, assuming that the veiled lady is the Queen, openly declares his love. Eboli's suspicions are thus confirmed. Furious at having the Queen for a rival, she tells Carlo that his father and Rodrigo are plotting against him. Rodrigo, tailing Carlo as requested, almost kills the scheming Eboli, but Carlo stays his hand. The two men, left alone, renew their resolve to help Flanders, and Rodrigo, wary of the Inquisition, persuades Carlo to hand over to him all documents relating to his involvement in an impending revolt there.

At a public auto-da-fé, Carlo boldly interrupts the ceremonies with a pro-Flanders demonstration, and draws a sword against his father. This time it is Rodrigo who disarms Carlo, and the Prince is led off to prison. The terrible burning of heretics ensues. The Catholic court does not hear a compassionate voice from heaven calling the souls of the victims to everlasting peace.

ACT III

King Philip, alone in his private chambers, reflects that wearing the crown does not empower one to command the love of a single human heart ("Ella giammai m'amo"). He summons the Grand Inquisitor to ask if he can morally execute his own son. The Inquisitor, old and blind but fearfully implacable, answers that God Himself did the same. He then demands the death of Rodrigo as well. The King bitterly assents to this, fearing himself the power of the Inquisition. Meanwhile, Eboli has gained access to Elisabeth's private jewel case, planted there an "incriminating" portrait of Carlo, and sent it to the King. Elisabeth faints when the King calls her an adulteress. Rodrigo rushes to her aid, realizing that she and Carlo are now in real danger and insisting that the two are innocent of any adultery. A repentant Eboli, left alone with Elisabeth, admits that not only is she herself in love with the Prince but that she has been the King's mistress for years. Elisabeth, with queenly dignity, banishes her. Eboli curses the beauty that has brought her to ruin ("O don fatale") and resolves to save Carlo from the Inquisition in the one day she has left before her banishment.

Rodrigo comes to Carlo's prison cell to tell him that he will soon be released; he has himself taken on all suspicion in the Flanders matter, and the documents have proved his implication ("Per me giunto"). In a moment he is fatally shot by an Inquisitorial gun pointed through the prison window. He dies telling Carlo to meet Elisabeth at the tomb of Charles V the next day ("O Carlo, ascolta"); he must live on for Flanders. [The King comes to the cell to pardon his son, but Carlo repulses him as the true murderer of Rodrigo.] Then the prison is stormed by a rebellious crowd roused by Eboli to set Carlo free. The Prince escapes, but the crowd is quelled by the sudden appearance of the powerful Grand Inquisitor.

In the moonlit monastery of San Yuste, at the tomb of Charles V, Elisabeth, steeled to see Carlo for the last time, reiterates the old friar's message: only in the tomb can one find peace ("Tu che le vanità"). She tells the Prince that he must forget her and live for Flanders; they will meet again in a better world (Duet: "Ma lassù"). But the King, now firmly in pursuit, finds them together and furiously turns them over to the Inquisition. Carlo fights his way toward the tomb, and suddenly the old friar—whom King Philip is astonished to see, perhaps rightly, as his father, Charles V—emerges and takes Carlo safely within, to the only place in this world where one can find peace.

❧

Verdi's heavily plotted French/Italian opera is hardly true to history (the historical Carlo, for example, was selfish, sadistic, and half-mad, and Verdi at one point in the opera's composition said ruefully, "Everything in this drama is false"), but is nonetheless powerfully true to life. The glory of Schiller's original play lies in its ideas, its dramatization of the tensions between liberalism and absolutism, and its sense of the complexities and ambivalences of political action. The glory of Verdi's opera lies in its five main characters—each of them seen in prismatic relationships with the other four, each limned in music of immense eloquence and compassion.

Verdi wrote the opera in French (as *Don Carlos*) for the Paris Exposition of 1867. Asked for a grand opera à la Meyerbeer, he overwrote, and the long work had to be cut for its first run of performances. Verdi subsequently made various shorter versions for Italian stages, and today the opera and its arias are generally referred to by their Italian titles. (A vocal minority prefers the French text, but few will claim that the opera should be performed with every bar of the French original restored.) When the opening scene at Fontainebleau is omitted, Carlo's aria is transferred to the first scene at San Yuste. One major cut, the Act III lament of father and son over the body of Rodrigo, was reworked by Verdi into the "Lacrimosa" of his *Requiem*. The *deus ex machina* ending, which many find unconvincing, and for which Verdi provided a (mostly musical) alternative, is to this day subjected to various dramatic "improvements" in performance.

Not surprisingly, *Don Carlo*, in any of its five different versions, was for decades thought problematic and unperformable. But in the years following

World War II several notable productions proved its viability and worth, and now the rich and somber work is rated by critics and public alike as one of Verdi's supreme masterpieces. The scene in King Philip's chambers (from "Ella giammai" to "O don fatale") is regarded by many Verdians as the greatest single scene in any opera.

Recording

Giulini / Caballé, Verrett, Domingo, Milnes, Raimondi
(EMI/Angel 1971)

Don Giovanni

(Don Juan)
Music by Wolfgang Amadeus Mozart
Text by Lorenzo da Ponte
First performance: Prague, 29 October 1787

ACT I

An overture establishes the ambivalent nature of the tragicomic work: the D-minor music that later will accompany the frightening appearance of a visitor from hell is followed by a D-major depiction, lighthearted and almost sexually explicit, of the exploits of the lecherous Don Juan.

At night in the garden of a palace in a city that is probably seventeenth-century Seville, the commoner Leporello complains that he must watch night and day outside the houses where his aristocratic master, Don Giovanni, takes his pleasure. Suddenly his master appears, masked and struggling with the lady he has ravished, or attempted to ravish, Donna Anna. In a moment her father, a royal Commendatore, is there, with his sword drawn. Giovanni kills the venerable man in the ensuing duel and escapes. Anna and her chivalrous fiancé, Don Ottavio, swear vengeance. (Through some of this tragic action, Leporello provides comic asides.)

As the dawn comes up, Giovanni bullies Leporello into silence, and is making his way to his nearby castle when, in front of an inn, his nostrils sense the presence of another conquest. He makes a hasty exit, however, when he sees that the lady is Donna Elvira, whom he has already loved and left, and who is in perpetual pursuit of him. Leporello attempts to console

Elvira with a happily heartless "Catalogue Aria": his master has enjoyed many conquests—2,065 so far, 1,003 in Spain alone!

Giovanni is still heading for his castle when he spots a rustic wedding party, on its way to the ceremony. He invites them all to celebrate with him beforehand, and as Leporello escorts the others, including the prospective bridegroom, Masetto, to the master's castle, the master makes a proposal to the prospective bride, Zerlina (Duet: "La ci darem la mano"). But before anything can happen, Elvira, a kind of Handelian angel to Giovanni's demon, catches up with him and, in a baroque arietta ("Ah, fuggi il traditor!"), hurries Zerlina away. She also rouses suspicions in Anna and Ottavio, on the trail of the masked rapist, until Anna is sure that it was Giovanni who attacked her and killed her father ("Or sai chi l'onore"). Ottavio is concerned at what this terrible desire for vengeance is doing to his fiancée ("Dalla sua pace").

In the castle, Giovanni prepares for at least ten more conquests ("Fin ch'han del vino"), while in the garden below Zerlina submissively assures her Masetto that she is still wholly his ("Batti, batti, o bel Masetto"). Three uninvited guests outside the castle request admission; they are masked, but their voices tell us they are Anna, Ottavio, and Elvira. As the strains of the famous Minuet begin, Leporello invites them inside. They pray to heaven to protect them, for the justice they must deal out terrifies them (Trio: "Protegga il giusto cielo").

Admitted to the castle, they join in the praises of liberty. (The word, very much in the air in Mozart's day, means something different to each of the seven characters.) Giovanni's private orchestra now plays the Minuet simultaneously with a Contredanse and a Ländler (the dances are another indication of the class-levels of the characters), and he leads Zerlina off to make his next conquest—but her screams alert the others. Giovanni attempts, without success, to put the blame on Leporello. The action freezes, as everyone sings about the vengeful tempest that is soon to strike.

Act II

This act, a kaleidoscope of changing moods, is a kind of recapitulation and resolution of the first, though we are given no indication of what happened after the face-off at the end of Act I.

Giovanni and Leporello begin the new series of episodes beneath Elvira's window (Trio: "Ah, taci, ingiusto core"). Each disguises himself as the other, and the servant leads Elvira away while the master serenades Elvira's maid ("Deh, vieni alla finestra"). Masetto and a peasant posse, thinking Giovanni is Leporello, ask where the master might be, intending to kill him; Giovanni sends the posse on a wild goose chase, beats Masetto up, and runs off. Zerlina comforts her battered swain by letting him feel, for medicinal purposes, where her heart is beating ("Vedrai, carino").

The five pursuers—Anna, Ottavio, Elvira, Zerlina, and Masetto—finally corner their prey (Sextet: "Sola, sola in buio loco"), only to find that the man they thought was Giovanni is Leporello—who slyly slips away from them. Ottavio asks the others to help him comfort the grieving Anna ("Il mio tesoro"). Elvira seems to see heaven crashing above—and hell opening beneath—the dissolute man she still loves ("Mi tradì").

Giovanni, exuberant after a night spent chasing girls, finds himself before the monumental statue of the dead Commendatore and, when the marble comes to life, brazenly forces a shivering Leporello to invite the statue to his castle for dinner.

Anna assures Ottavio that, despite her grief, she still loves him ("Non mi dir").

Giovanni is dining luxuriously in his castle as his orchestra plays three tunes—successively this time—from operas of Mozart's day. Leporello, stuffing his mouth with food, easily identifies each tune (apparently he is an opera fan), especially the last, which is from Mozart's *Nozze di Figaro*. Elvira makes an unsuccessful last-minute attempt to persuade Giovanni to change his ways—and the statue of the Commendatore appears and drags Giovanni, defiantly unrepentant even as the flames rise around him, to his damnation. (Through some of this tragic action, Leporello makes comic asides.)

The six remaining characters advance to the footlights, quickly plan their separate futures, and point the moral for the audience: "This is the way evildoers end. The death of sinners always suits the life they led."

♣

We need not take that message any more seriously than would any *Don Juan* audience through the centuries watching a morality play at a carnival, for the opera—a very sophisticated work of art—constantly acknowledges its indebtedness to a century or more of puppet plays, popular entertainments, and literary works treating the Don Juan theme, as well as to earlier traditions of symphonic, ecclesiastical, and occasional music, and especially to the two kinds of opera Mozart had already begun, in his *Nozze di Figaro*, to combine—the dignified, aristocratic *opera seria* and the light, popular *opera buffa*. (Anna represents the former and Zerlina the latter genre, while Elvira, tragic and at the same time a little dotty, is what Mozart called *mezza carrattere*, half way between the two.)

We have never been able to form an adequate idea of what *Don Giovanni* is, for it defies classification. Da Ponte seems to have had a comedy in mind, but Mozart, who may have taken a hand in shaping the text (as he most certainly did with other operas), saw to it that in his music the comic was balanced by, and often commingled with, the tragic. This remarkable ambivalence to some extent accounts for the opera's enduring fame. In Latin countries, it has generally been thought a comedy thrown slightly out of whack by its composer's insistence on empathizing with his characters; in Germanic countries it is almost invariably played as a tragic drama in which a hero like a force of nature rises heroically to challenge supernature—a figure to be compared with Hamlet or Faust.

There is scarcely an artist of genius—from Goethe and Wagner through Kierkegaard to Shaw and Stravinsky—who has not expressed his admiration for *Don Giovanni*, and there is scarcely a number in the opera that is not quoted from in the music, art, literature, and even cinema of the years to follow, from Beethoven's use of Leporello's opening "Night and day I'm worked to death" (as a gibe at his publishers) in the Diabelli Variations through Chopin, Offenbach, Wilde, and Joyce to the delicious use of "Il mio tesoro" in the film *Kind Hearts and Coronets*, and beyond. Perhaps E. T. Amadeus Hoffmann, he of the tales, paid the best and simplest tribute to *Don Giovanni* when he called it "the opera of all operas."

Recording
Giulini / Sutherland, Schwarzkopf, Sciutti, Alva, Wächter, Taddei,
Frick (EMI/Angel 1959)

Don Pasquale

Music by Gaetano Donizetti
Text by Gaetano Donizetti and Giovanni Ruffini
First performance: Paris, 3 January 1843

ACT I

An overture introduces us to some, but by no means all, of the best tunes to come in this last of the famous *opere buffe*.

Old Don Pasquale is resolved to marry and thereby disinherit his rebellious nephew Ernesto. His friend Dr. Malatesta tells him that he has a sister, convent-trained, who would be an ideal wife ("Pura siccome un angelo"). Actually the "sister" is the very Norina that Ernesto is in love with.

Norina, laughing over the tales of chivalry she is reading ("Quel guardo il cavaliere"), agrees to cooperate with Malatesta in teaching Don Pasquale to act his age.

Act II

Ernesto bewails his fate until he is let in on the plot. Don Pasquale, entranced by the "sister," proposes marriage and endows her with half his worldly goods. She turns instantly into a terrible termagant, running up bills to stratospheric heights.

Act III

In one of her now customary spats with Don Pasquale, Norina slaps his face—and begins to fear that the joke has gone too far. When he finds a note from a "lover" that she has dropped on purpose, asking for an assignation in the garden that night, he enlists the services of Malatesta in surprising her there.

It is of course Ernesto in the garden ("Com' è gentil"), and he and Norina pledge their love (Duet: "Tornami a dir"). The three conspirators reveal the roles they have played in bamboozling Don Pasquale, and he allows the lovers to marry—with half his worldly goods.

♣

One of the last of Donizetti's seventy-odd operas, *Don Pasquale* finds the master at the peak of his comic form, still able to lift the comedy above the level of *opera buffa* with just the right touches of seriousness and romance in the final act. Writing with Mozartian swiftness, Donizetti brought *Don Pasquale* in in three weeks, possibly even less. Richard Strauss, with a noisier orchestra, more time at his disposal, and much more complexity in his approach, hardly came within hailing distance of Donizetti when, in *Die Schweigsame Frau*, he tried the same subject.

Recording
R. Abbado / Mei, Lopardo, Allen, Bruson (RCA 1994)

Elektra

Music by Richard Strauss
Text by Hugo von Hofmannsthal (after Sophocles)
First performance: Dresden, 25 January 1909

In the royal palace of Mycenae, Princess Elektra is kept loveless and in rags in the courtyard, and is thought spiteful, if not mad, by the serving women. Left alone, she invokes the spirit of her father, Agamemnon, who years before was killed—with an axe—by her mother, Klytämnestra. Elektra looks forward obsessively to the day when Orest, her exiled brother, will return to avenge their father and slay their mother. (Her younger sister, Chrysothemis, complies with palace policy, hoping eventually to marry and have children.) Elektra confronts her cruel mother, who is haunted by evil dreams and omens, but relieved, even exultant, when news comes that her potentially dangerous son Orest is dead. Elektra resolves then to act alone, and is frantically digging for the axe that killed her father when Orest suddenly appears. In the classic tradition of Greek tragedy, she recognizes him only gradually, and they share a moment of tenderness before he enters the palace, kills their mother, and then, when their mother's lover Aegisth approaches, kills him as well. Elektra, hearing the screams from within the palace, dances in manic ecstasy till she falls dead in the courtyard.

♣

A starker and ultimately more compelling work than the earlier *Salome*, *Elektra* is Sophocles informed by Freud, heightened by Hofmannsthal, and set to music of almost intolerable savagery. Only the heaviest voices can ride the crest of a vast orchestra worked to its utmost capacity. Strauss, conducting, may have said "Louder, louder, I can still hear the singers!", but, while the glittering *Salome* has begun to fade, *Elektra*, for all its overstatement, can in a great performance touch the soul with something like a Greek catharsis.

Recording

Solti / Nilsson, Collier, Resnik, Stolze, Krause
(Decca/London 1966)

L'Elisir d'Amore

(The Elixir of Love)
Music by Gaetano Donizetti
Text by Felice Romani (after Eugène Scribe)
First performance: Milan, 12 May 1832

ACT I

In an Italian village, Adina, rich and pretty, reads the story of Tristan and Isolde while Nemorino, poor and shy, despairs of ever winning her love ("Quanto è bella"), and when the swaggering Sergeant Belcore sets his cap for her, she tells the doting boy she can never love him ("Chiedi all'aura"). As luck would have it, the spectacular quack Dr. Dulcamara arrives selling panaceas, and Nemorino hopefully buys, and drinks, the very elixir that, he is told, once made Tristan irresistibly attractive to Isolde. But the potion will take effect only in twenty-four hours (enough time for the doctor to hightail it out of town), and Nemorino, in desperation, learns that Adina is going to marry the sergeant that very day.

ACT II

As the wedding preparations get under way, Nemorino, encouraged by the sergeant, enlists in the army to get money for another bottle of elixir. And at last the potion seems to work, for the village girls, having heard that Nemorino has just inherited a fortune, cluster amorously around him. Nemorino is touched to see that Adina is affected by this ("Una furtiva lagrima"), and soon finds her falling in love with him (though neither of them knows anything of the money that is now his). Adina even buys back Nemorino's enlistment papers ("Prendi: per me sei libero"). So the wedding proceeds with a different bridegroom, the quack doctor does a roaring business selling elixirs, and the sergeant, equipped with a bottle, will probably do better next time.

♣

L'Elisir is perfection. Number after number is lovingly shaped by a theatrical sense that would be the envy of even the best Broadway composer-librettist team. Donizetti knows just when to deepen the comedy to telling effect, and Romani just how to keep the audience interested in watching a wealthy, pretty, literate girl realize that a boy who (she thinks) has nothing to offer is in fact the one who will offer her what she most needs—simple and adoring love.

Recording

Bonynge / Sutherland, Pavarotti, Cossa, Malas
(Decca/London 1979)

Die Entführung aus dem Serail

(The Abduction from the Seraglio)
Music by Wolfgang Amadeus Mozart
Text by Gottlieb Stephanie the younger
First performance: Vienna, 16 July 1782

ACT I

An overture in Turkish style (which was all the rage in Vienna in 1782) segues into . . .

. . . the song of Belmonte, a young Spanish nobleman, who has arrived at the seaside palace of Pasha Selim, ostensibly to offer architectural services but really to rescue his sweetheart, Constanze ("Hier soll ich dich denn sehen?"). The lady has been captured by pirates, along with her saucy maid Blondchen and Belmonte's saucier servant, Pedrillo. All three have been sold as slaves to the Pasha and—unluckily for Pedrillo, who is in love with Blondchen—the ladies are being kept in a seraglio.

The palace overseer, Osmin, picking figs in the garden, refuses Belmonte entry, dismissing him with the special disdain he reserves for foreigners. But Pedrillo slips out on the sly to assure Belmonte that Constanze has not been touched, and Belmonte assures Pedrillo that he has a ship ready for their escape. He tries to quell his beating heart ("O wie ängstlich") and hides when the Pasha arrives in a boat with Constanze. The Pasha, polite but formidable, hopes to win her heart rather than force her into submission, but she remains steadfastly faithful to the man she loves and still thinks is far across the sea ("Ach, ich liebte"). Unable to see his Constanze, the young "architect" nonetheless receives the Pasha's permission to enter the palace, though he has to push and shove his way, with the help of his plucky servant, past the obstinate Osmin.

ACT II

Inside the seraglio, Blondchen, English-born, wittily keeps the lustful Osmin at bay (he regards the English as fools to let their women go so fast and free). But Constanze is overwhelmed with sadness ("Traurigkeit") and resolutely tells the Pasha, when he gives her only one more day to submit, that he can torture her but she will remain constant ("Martern aller Arten"). Pedrillo drugs Osmin with wine (Duet: "Vivat Bacchus"), and the two pairs of lovers joyfully meet in the seraglio. The ladies are indignant that the men should even think they might have been unfaithful (Quartet: "Ach, Belmonte!"), but reconciliations lead to pledges of eternal fidelity.

ACT III

That night, Pedrillo, watching outside the palace, sings a Moorish song ("Im Mohrenland") as a signal that the coast is clear, but the four would-be escapees are caught by Osmin, who is overjoyed at the pleasant prospect of hanging them ("O, wie will ich triumphieren").

Brought before the Pasha, Belmonte, hoping for mercy, reveals that he is the son of the aristocratic Lostados. This seals his fate: the Pasha replies, "Your father, that barbarian, took away my beloved, my honor, and my fortune, and sent me into exile." Belmonte and Constanze are resigned to die nobly together (Duet: "Welch ein Geschick!"), but the Pasha has a magnanimous change of mind: "I detest your father too much to do as he does. Take your leave, take Constanze, and tell your father that you were in my power and that I have set you free." Osmin pleads with the Pasha to have all four Europeans burned, hanged, beheaded, impaled, drowned, and flayed, but the four leave in freedom, inviting the audience to ponder this tale of humane and generous forgiveness.

♣

Vienna's new emperor, Joseph II, noting with regret that his subjects wanted only Italian opera, established a company for the production of German-language works, and the long-familiar *Singspiel* (musical comedy with spoken dialogue) became the basis for a new, indigenous opera tradition. The twelve-year-old Mozart had already tried his hand at the *Singspiel* with the one-act *Bastien und Bastienne*. Fourteen years later, with *Die Entführung*, Mozart returned to the genre, armed with *opera seria* experience and determined not just to turn the heads of the Viennese, mad for all things Turkish, but also to raise the lowly *Singspiel* to new and unexpected heights. (We know much about the genesis of *Die Entführung* from the surviving correspondence between Mozart and his father, which is also filled with pleas from the young composer to be allowed to marry a girl named Constanze.)

Sir Thomas Beecham, the work's most eloquent interpreter, thought the finest parts of the score were "the ensemble pieces, of which the finale to the second act is the crown," but the most famous moment is Constanze's *opera seria* aria "Martern aller Arten," a triumphant, all-stops-out set piece in which four solo instruments defend the soprano from a fate worse than death, and she sends her voice spinning through some of the most difficult coloratura heroics in the repertory. It is a pivotal moment: never again could Mozart's operas be simply classified. He was out to forge from the traditions of separate genres new kinds of drama for the musical stage.

Mozart is almost certainly responsible as well for the surprising ending that turns the fearful Pasha (who only speaks in the opera) into a symbol of magnanimity and forgiveness, anticipating the sublime conclusion of *Figaro* and the central idea in *La Clemenza di Tito*. For all its lightheartedness, *Die Entführung* is a work of serious import and has about it something of the Enlightenment feeling that was to fill *The Magic Flute*.

Recording

Beecham / Marshall, Hollweg, Simoneau, Unger, Frick
(EMI/Angel 1956)

Eugene Onegin

Music and text by Peter Ilyich Tchaikovsky
(after Alexander Pushkin)
First performance: Moscow, 29 March 1879

Act I

On a country estate in nineteenth-century Russia, two young sisters, Tatiana and Olga, are visited by Olga's beau, Lensky, and his friend Eugene Onegin. The shy Tatiana is smitten with the sophisticated Onegin.

That night she pours out her heart to him in a letter declaring her love.

A few days later, Onegin quietly but condescendingly tells Tatiana that marriage is not for him and that she should be more circumspect about expressing her feelings. She is utterly humiliated.

Act II

At a name-day party for Tatiana, the bored Onegin openly flirts with Olga, and Lensky challenges him to a duel.

Beside a snowy river, Lensky bids farewell to his happiness. Onegin kills him in the duel.

Act III

Three years later, in an elegant St. Petersburg mansion, a world-weary Onegin sees Tatiana, now the Princess Gremin, and is told by her husband that she has brought him happiness beyond measure.

Now it is Onegin who, clinging to his one chance for happiness, has written a letter. Tatiana receives him, confesses that she still loves him, weeps for what might have been, but finally leaves him to his despair.

♣

Tchaikovsky's "Lyrical Scenes" from Pushkin depict the characters and situations with a tenderness and compassion far removed from the poet's cynical original. The composer had himself received a letter from a naive admirer who was in love with him, and had politely refused her. But eventually he married her for appearance's sake (he was homosexual) and, in the course of writing *Onegin*, was driven nearly to suicide. It is small wonder that in his hands Pushkin's ironic verses were made to express sympathetically the sufferings of lives thrown into torment by wrong decisions. Lensky's aria before the duel, full of pain, and that of Prince Gremin, in which Onegin is given a vision of a happiness that can never be his, reflect the composer's own moods as much as does Tatiana's extended "Letter Scene," a melodious and masterly depiction of a soul trembling with emotion. In Russia, *Eugene Onegin* has from its premiere been the most popular of all operas; in other countries it has finally conquered a public that once thought the composer's last three symphonies, much more extroverted works, the summit of his achievement.

Recording
Rostropovich / Vishnevskaya, Atlantov, Mazurok, Ognivtsev
(EMI/Angel 1970)

Falstaff

Music by Giuseppe Verdi
Text by Arrigo Boito (after Shakespeare)
First performance: Milan, 9 February 1893

ACT I

At the Garter Inn in Elizabethan Windsor, a furious Dr. Caius accuses the fat knight Falstaff of breaking into his house and wrecking his property. Unperturbed, the impecunious Falstaff sets his sights on the wives of the wealthy citizens Ford and Page. His lowlife sidekicks Bardolph and Pistol refuse to help him in his dishonorable enterprise, and he lectures them on honor ("L'Onore!"), then batters them with a broom.

In the garden of Ford's house, the merry wives of Ford and Page, with their sly factotum Mistress Quickly and Ford's young daughter Nannetta, plan to punish Falstaff for the amatory letters he has sent them. Unbeknownst to the four ladies, five men—Ford, Bardolph, Pistol, and the two rivals for Nannetta's hand, old Dr. Caius and young Fenton—are similarly conspiring. (At scattered intervals in the planning, Fenton and Nannetta steal brief moments of happiness together.)

ACT II

At the Garter Inn, Mistress Quickly invites Falstaff to visit Ford's wife "between two and three," when her husband is away. Soon after, Ford, launched on his own plot, comes to Falstaff disguised as a certain Mr. Brook, and pays him handsomely to seduce the woman he says he can't make any headway with—Mistress Ford. While Falstaff is primping, Ford wonders if he has already been cuckolded ("È sogno? o realtà?").

At Ford's house, Falstaff is wooing the wife when the husband arrives with a posse and with murderous intent. Falstaff hides in a laundry basket, and the ladies foil the gentlemen's plot by having the fat knight dumped unceremoniously out the window and into the Thames. (In the midst of all this, Fenton and Nannetta steal more moments of happiness and are detected by her angry father, who wants her to marry the wealthy Dr. Caius.)

ACT III

Outside the Garter Inn, a drenched Falstaff warms himself with mulled wine. Mistress Quickly comes to arrange another assignation with Ford's wife, this time in Windsor Forest, at Herne's Oak at midnight; to scare away anyone who might happen by and disrupt the tryst, Falstaff is told to come dressed as the "Black Hunter" who haunts the place. (This time, all the men and women are in on the plot to humble the fat knight.)

At Herne's Oak, the horned Falstaff is set upon by the others, dressed as sprites, until he repents of behavior unsuited to one of his age and girth. (The two lovers do not in this act have to snatch scattered moments together; in their fairy costumes they both get arias to sing.) Amid the disguises, Ford marries his daughter off, not to Dr. Caius as he thinks, but to Fenton. Ford is further confounded when he discovers that he has betrothed Dr. Caius to the red-nosed Bardolf. Falstaff leads them all in singing "All the world's a jest, and he who laughs last laughs best."

♣

Verdi, the composer of operatic tragedies, writes *finis* to his long career with a burst of laughter—set, *mirabile dictu*, to a fugue. *Falstaff* is the work of a man on the threshold of eighty, paradoxically filled with youth, with all his musical powers on the alert, returning to write one last opera "just for my own pleasure." But in fact the opera—kaleidoscopic, bubbly, and beautifully crafted—has given pleasure to many more people, once they have recovered from the shock it initially delivers. This is not the massive *Aida* or the impassioned *Otello*. This is a swift-flowing stream that crests for moments in bits of arias like those in *Traviata* and *Trovatore*, only to be swept along a moment later in a current as irresistible as the force of life itself. Verdi saw to it that his faithful librettist Boito fashioned a Falstaff who was not just the duped clown of Shakespeare's *The Merry Wives of Windsor* but also the more complex figure from the two *Henry IV* plays. At the end of the finished score, Verdi wrote an affectionate note, "Farewell, old John," to his last operatic character, a figure in whose human frailty and indomitability he was grateful to see something of himself.

The opera is a true ensemble piece, and yet Verdi not only individualizes the characters but shows real feeling for them. And every role is a singer's role: in the unlikely part of the blustering Ford, the young Lawrence Tibbett was catapulted to stardom. The work is also very much a conductor's opera, and it was largely through Toscanini's incomparable early performances that a somewhat bewildered public came to understand how, as Kenneth Clark said in another connection, an old, even a very old, man can add "something of immense value to the sum of human experience."

Recording

Toscanini / Nelli, Merriman, Stich-Randall, Elmo, Madasi,
Valdengo, Guarrera (RCA 1950)

La Fanciulla del West

(The Girl of the Golden West)
Music by Giacomo Puccini
Text by Guelfo Civinini and Carlo Zangarini (after David Belasco)
First performance: New York, 10 December 1910

ACT I

At the Polka Bar in the Cloudy Mountains of gold-rush California, Minnie the gun-toting bar owner rejects the advances of sheriff Jack Rance and falls for the handsome Dick Johnson. Meanwhile, the gold-miners, all of them at least a little in love with Minnie themselves, are on the look-out for the bandit Ramerrez.

ACT II

Johnson comes to Minnie's cabin and gives her her first kiss. Snowed in, he has to stay the night. Rance and some of the miners call at the door to tell Minnie that they have discovered from Johnson's half-breed mistress that he is actually the bandit they have been seeking. When they leave, Minnie orders Johnson out into the storm, where he is shot by the posse. Distraught, Minnie pulls him back inside the cabin and hides him in the loft. When Rance comes to investigate, Johnson's blood dripping from the rafters betrays his presence. Minnie in desperation agrees to marry Rance if he can beat her at cards; if not, Johnson must go free. She wins the wager by cheating on the last hand.

ACT III

Amid the great sequoias, Rance's men capture Johnson and are about to lynch him. He asks them not to tell Minnie of his fate ("Ch'ella mi creda libero"), but in a matter of minutes she rides in on horseback and, reminding the miners of all she has done for them, convinces them to let her start a new life with the man she loves, somewhere beyond California.

♣

The days are gone at last when Puccini's gold-rush opera seemed laughable to audiences accustomed to the "realism" of Hollywood Westerns. The opera can now be seen for what it is—a skillful blending of Debussyesque harmonies and Straussian sonorities in Puccini's ripest style, with a heroine who, for the first time in the composer's output, survives, and with the best of Puccini's familiar *morbidezza* reserved, not for the lovers, but for the desperately devoted, childlike miners.

Recording

Mehta / Neblett, Domingo, Milnes
(Deutsche Grammophon 1977)

Faust

Music by Charles Gounod
Text by Jules Barbier and Michel Carré (after Goethe)
First performance: Paris, 19 March 1859

Act I

An orchestral prelude depicts in quasi-fugal terms the intellectual labors of Faust, a world-weary polymath in sixteenth-century Germany. Then a rising scale on the harp transports the listener to Gounod's nineteenth-century world of sentimental melody.

The aged Faust, alone in his study as Easter dawns, is about to raise a cup of poison to his lips when his hand is stayed as he hears, first, the voices of young girls hymning the beauty of nature and then the song of young men following the lark to their fields, praising God. The very word "God" infuriates Faust and, cursing science, faith, youth, and love, he calls on Satan. Méphistophélès, the rogue among devils, promptly appears, gallantly dressed with sword and plume, and offers the old philosopher, in exchange for his soul, gold, glory, and power. Faust asks instead for the pleasures of youth and love ("A moi les plaisirs"). Mephisto conjures up a vision of the virginal Marguerite. Faust quickly signs over his soul and, miraculously rejuvenated, sets off with the demon in search of his new dreams.

At a beer-drinking German fair ("Vin ou bière"), Marguerite's brother Valentin, about to leave for the wars, entrusts his sister to the care of her youthful admirer, Siébel ("Avant de quitter ces lieux"). Wagner, a student, begins a song about a rat and is interrupted by Mephisto, who offers the crowd a better song, about the Golden Calf ("Le veau d'or"). For a moment, he casts a spell on the merrymakers. But Valentin knows that an evil power is at work when Mephisto predicts his death and sardonically toasts his sister with magically produced wine. When his blade shatters against an invisible circle Mephisto has described in the air, Valentin inverts his sword hilt to make the sign of the cross and leads the crowd in exorcizing the devil ("Chorale of the Swords"). But the devil is not down for long; he sets the whole crowd swirling to magical waltz rhythms ("Ainsi que la brise légère") and, in a quiet moment in the midst of the madness, arranges for Faust to offer his arm to Marguerite ("Ne permettrez-vous pas"). She politely declines.

Act II

That evening, in Marguerite's garden, young Siébel gathers flowers that, as the devil had predicted they would, fade at the touch of his hand—until he dips that hand in holy water ("Faites-lui mes aveux"). Faust is led by Mephisto to the enclosure, which so overwhelms him with its innocence ("Salut! demeure chaste et pure") that he has momentary qualms about the impending seduction. Mephisto produces a casket of jewels—a better gift, he wagers, than Siébel's flowers. Marguerite comes through the gate and sings an old ballad at her spinning wheel ("Il était un roi de Thulé"), thinking quietly about the handsome man she has just met. Then she finds the casket of jewels and, surprised at the feelings they prompt in her, bedecks herself ("The Jewel Song"). Mephisto, with some feelings of revulsion, forces his attentions on a gossipy old neighbor, Martha, so that Faust can walk with the shy Marguerite through the garden, which Mephisto has put under a spell (Duet: "Laisse-moi contempler ton visage" and "O nuit d'amour"). Marguerite, trembling on the brink, implores Faust to leave ("Ah partez!"), but the devil induces him to stay and listen to what she says from her window to the stars ("Il m'aime!"). Faust, aflame with passion, rushes into the house, while Mephisto, at last showing his sinister side, explodes in mocking laughter.

Act III

[Marguerite, abandoned by Faust and alone in her room, is taunted by village girls under her window. Her sorrow ("Il ne revient pas") is partially assuaged by the faithful Siébel ("Si le bonheur").]

Méphistophélès terrorizes Marguerite in church as she tries to pray. The choir thunders out a "Dies Irae." She falls in a faint.

Valentin returns from the wars with his fellow soldiers ("The Soldier's Chorus"), learns from Siébel of his sister's fall from grace, and is lured by a mocking Mephisto ("Vous qui faites l'endormie") into fighting a duel, in which he is killed by Faust. He curses Marguerite as he dies, and, while the villagers watch in horror, her mind gives way.

[On an abandoned night in the Harz Mountains, Méphistophélès tries to distract the guilt-ridden Faust by conjuring up the beautiful women of antiquity ("The Walpurgis Night Ballet"). In the midst of the revels, Faust seems to see Marguerite with a thin line of blood around her neck. He cries out in horror and demands to be taken to her.]

Marguerite is in prison, weak, mad, and condemned to death for the murder of her baby. Faust awakens her to memories of their past together (Duet: "Oui, c'est moi!"), but she repulses him when Méphistophélès appears, and, dying, implores heaven to help her (Trio: "Anges purs, anges radieux!"). "Damned!" the demon decrees as she falls lifeless to the ground. "Saved!" the angels proclaim in contradiction, and the prison cell is filled with an affirmation of mortal resurrection and rebirth.

♣

The music critic W. J. Henderson once told in chagrin the fanciful tale of a visitor wandering, eons hence, through the ruins of what was once New York City and asking what a certain noble edifice might have been. He is told that it was not the *Festspielhaus*, the "festival playhouse" as in Wagner's Bayreuth, but the famous *Faustspielhaus*—"the house where they played *Faust*"—endlessly. Gounod's piece suited exactly the expectations of generations of operagoers at the old Metropolitan.

This sweetly Gallic *Faust* does not compare in complexity and daring with Goethe's vast German drama, but then what operatic *Faust* does? Certainly not those of Berlioz, Boito, and Busoni, despite their individual touches of brilliance. Gounod, contrary to popular belief, has set to music virtually the whole of Goethe's *Ur-Faust*, the German's first thoughts on the subject. But his French chef d'oeuvre actually took its inception from Michel Carré's boulevard play, *Faust et Marguerite*, not from Goethe, and it was first conceived, not as the grand opera it was to become, but as an *opéra-comique*, a small-scaled bourgeois entertainment with spoken dialogue.

It was at the time a brave work, thought "difficult" and "German," and a pioneering work, refining and perhaps redefining Meyerbeer's till-then unchallenged grand-opera concept of what opera should be. In Marguerite, Gounod virtually created the species of soprano now known as lyric, and in Faust he substituted, possibly for the first time in France, tenorial lightness and sweetness in place of Meyerbeerian brawn. Thereafter the shadows of Marguerite's garden have cast their languid influence across the stage works of Bizet, Saint-Saëns, Massenet, Delibes, and Lalo, not to mention some of the instrumental music of Franck, Fauré, and d'Indy.

The score is a seemingly endless succession of melodies, all familiar, some (the Waltz and the Soldier's Chorus) perhaps too familiar, others (Siébel's two ariettes) far less familiar now than they were in generations past. Valentin's famous aria was first composed in London for the baritone Charles Santley who, in need of a display piece, suggested that Gounod adapt the sentimental melody in the prelude as an introductory aria for him. Gounod casts a remarkable spell in the long, luminously scored, impeccably paced scene in Marguerite's garden, where Faust's elegant cavatina (with its famous and fearfully exposed high C, a magical moment at the old Met for the young Giuseppe di Stefano) is followed by Marguerite's delicately tinted Gothic ballad and sparkling Jewel Song, by the skillful quartet in which a humorous seduction is interwoven with a serious one as the four characters make their way in and out of the shadows, by the love duet that until *Tristan* was thought the epitome of yearning eroticism, and above all by the ecstatic song of Marguerite at her window, singled out by Berlioz as the finest moment in the score. Elsewhere, the first meeting of Faust and Marguerite forecasts, in music that is a natural extension of the spoken word, the best of Massenet, while the solos of Méphistophélès are masterly bits of musical characterization, and the final trio one of the most effective pieces ever written for the stage.

On the other hand the popular ballet music, written ten years after the premiere to satisfy the requirements of the Paris Opéra, prolongs the opera unnecessarily and almost inevitably strikes a vulgar note. (It may in fact have been written by Delibes, whose name appears on one of the scores preserved in the Opéra archives, or by Saint-Saëns, who was approached by the Opéra to supply ballet music when Gounod initially refused to do so. The final orchestral measures were added by another hand as well, perhaps to accompany an onstage apotheosis for a production at the Opéra. *Faust* still awaits the kind of scholarly attention Offenbach's *Contes d'Hoffmann* has been given in recent years.)

After a rather precipitous drop in popularity in the 1960s, when audiences could no longer take Goethe's mythic situations as literally as Gounod asked them to do, and when the double standard in sexual morality was beginning to give way, *Faust* has, at the end of a century starved for melody, staged a surprising comeback. "You can beat it down," said one chagrined devotee of dissonance, "but it won't die!"

Recording

Rizzi / Gasdia, Mentzer, Hadley, Agache, Ramey (Teldec 1994)

Fidelio

Music by Ludwig van Beethoven
Text by Joseph Sonnleithner and Georg Friedrich Treitschke
First performance: Vienna, 20 November 1805

ACT I

A brisk overture with searing strings and urgent kettledrum beats conjures up the heroic world of the opera to follow.

In the courtyard of an eighteenth-century prison near Seville, Marzelline, the jailer's daughter, is pestered by her would-be suitor, Jaquino, when all she really wants is to marry Fidelio, a young man much more mature in his outlook who has come to work at the prison. Her father, Rocco, approves of the match (Quartet: "Mir ist so wunderbar"), but Fidelio shows more interest in hearing about the prisoner who has been kept in solitary and on starvation rations for two years.

The governor, Don Pizarro, inspects the daily post and is startled to read that the Minister of Justice has discovered his secret: among his prisoners are "victims of arbitrary oppression"; the Minister will arrive tomorrow to investigate. Pizarro decides to do away with the solitary prisoner while there is still time ("Ha! welch' ein Augenblick!"). Rocco refuses to kill him, and Pizarro, contemptuous of such weakness, tells the jailer simply to dig the grave below; he will descend to kill the prisoner himself. Fidelio overhears this in horror ("Abscheulicher!") and prays that heaven will strengthen him—or rather her, for young Fidelio is actually a woman, Leonore, who suspects that the prisoner in solitary may be her husband, Florestan. She has come in disguise to find him and rescue him if she can. She asks Rocco to let the prisoners out into the courtyard to feel the sun on their faces ("The Prisoner's Chorus"), but her Florestan is not among them. She then asks, and receives, permission from Rocco to accompany him to the prison depths when he descends to dig the solitary prisoner's grave.

ACT II

An orchestral introduction takes us through the terrifying depths of the prison, where a voice rings out, "God! What darkness here! And what a deadly silence!" It is Florestan, chained to the wall, a just man silenced in the springtime of his life ("In des Lebens Frühlingstagen"). Feverishly he seems to see Leonore coming like an angel to save him, but he faints away, his head buried in his hands. Leonore, descending with Rocco, is so moved at the sight of the prisoner that she resolves to risk everything to free him even if he turns out not to be her husband. When he revives, she recognizes him (but is not recognized herself) and offers him bread and wine. Pizarro appears, intent on doing away with the jailer and the "boy" when he is finished with the prisoner. He lunges at the defiant Florestan, and Leonore rushes between them, shouting "First kill his wife!" She holds Pizarro off with a pistol and at that moment, as if called forth by her courage, a trumpet above announces the arrival of the Minister. Pizarro rushes away, and Leonore and Florestan fall into each others' arms thanking God (Duet: "O namenlose Freude").

[The orchestra plays the greatest of the four overtures Beethoven wrote for this opera, the "Leonore" Overture No. 3.]

On the castle parade ground, a massive drawbridge is lowered, and the prisoners run into the arms of their families as the Minister, "a brother come to help his brothers," declares a general amnesty. Pizarro is led away to judgment, Leonore herself removes the chains from Florestan's hands, and all joyously sing the praises of the wife who has saved her husband.

♣

Fidelio is based on an actual incident from the Reign of Terror in France, and its subject had already been dramatized and set to music several times before Beethoven turned his hand to it. His opera may now be better known than ever before, after a century in which political prisoners have suffered so terribly. Famous performances of it have marked the moral history of Europe in this writer's lifetime. *Fidelio* has come to be music's supreme expression of the equality and brotherhood of all humankind, the loving interdependence of man and woman, the just providence of God, and above all, the resilience of the human spirit in the face of oppression and tyranny.

Musically, Beethoven's only opera seems craggy and, even after many revisions, unfinished. He makes ferocious demands on his singers and some of his instrumentalists, and moves in the course of the work from homely *Singspiel* (the early scenes between Marzelline and Jaquino) to music drama (Leonore's great aria) to melodrama (the grave-digging scene, where Leonore and Rocco speak over sinister music) to oratorio (the whole of the final scene).

Beethoven declared *Fidelio* dearer to his heart than any of his other works because composing it had caused him so much difficulty. But there are other reasons for its being intensely personal to him. There is a striking correspondence between the words of Florestan's cry of pain in the silence of his prison and the testament Beethoven wrote at Heiligenstadt when he realized that he was going deaf: "Submission, absolute submission to your fate—only this can make you capable of the sacrifice duty demands of you." *Fidelio*, with its emphasis on submission to suffering, marks a midpoint in what J. W. N. Sullivan calls Beethoven's spiritual development—between the early symphonies, where the composer finds the meaning of life "in spite of suffering" and the last piano sonatas and string quartets, where he finds that meaning "through suffering," accepted almost as a blessing.

The religious element in *Fidelio* has often been overlooked. While some commentators have thought the sounding of the trumpet at the moment of rescue a symbol of the trumpet of the Last Judgment, and the last scene an enactment of the day of Judgment, few have gone on to see in Leonore's bringing bread and wine to her imprisoned husband, and in his repeated thanks, a reenactment of the Eucharist (the word is Greek for "giving thanks"). Most touching of all is Leonore's decision to rescue the solitary prisoner even if he turns out *not* to be her husband: Jesus said that He would be merciful to those who gave food to the hungry and drink to the thirsty, and came to those in prison, even if they did *not* know that in doing so to the humblest human creature they were doing so to Him. "Again and again," says Ernest Newman, Beethoven "lifts us to a height from which we reevaluate not only all music, but all life, all emotion, and all thought."

Recording

Klemperer / Ludwig, Vickers, Frick, Berry, Crass
(EMI/Angel 1962)

La Fille du Régiment

(The Daughter of the Regiment)
Music by Gaetano Donizetti
Text by J.-F.-A. Bayard and J. H. Vernoy de Saint-Georges
First performance: Paris, 11 February 1840

ACT I

A flavorsome overture sends a Napoleonic regiment marching through the Tyrolean Alps.

The brave soldiers of the Twenty-first Regiment handily defend a Swiss village and the old Marquise of Birkenfeld, who lives in a nearby castle. Marie, an orphan girl brought up by the doting regiment and its jolly sergeant Sulpice (Duet: "Au bruit de la guerre"), has been saved from falling off an Alp by the handsome Swiss mountaineer Tonio. She leads the grateful regiment in a rousing round ("Écoutons, écoutons"). As it has long been understood that only a grenadier can marry Marie, the smitten Tonio enlists in the regiment ("Pour mon âme"). But the Marquise, claiming to be the girl's aunt, takes her away to what she considers a more suitable environment.

ACT II

Marie is bored at the castle, learning manners and minuets, affianced by the Marquise to the fatuous son of the Duchess of Krakenthorp, and cheered only by the temporary presence of Sulpice, with whom she sings rataplans. The other soldiers all but invade the castle to rescue her. Tonio is in fact prepared to elope with her—till the Marquise reluctantly reveals that Marie is her long-lost daughter, born out of wedlock. Marie feels that she cannot go against her own mother's wishes in the matter of marriage, but her attachment to her regimental "fathers" so moves the Marquise that she blesses the lovers' union, and all but the disgusted duke and his ridiculous mother join in a rousing "Salut à la France."

♣

Donizetti's tuneful French trifle has served sopranos from Jenny Lind through Adelina Patti to Lily Pons, who interpolated the "Marseillaise" during World War II performances, and Joan Sutherland, who gamely allowed her tenor, the young Luciano Pavarotti, to take the spotlight and earn his operatic spurs with nine exuberantly tossed off high Cs in "Pour mon âme" —an aria which had been cut from the score for generations.

Recording
Bonynge / Sutherland, Pavarotti (Decca/London 1967)

Die Fledermaus

(The Bat)
Music by Johann Strauss II
Text by Carl Haffner and Richard Genée
First performance: Vienna, 5 April 1874

ACT I

An exuberant overture runs through a few of the operetta's fifty or so familiar melodies.

Gabriel von Eisenstein, a rich Viennese gentleman involved in a bungled lawsuit, is convinced by his rascally friend Falke that he can postpone reporting to jail long enough to attend a party at the eccentric Prince Orlofsky's. Unbeknownst to him, his wife, Rosalinde, plans to attend the same party disguised as a Hungarian countess, and, unbeknownst to them both, their maid Adele will be there as Mlle. Olga. After Eisenstein leaves for the party, the prison governor, Frank, arrives, assumes that Alfred, a tenor who has been serenading Rosalinde, is her husband, and hauls him off to jail.

ACT II

At the party, Falke tells Prince Orlofsky that he has staged the whole evening as a farce, "The Bat's Revenge," to pay Eisenstein back for having humiliated him after a previous party, leaving him fast asleep in public in a bat's costume. In the course of the evening, with everyone in disguise, Eisenstein, all unaware, matches wits with his own maid and his own jailer and flirts with (and loses his watch to) his own wife—for Falke has invited them all. Everyone gets merrily and then sentimentally tipsy on champagne, and at six in the morning Eisenstein hurries off to report to jail.

ACT III

Virtually the entire cast ends up in jail for one reason or another, to the consternation of the besotted turnkey Frosch. Eisenstein is furious to think that his wife may have dallied with Alfred—only to have her produce the watch as proof of his own dallying. So "The Bat's Revenge" hurries to its conclusion: everyone forgives everyone else and blames what has happened on the champagne.

♣

A perennial New Year's Eve event at the Wiener Staatsoper and other great houses, *Fledermaus* is the most operatically stageworthy of all light entertainments—though Lehár's *The Merry Widow*, Offenbach's *Orpheus in the Underworld*, and Sullivan's *The Mikado* are rest-of-the-year contenders for that title. Through the first two acts at least, Strauss' *gemütlich* offering is a succession of melodies the like of which any composer would give his eyeteeth to have penned—and many have said as much. For the wide world, *Fledermaus* epitomizes the Vienna of Emperor Franz Joseph, and its haunting strain "Glücklich ist wer vergisst" ("Happy is he who forgets what can't be changed") is a lasting reminder of the gaiety that, we like to believe, once was. Another line from the libretto comments unexpectedly on the characters' peculiar problems: "Ha, welch ein Fest, welche Nacht voll Freud!" ("Oh, what a party, what a night full of Freud!").

Recording

Karajan / Gueden, Koth, Resnik, Kmentt, Zampieri, Berry, Wächter, with guest appearances by Nilsson, L. Price, Sutherland, Tebaldi, Welitsch, Berganza, Simionato, Björling, del Monaco, Bastianini, et al. (Decca/London 1960)

Der Fliegende Holländer
(The Flying Dutchman)
Music and text by Richard Wagner (after Heinrich Heine)
First performance: Dresden, 2 January 1843

ACT I

A stormy overture depicts the eternal sea that the Dutchman is doomed to sail and the love of Senta that finally redeems him.

A Norwegian ship is driven by a storm into a sheltering fjord. The Steersman falls asleep on watch ("Mit Gewitter und Sturm"), and another ship, with blood-red sails, draws up alongside; seven years have passed since it last reached land. Its ghostly captain, the Flying Dutchman—condemned, for a proud boast hurled in the face of a storm, to sail the seas until the day of Judgment—steps ashore. He will now be given another chance to find a love that will redeem him from his curse ("Die Frist ist um"). The Norwegian captain, Daland, is tempted by the Dutchman's store of treasure and offers him the hand of his daughter, Senta. The two ships sail under suddenly clear skies into port.

Act II

In port, Senta, spinning with the other girls beneath a picture of the Dutchman, obsessively tells his tale and declares that she is the woman who will save him. Her suitor Erik, a hunter, is convinced that some devil has taken possession of her. The Dutchman enters, looking exactly like the picture, and there is a moment of stunned shock as he and Senta realize that their fates are intertwined. Oblivious of her father's bourgeois concerns, the two pledge themselves eternally to each other.

Act III

In the harbor where the two ships are anchored side by side, the Norwegians' lusty chorus ("Steuermann, lass' die Wacht!") is answered by supernatural manifestations from the Dutchman's haunted craft, and the people flee in terror. Erik makes a last effort to save Senta, and the Dutchman, seeing her with another man, despairs and orders his crew to set sail. Senta, determined to save him from his eternal punishment, leaps into the sea. The haunted ship sinks, and the ghostly figures of the Dutchman and his redeeming woman appear, flying over the waters.

♣

The story of the Flying Dutchman, inspired perhaps by fanciful accounts of Vasco da Gama's voyages, by the ever-popular Faust story, and by the legend of the Wandering Jew, surfaced in the nineteenth century, along with the tales of Dracula and Frankenstein's monster, as if to prove that new myths could still emerge in an industrial age. Wagner's account of his first hearing the tale from sailors on a stormy sea voyage cannot be fully credited, but it was with *Der Fliegende Holländer* that he found himself, after three unsatisfactory starts, as a composer for the stage. It was the mythic element in the subject that fired his imagination. He flooded the tale with music that evokes the sea, and the figures of the Dutchman and Senta—the misunderstood hero and the redeeming woman, the romantic "stranger from nowhere" and the "eternal feminine"—became the pattern for virtually all of his subsequent pairs of lovers. Wagner originally thought of the opera in terms of one uninterrupted act, and some recent productions have found that the obsessed, single-minded opera gains in power thereby.

Recording
Keilberth / Varnay, Lustig, Traxel, Uhde, Weber
(Decca/London 1955)

La Forza del Destino
(The Force of Destiny)
Music by Giuseppe Verdi
Text by Francesco Maria Piave (after el Duque de Rivas)
First performance: St. Petersburg, 10 November 1862;
second version, Milan, 27 February 1869

Act I

An overture sends the repeated note of destiny in pursuit of themes associated with Don Alvaro and his lost Leonora.

In eighteenth-century Seville, Leonora di Vargas, an aristocratic lady, is about to elope with Alvaro, a prince of Spanish-Incan blood, when her father, who has disapproved of the match, surprises them. Alvaro, as a sign of good faith, throws his pistol away and it goes off, fatally wounding the old man, who dies cursing his daughter.

Leonora, separated from Alvaro in the ensuing flight, comes disguised as a boy to an inn at Hornachuelos, under the protection of the muleteer Trabuco. Don Carlo, Leonora's brother, intent on saving the family honor by hunting down and killing his sister and the man he regards as her half-breed lover, arrives at the same inn disguised as a student ("Son Pereda"). The perceptive gypsy girl Preziosilla sizes up the situation and takes the brother to bed, allowing the sister to escape.

Leonora reaches her final destination, the cliffed monastery of Our Lady of the Angels. After an initial rebuff by the rude Fra Melitone, she is recognized and kindly received by Padre Guardiano, who offers her sanctuary in a solitary hermitage farther up the cliff. The monks, unaware that the hermit is a woman, call down an anathema on anyone who violates the sanctuary, and Leonora joins them as they pray for the Virgin's protection ("La Vergine degli Angeli").

ACT II

Several years have passed. Don Alvaro, believing Leonora long since dead ("O tu che in seno agli angeli"), has achieved eminence as a soldier in Italy during the Wars of Austrian Succession. There he rescues a Spanish officer from a pack of brawlers. By a twist of fate, the rescued Spaniard is Don Carlo, Leonora's brother. The two men swear friendship, neither knowing who the other is.

Alvaro is seriously wounded in the Battle of Velletri, and, with death imminent, he entrusts some papers to Carlo (Duet: "Solenne in quest'ora"). Carlo, suspecting that his new friend might be the hated Alvaro, has his suspicions confirmed when he finds a portrait of Leonora among the papers. When the surgeon announces that Alvaro will live, Carlo exults that he can at last avenge his father's death and his sister's dishonor.

At a military encampment near Velletri, three more figures from Spain show up in Italy—Trabuco as a peddler, Preziosilla as a camp-follower, Fra Melitone as a blustering and unwelcome chaplain. [In the camp, Carlo challenges the recovered Alvaro to a duel. Alvaro refuses, protesting his innocence of any wrongdoing, but is moved to fight when he learns that Leonora is still alive and that Carlo intends to find her and kill her. In the first version of the opera, they fight a duel, and Alvaro thinks he has killed Carlo. In the second version, the two are separated by their fellow soldiers, and Alvaro decides to seek peace of mind in a monastery.]

ACT III

More years have passed. At the monastery of Our Lady of the Angels, Fra Melitone, returned to Spain from his chaplaincy abroad, grudgingly doles out soup to the poor and complains that they have been spoiled by "the good Padre Rafaele." Don Carlo, still on the track, demands entrance at the gate and calls for the beloved priest, rightly suspecting that he is Don Alvaro. Despite Alvaro's resistance, Carlo's insults have their effect (Duet: "Invano, Alvaro"), and the two rush from the monastery with drawn swords, each intent on killing the other.

At her lofty hermitage, Leonora has never, through all the intervening years, found peace ("Pace, pace, mio Dio!"). The pursuer and the pursued seek out this remote place for their duel, and Alvaro fells Carlo. The dying man calls for a priest, and Alvaro, having bloodied his hands, appeals to the unknown "hermit" to hear the confession. Leonora, shouting from within that she cannot, rings a bell to summon Padre Guardiano from the monastery below, and then, in one terrible moment, recognizes Alvaro and rushes past him to aid the man he has slain. Carlo, unforgiving to the last, fatally stabs his sister. [Alvaro (in the first version) is so overwhelmed by the force of destiny that he flings himself off the cliff, calling on heaven to annihilate the human race.] Alvaro (in the second version) is persuaded by Padre Guardiano to trust in heaven, where Leonora now awaits him.

♣

Only the first version, commissioned by and premiered in St. Petersburg, is true to the title of this opera that—after tracing the paths of its characters across the map of Europe for several years—finally explodes in terrible ironies: the Incan prince turned Byronic soldier turned humble priest violates, out of compassion, the sanctuary of the very woman he has been searching for, and thus brings down upon his head the anathema so massively intoned years before by the monks of the monastery where he has found refuge. Alvaro is destroyed by the very religion he has served. And his Leonora is killed by her vengeful brother, not only because the brother has sworn to save the family honor, but because the brother presumes that his sister and his enemy have been living in sin under the cover of religion. In the first version of *Forza*, it is a *destino*, a cruel fate, not a provident God, that directs the courses of human lives.

In the second version, premiered at La Scala six years later, Alvaro is persuaded by a wise old man of vibrant faith to find meaning in Christian forgiveness. Verdi may well have made the change after meeting Alessandro Manzoni, the wise old man of vibrant faith for whom he eventually wrote the *Requiem*. ("If mortal men could be adored," Verdi said, "I would have knelt before him.") The music in this second ending is very fine, and grows thematically out of what has gone before, but the drama does not. Until very recently the second ending has been favored. That may now be changing.

Forza has often been criticized as sprawling and incoherent. Yet Verdi called it his "opera made of ideas." Written for Russia, it is no more sprawling or incoherent than the great Russian novels and pageant operas that preceded and followed it. Like those pieces, it gives almost as much attention to the three commoners who survive the force of destiny as to the three aristocrats who are destroyed by it. And, like the *mélodrame à grand spectacle* newly arrived on French stages, it marks the end of the long reign of the unities of time, place, and action in European drama. It also attacks head-on the old certainties imposed by an inflexible social order and an unquestioned religion. It is, in short, what Verdi claimed it was.

Forza's music is as varied as its characters. That given the commoners is not always of the highest quality; that assigned to the nobility (listen to Rosa Ponselle's "La Vergine degli Angeli") is often surpassingly beautiful. But all of the music is throbbing with life, and that—the whole checkered play of life—is what Verdi was after in this remarkable work.

Recording

Gergiev / Gorchakova, Borodina, Grigorian, Putilin, Kit, Zastavny
(first version, Philips 1997)
Levine / Price, Cossotto, Domingo, Milnes, Giaiotti, Bacquier
(revised version, RCA 1976)

Four Saints in Three Acts

Music by Virgil Thomson
Text by Gertrude Stein
First performance: Hartford, 8 February 1934

Acts I–IV?

No operagoer need know anything in advance about the plot of *Four Saints in Three Acts*, an opera with four times four saints and something more or something less than three acts. It appears to take place in the sixteenth-century Spain of St. Teresa of Avila and St. Ignatius Loyola. Their mystical experiences (his famous "Pigeons on the grass alas" is his vision of the Holy Ghost), and the quasi-minstrel-show contributions of a Compère and Commère, lift the piece to unworldly realms where it signifies, if anything, the absolute craziness and sheer joy of commitment to religious life. Henry W. Simon calls it "wilfully naïve" and says with admirable frankness, "It closes with the only two lines I completely understand. Compère . . . announces: 'Last Act.' And the chorus answers loudly: 'Which is a fact.'"

❧

The opera's subtitle, "An Opera To Be Sung," was clearly chosen by design, as many operas of its period were unsingable, and Thomson wanted this one to be performed. The music is a charming mixture of hymn styles, with Southern Baptist predominating, and during the work's first run—on Broadway, with choreography by Frederick Ashton and John Houseman, it was performed, at the composer's insistence, by an all-black cast chosen largely from Harlem churches "for beauty of voice, clarity of enunciation, and fine carriage." Thomson was delighted by "their understanding of the work. They got the spirit of it, enjoyed its multiple meanings, even the obscurities." The opera is still performed with black singers, but fire laws no longer permit the use of Dadaesque cellophane scenery such as graced the original production.

Avant-garde in its day, *Four Saints* has scarcely dated at all, and may have pointed a path to the future—opera that depends less on plot and more on the communication of states of mind through theatrically inventive combinations of divergent (including non-Western) musical forms. It can also lay claim to being the best American opera, its only rival being *Porgy and Bess*, premiered the next year. The more conventional Gershwin work has gone on to conquer the world, whereas *Four Saints* can still draw uncomprehending and even scathing reviews on the rare occasions when it ventures abroad. An offended and presumably unchurched English critic called it, in a review filled with mistakes, "not only incoherent but irresponsible." On the other hand, Andrew Porter described it as "a wonderful vision of holiness rendered —not without jokes, not without wit—in transfigured American speech and transfigured American song."

Recording

Thomson / Robinson-Wayne, Matthews (RCA 1947, abridged)

Die Frau ohne Schatten

(The Woman Without a Shadow)
Music by Richard Strauss
Text by Hugo von Hofmannsthal
First performance: Vienna, 10 October 1919

ACT I

Keikobad, the father god of the Spirit World (who remains unseen throughout the opera), sends his Messenger down to the Middle World, to the Nurse of his translucent daughter, who has married the Emperor there: the beautiful Empress must be told that if she does not in three days cast a shadow (that is, conceive a child and so become fully human) she will be recalled to the Spirit World, and her Emperor will be turned to stone.

While the Emperor is away searching for the faithful falcon that first led him to his Empress twelve moons before, the Empress prevails upon her Nurse to take her further below, to the Lower World of suffering humans to find a woman willing to part with her shadow.

They arrive at the home of Barak, a selfless Dyer, who hopes to have children, and his unfulfilled Wife, who would gladly forego having them. The Nurse uses magic to separate the Dyer and his Wife that night, though the distant voices of watchmen are heard crying out to all the husbands and wives who lie in each others' arms, "Love one another."

ACT II

In the Lower World, the Empress feels sympathy both for the Dyer's Wife, who out of love for her husband resists the Nurse's offer to buy her shadow, and for the Dyer, who provides food for poor children and tenderly cares for his three malformed brothers.

In the Middle World, the Emperor is led by his guardian falcon ("Falke, Falke") to the realization that his Empress has been to the Lower World; he presumes that she has been unfaithful, and is tempted to kill her.

Similarly, in the Lower World, the Dyer is tempted by the malicious Nurse to kill his Wife; she even provides him with a sword. But the sword is magically snatched from his hand, and the earth opens and swallows both the Dyer and his Wife. The unseen Keikobad's power is at work.

Act III

The Dyer and his Wife repentantly seek each other beneath the earth ("Mir anvertraut"). A voice invites him, and then her, to mount a winding staircase.

Meanwhile, the Nurse and the Empress are magically drawn in a boat upward to Keikobad's kingdom, where the Messenger condemns the Nurse to wander the Lower World forever in punishment for her hatred of humankind, while the Empress is given a crucial test: if she drinks from a suddenly appearing spring, the shadow of the Dyer's Wife will be hers. But out of sympathy for the human suffering she has witnessed, she will not do so, even when she is given a vision of her Emperor gradually turning to stone. She says she is willing to die with him. At this overwhelming expression of selfless compassion for humanity, Keikobad floods the world with light, and the Empress casts the shadow that frees her Emperor from his imminent fate.

The two couples find each other by a cascading spring, as the voices of the children they will have sing a radiant epithalamium.

♣

The massive, four-hour, allegorical *Die Frau ohne Schatten* is Strauss' Wagnerian homage to Mozart's *The Magic Flute*, and to his dying day he claimed it was his favorite among his operas. The score is luxuriantly unMozartian—opulent, complex, sweeping, and full of fine effects, yet for a *Zauberoper* it is strangely lacking in magic, and for once Strauss gives his male characters the most memorable moments—the expansive but relatively simple melodies sung by the Emperor in the second act and the Dyer in the third.

Ultimately, the opera is loved by those who are convinced by Hofmannsthal's libretto and hated (not too strong a word) by those who are not. And yet the libretto makes a cogent statement of the spiritual belief that illuminates every text Hofmannsthal wrote for Strauss from *Der Rosenkavalier* onward—his theory of *das Allomatische*, the capacity of the selfless and loving individual to transform not just the lives but the natures of others who are less giving and less perceptive. That is the role played by the Marschallin and Arabella in their operas, and by both the Empress and the Dyer here. *Ariadne* too is about such transformations, as the librettist had patiently to explain to the composer.

The libretto for *Frau* borrows so profusely (and enigmatically) from world mythologies that Hofmannsthal wrote a novella to explain it. Clearly the opera is, on one level, about Austria after World War I—its troubled social strata and its need for children after a whole generation of young men had died in battle. But *au fond* this transcendent opera is a proclamation that a good man and a good woman can transform the fabric of others' lives. That is why Barak, the only character in the cast to have a name, is by profession a Dyer.

Recording
Solti / Varady, Behrens, Domingo, van Dam (Decca/London 1989)

Der Freischütz
(The Free-Shooter)
Music by Carl Maria von Weber
Text by Johann Friedrich Kind
First performance: Berlin, 18 June 1821

ACT I

An overture contrasts the sinister music of the devil's haunt, the Wolf's Glen, with the redeeming music of the heroine Agathe.

At a Bohemian inn, Max, a marksman, is unsuccessful in a shooting match, and Kuno, his employer, tells him that he is thereby disqualified from marrying his daughter, Agathe. The despairing Max is then induced by Kaspar, an invariably successful marksman who has secretly sold his soul to the devil, to meet him in the dreaded Wolf's Glen at midnight: under the devil's influence, Max will cast, as Kaspar has, seven bullets that, free of ballistic constraints, will always find their mark.

ACT II

Agathe—her brow injured by the sudden ominous fall of an ancestral painting—tells her cousin Ännchen that a hermit has warned her of impending danger. She worries about Max and prays for him ("Leise, leise"); then she is shocked to hear from him that he intends to visit the Wolf's Glen.

Within the Glen just before midnight, Kaspar rouses the voice of the devil Samiel and pleads with him to accept Max's soul in place of his. Then at midnight Max makes his way to the terrifying place, and the seven bullets are cast to seven supernatural manifestations. (Kaspar does not tell Max that Samiel always reserves the seventh bullet for himself.) The two marksmen drop fainting to the ground when, at the seventh of the forest horrors, Samiel appears!

ACT III

Max has used six of his seven bullets, and, victorious at every match, has more than won the right to wed his Agathe. She, with trust in heaven ("Und ob die Wolke"), has dreamed that she was a white dove shot by Max, but that when she fell to earth she was restored to her own form, and a black bird lay dead at her feet. The bridesmaids discover another omen: a box delivered by the florist contains, not the expected wedding bouquet, but a funeral wreath. They quickly fashion a new wreath from flowers blessed by the hermit.

At the shooting match, the taget chosen is a white dove. Max aims, and Agathe cries out to him not to shoot. As he fires, she falls down as if dead, but she has been protected by the hermit's wreath on her brow, and it is Kaspar who falls dead: claimed by the devil, he has received the seventh bullet. Max confesses that he and Kaspar have made a diabolical compact and is almost banished forever, but the hermit appears from the forest to intervene on his behalf: Max and Agathe will marry in another year.

♣

In the original *Gespensterbuch*, the Freischütz, the "marksman who shoots with bullets free of ballistic constraints," fatally shoots his fiancée and ends up in a madhouse. Several composers attempted relatively upbeat operas on the grim tale, but it was Weber who, with superior skill, fashioned it into the first German romantic opera, an instant success and eventually something of a national symbol. It exerted a strong influence on the early works of Wagner, who saw it as a child and often conducted it as a young adult.

In German-speaking lands, *Freischütz* still holds the stage, its Wolf's Glen scene a goosebumpy delight for generations of children. Elsewhere those aware of the work's importance in operatic history constantly lament its absence, and that of Weber's *Oberon* and *Euryanthe* as well, from the standard repertory, but the general public has failed to show much interest in any German romantic opera before Wagner. Myth is now regarded with awe, while folklore is often dismissed as kitsch. The loss is ours: Weber's score is a miracle.

Recording

C. Kleiber / Janowitz, Mathis, Schreier, Weikl, Adam
(Deutsche Grammophon 1973)

La Gioconda

Music by Amilcare Ponchielli
Text by Arrigo Boito, as "Tobia Gorrio" (after Victor Hugo)
First performance: Milan, 8 April 1876

ACT I: THE LION'S MOUTH

An overture pits the blind mother's "Rosary" theme against the mocking music associated with the evil Barnaba.

In the courtyard of the Doge's palace in Venice, Barnaba, a street singer who spies for the Inquisition, is unable to win the affections of Gioconda, another street singer, and tries to have her blind mother burned as a witch. But he is prevented from doing so by Enzo, a handsome Genoese exile, and by his lover, Laura, wife of the powerful Inquisitor, Alvise. Gioconda's mother (La Cieca) gratefully gives Laura a rosary. Barnaba has his revenge by dropping a denunciation of Enzo into "the Lion's Mouth," a stone slot reserved for Inquisitorial purposes.

ACT II: THE ROSARY

Aboard his ship, anchored in a Venetian lagoon, Enzo awaits an evening in the arms of Laura ("Cielo e mar"), but her husband's ship arrives soon after hers, cued by Barnaba, who has set the trap. Gioconda, who is also in love—ferociously—with Enzo, tries to kill Laura, but enables her to escape when she sees in her hand the rosary her blind mother had given her. Enzo, to forestall arrest by Alvise, sets fire to his ship.

ACT III: THE CA' D'ORO

In Venice's resplendent "House of Gold," Alvise entertains his guests with a ballet, "The Dance of the Hours," gloating that his unfaithful wife, whom he has forced to drink poison, is dying behind the scenes. But his plan is foiled: Gioconda, among the entertainers present, has provided a potion that only simulates death. Enzo, believing Laura dead, tries to stab the murderous Alvise and is arrested. Gioconda, overwrought, offers herself to Barnaba if he can contrive to set Enzo free.

ACT IV: THE ORFANO CANAL

Gioconda, through her street connections, has had the slumbering Laura brought to her dilapidated palazzo on a canal full of corpses, and has sent for

Enzo. She contemplates suicide ("Suicidio!"): out of love for Enzo she will enable him to escape with the woman he loves, while she herself must surrender to the lust of the despicable Barnaba. When the lovers have gratefully flown, and Barnaba arrives to claim his reward, Gioconda stabs herself. Barnaba tries to have the last word, shouting that he has drowned her mother (presumably in the Orfano canal), but Gioconda can no longer hear him.

❧

Still a warhorse in Italy and America, largely ignored elsewhere, *La Gioconda* has always had insistent admirers ready to defend its every preposterous plot twist and singers eternally grateful for its six starring roles à la Meyerbeer. Zinka Milanov's famously floated high B-flat in the first act has rightly been called "the stuff of which legends are made." And "The Dance of the Hours," despite numerous travesties, remains opera's best-known ballet music.

Recording

Previtali / Milanov, Elias, Amparan, di Stefano, Warren, Clabassi
(Decca/London 1957)

Giulio Cesare

(Julius Caesar)
Music by George Frideric Handel
Text by Nicola Francesco Haym
First performance: London, 20 February 1724

Act I

A quasi-fugal overture places the pyramids squarely in Handelian London.

Caesar, landing in Egypt, is presented with the severed head of his rival Pompey and turns away in grief. Pompey's wife and son (Cornelia and Sextus) swear revenge. Meanwhile, Egypt's regent Cleopatra allies herself with Roman Caesar against her own brother, Ptolemy, who is responsible for the atrocity. Caesar is wary of the devious Egyptians ("Va tacito"), and rightly so, for their general Achillas, smitten by the beauty of Pompey's widow, tells Ptolemy he will kill Caesar if he can have her as his reward. Pompey's son is conveniently imprisoned for defending his mother, and the hapless lady is placed in a harem on reserve for Achillas.

Act II

Cleopatra, disguised, sets her cap for Caesar ("V'adoro, pupille"), but he is called away to quell an insurrection, and later is reported to have been drowned. Ptolemy, despite the promise he made to Achillas, tries without success to force Pompey's widow to his lust ("Si, spietata").

Act III

Ptolemy's armies are victorious against Caesar's, though Achillas is mortally wounded in the battle. Cleopatra is taken prisoner ("Piangerò la sorte mia"), but Caesar, who has swum to safety, reappears with reinforcements to save her. Ptolemy is justly dispatched by Pompey's son, Cleopatra is crowned queen, and a *pax Romana* is bestowed on troubled Egypt.

❧

Giulio Cesare is seldom referred to by its original title, *Giulio Cesare in Egitto* (Julius Caesar in Egypt), but the longer title is a clearer index to its content, for Handel's opera limits itself to the events later dramatized in Shaw's *Caesar and Cleopatra* and never touches on those Shakespeare made into his *Julius Caesar*. (The summary given here outlines only the most important of the many plot developments in this pseudohistorical, eminently baroque opera.)

Giulio Cesare, in which both Caesar and Ptolemy were originally sung by castrati, exists in a number of versions, boasts a plenitude of splendid (if protracted) arias for soprano, alto, bass, and—today—countertenor, and has effectively spearheaded the Handel revival of the late twentieth century. But it seems only a matter of time till such still finer Handel pieces as *Tamerlano*, *Alcina*, and *Semele* (not to mention some of the great oratorios now successfully staged as operas) surpass it in public acceptance. Meanwhile, long live *Giulio Cesare*!

Recording

Jacobs / Schlick, Rorholm, Larmore, Fink, Ragin
(Harmonia Mundi 1991)

Hansel and Gretel

Music by Engelbert Humperdinck
Text by Adelheid Wette (after the Brothers Grimm)
First performance: Weimar, 23 December 1893

ACT I

An overture patterned after that of *Die Meistersinger* sets the mood for this German fairy tale.

In their poor cottage, Hansel and Gretel accidentally break the pitcher and spill the milk, and are sent by their angry mother into the forest to look for food. Their father, returning from a successful day selling brooms, is appalled: there is a Witch in the forest who lures children into her cottage and bakes them into gingerbread. The parents hurry off to find their little boy and girl.

Picking berries in the forest, Hansel and Gretel lose their way. The Sandman strews sand in their eyes, and they kneel to say their night prayers. The fourteen angels in their prayer descend to protect them as they fall asleep.

ACT II

The next morning the Dew Fairy washes the sand from the children's eyes, and they wake to see a gingerbread house with a fence made of gingerbread people. Desperately hungry, they nibble at the house, and the Witch appears. She immobilizes Hansel with a magic spell, puts him in a cage, and sets Gretel to fattening him up. But the resourceful girl uses the Witch's wand to free her brother, and the two of them push the Witch into her own oven. The oven explodes, and Hansel and Gretel find themselves surrounded by all the children who had formed the gingerbread fence, still bound by the Witch's spell and softly calling, "Oh, touch me, let me wake." As Hansel and Gretel touch each figure, a child is set free. Their parents arrive and view the scene with wonder. Two boys triumphantly pull the Witch from the oven's remains; she has been baked into gingerbread herself. The father then leads all the children in the prayer his own children sang, now equipped with the moral: "When past bearing is our grief, God the Lord will send relief."

♣

Humperdinck's sister, Adelheid Wette, first wrote the libretto of *Hänsel und Gretel* for her own children to perform, and in expanding it to operatic length, the composer, one of Wagner's assistants at Bayreuth, affectionately blended the Master's style with familiar nursery songs from the *Knaben Wunderhorn* collection. Children love *Hansel and Gretel* for the story (chock-full of fairy-tale archetypes) and for the tunes they, if they were lucky, first learned in kindergarten. Their parents, if they know their Wagner, will spot amusing references to *Parsifal* and the *Ring*, and perhaps too they will fight to keep the tears back at the moment when human contact sets all the gingerbread children free. Operagoers will know that the role of the Witch has sometimes been used by operatic ladies to spoof the mannerisms of other operatic ladies. *Hansel and Gretel* spread quickly around a world weary of verismo violence, and was the first opera to be broadcast complete from the Metropolitan Opera stage, on Christmas Day, 1931.

Recording
Pritchard / Cotrubas, von Stade, Söderström, Te Kanawa, Ludwig, Nimsgern (CBS/Sony 1978)

Les Huguenots
Music by Giacomo Meyerbeer
Text by Eugène Scribe and Émile Deschamps
First performance: Paris, 29 February 1836

Act I
A prelude built upon the Protestant chorale "A Mighty Fortress Is Our God" introduces this story of religious strife.

In 1572, in Touraine, the Huguenot Raoul is lavishly entertained by the pleasure-loving Catholic nobleman Nevers, while Marcel, Raoul's crusty retainer, sings about blowing papist heads off. The young Huguenot tells the assemblage that he has fallen in love with an unknown lady he has rescued from danger—and then he is shocked when he sees that very lady meet Nevers secretly in his garden. He assumes she is Nevers' mistress, but she is in fact Valentine St. Bris, a Catholic who is affianced to Nevers. She has come to ask him to release her from her promise, which he reluctantly does. Meanwhile Raoul receives from the page boy Urbain an anonymous note requesting him to meet another lady; he is to follow Urbain blindfolded.

ACT II

Raoul is taken to the streamside garden of the royal chateau of Chenon-ceaux, into the presence of the Queen, Marguerite de Valois. Graciously she calls the most influential Catholics and Huguenots together, hoping to end the hatred between them by uniting Raoul and Valentine. But Raoul can only think of Valentine as Nevers' mistress and publicly refuses to marry her. The Catholic party is deeply offended, but the Queen forbids any violence.

ACT III

At the Pré-aux-Clercs in Paris, Valentine, at her father's insistence, is mar-ried to Nevers. Her father is now determined to kill Raoul, but the attempt to ambush him is foiled when Valentine gets a warning to him through his servant Marcel. Further violence between Huguenot soldiers and Catholic students is prevented when the Queen comes riding in on horseback. Raoul finally realizes that he has misjudged Valentine—just as she is ceremoniously conveyed down the Seine, married to another.

ACT IV

On St. Bartholomew's Eve, Raoul comes desperately to Nevers' palace to see Valentine, and has to hide behind a curtain as her father enters with his fellow Catholics. There Raoul overhears the Catholic plan, ordered by Cath-erine de Medici, to massacre all the Huguenots in the city that night. Valen-tine, revealing her love for Raoul, keeps him from rushing out into the slaugh-ter, but when the tocsin sounds he leaps out the window and is shot dead.

ACT V

[In the longer version, Raoul is not shot when he leaps, but rushes to warn his fellow Huguenots—and to marry Valentine when Nevers is killed. She converts to his faith, and Marcel blesses their union, while a terrible scene of carnage rages in the church behind them. Then the three are hauled off to a Paris quay, where they are shot by a pack of soldiers led by, ironically, Valentine's father. This time the Queen is unable to stop the slaughter, which continues its course as the curtain falls.]

♣

Les Huguenots, a sensation at its 1836 premiere at the Paris Opéra, was cho-sen in 1842 to open the current house at Covent Garden, and, with its seven starring roles, it ran up more performances in the first years of the old Met-ropolitan than any other opera. (Three other pieces by Meyerbeer—*Robert le*

Diable, *Le Prophète*, and *L'Africaine*—were almost as popular.) In the early years of the twentieth century the Metropolitan charged a then outrageous seven-dollar top for a *Huguenots* "night of the seven stars." In London and New York, predominantly Protestant cities, Meyerbeer's operas, which invariably cast Catholics as the villains, didn't have the same *épater-la-bourgeoisie* effect they had in Paris. But there was spectacle enough to sell out houses night after night.

No opera exemplifies so well as *Les Huguenots* the French grand opera that the nineteenth-century public considered, despite the much finer work of Verdi and Wagner, the ultimate operatic experience. And no opera so quickly plummeted out of sight after World War I. *Les Huguenots* has not been done at the Metropolitan since 1914. A brilliantly cast 1962 revival at La Scala, in Italian, did not restore the work to permanent favor. Yet there is always the chance that, if seven starry voices come along at the same time . . .

Les Huguenots boasts a famous aria in the Queen's "O beau pays" and a fourth act that, with its "Consecration of the Swords" and frenetic love duet, is riveting enough to have impressed even that notorious Francophobe, Richard Wagner. On the other hand, the opera opens with a religious prelude that, in Ethan Mordden's words, "has to be heard not to be believed," and finds room in a long evening for nude bathers at Chenonceaux (with the page boy as peeping Tom), a nun's Ave Maria chorus and two irrelevant gypsy ballets in the Pré-aux-Clercs, more nuns (to supply soprano and alto parts) at the plotting of the massacre, further ballet divertissements in the often-cut fifth act, and at least one climactic massacre too many. Wagner perceptively called Meyerbeer's operas "effects without causes." They were Hollywood spectacles before Hollywood. But *Les Huguenots*, the best of them, will always have Paris—and that impassioned Act IV duet.

Recording

Gavazzeni / Sutherland, Simionato, Cossotto, Corelli, Ganzarolli, Tozzi, Ghiaurov (Melodram 1962, in Italian)

Idomeneo

Music by Wolfgang Amadeus Mozart
Text by Giambattista Varesco (after Antoine Danchet)
First performance: Munich, 29 January 1781

ACT I

An overture, one of the earliest instances of seascape music, also provides one of the earliest instances in opera of thematic reminiscence: a five-note descending figure, possibly associated with nature's cruelty, will recur in many guises in the opera to follow.

The Trojan princess Ilia, a captive in Crete, is tenderly treated by the young prince Idamante and regarded with jealous fury by Elettra, the visiting Greek princess. Idomeneo, the Cretan king, who has been away for ten years fighting in the Trojan War, survives a shipwreck off his own coast. But he is devastated when Idamante, his son, comes first to his aid, for in the midst of the storm he had vowed to Neptune that, if saved, he would sacrifice the first living thing he would meet on shore.

ACT II

Ilia has found in Idomeneo a father to replace the one she lost at Troy ("Se il padre perdei"), but Idomeneo has not fulfilled the vow he made to Neptune ("Fuor del mar"), or even told his people about it. On the advice of his counselor, Arbace, he decides to send his son safely out of the kingdom: Idamante will take Elettra back to Greece. The ship is about to sail ("Placido è il mar") when Neptune, demanding payment, sends a sea monster to stop the voyage and terrorize the island of Crete.

ACT III

Ilia asks the breezes ("Zeffiretti lusinghieri") to tell Idamante of her love. Elettra can hardly contain her jealousy. Idamante, hurt that his father treats him so strangely, resolves to slay the sea monster or be slain himself (Quartet: "Andrò ramingo e solo"). Idomeneo finally reveals to his angered and uncomprehending populace that the victim Neptune requires is his own son (Chorus: "O voto tremendo"). Idamante, having killed the monster, willingly bows his head to his father's sword, but Ilia rushes forth to die in his place. Suddenly the god Neptune, moved by the nobility of the two young people, decrees through his oracle that Idamante will henceforth rule instead of his father. Elettra is driven mad by this turn of events, attacked by the same furies that had destroyed her brother Orestes ("D'Oreste, d'Aiace"). Idomeneo welcomes the return of peace to the kingdom that his son will now rule ("Torna la pace").

♣

Idomeneo, Re di Creta, restored to popularity in the last quarter of the twentieth century, was the young Mozart's brilliantly successful attempt to restructure the genre he was invited, on commission from the Elector of Munich, to compose in—*opera seria*. A remarkable sense of musical continuity prevails from the very start: the overture segues into the first aria, and that aria melts into the first recitative. There is in addition an embryonic use of what later came to be called leitmotifs—beginning, again, with the overture. And throughout the opera, ensembles and choruses assume the roles that in older *opere serie* were given to lengthy and undramatic *da capo* arias. The arias in *Idomeneo* are considerably shorter than those of, say, Handel, and rank among the finest in all of Mozart's output. Finally, Mozart was writing for what was thought in 1781 to be the best orchestra in the world, the Mannheim ensemble, and his orchestration throughout is of a wholly new loveliness.

All the same, there are problems. The opening situation (reminiscent of that in Verdi's *Aida*) is never developed dramatically. Ilia's intervention in Act III, which should be the high point of the action (as a similar situation is in Beethoven's *Fidelio*), is rendered only in recitative. The work is unconscionably long, and two of the best numbers, which come late in the evening, Mozart was persuaded to cut for the premiere; the deplorable tradition of continuing these cuts continues, when a common-sense overview of the score would dictate that any cuts to be made should come from the closing ballet and from the still-tentative and somewhat Gluckian first act.

We know from Mozart's widow that to the end he loved *Idomeneo* most of all his works for the stage, perhaps because it marked his full emergence, at the age of twenty-five, as a mature man and composer. The opera's subject, a symbolic story in which a young man remains unquestioningly faithful to his demanding father and eventually reaches the fullness of his manhood, must have appealed to Mozart strongly. There were personal reasons as well for his choosing, ten years later, the subject of his other great *opera seria*, *La Clemenza di Tito*. In both works, Mozart deals with subjects from antiquity, not with the baroque pomposity they had been given in the previous hundred years, but with tenderness, personal feeling, unfailing taste, and striking originality.

Recording
Pritchard / Popp, Gruberova, Baltsa, Pavarotti, Nucci
(Decca/London 1983)

L'Incoronazione di Poppea

(The Coronation of Poppea)
Music by Claudio Monteverdi
Text by Giovanni Francesco Busenello
First performance: Venice, 1642

ACT I

[Cupid tells Fortune and Virtue that he is king of the world, as the following drama will prove.]

The Roman emperor Nero enjoys a night of lovemaking with the beautiful and ambitious Poppea while her husband, Otho, fumes outside. Poppea's nurse Arnalta tells her that she is courting disaster. Nero's humiliated wife, Octavia, is advised by the philosopher Seneca to take refuge in Stoicism. Seneca is less successful in advising Nero: the emperor's anger is aroused, and Poppea suggests that he put Seneca to death. She then dismisses her husband, the last obstacle on her way to the throne. He, near despair, transfers his affections to the loving Drusilla (though Poppea still rules his heart).

ACT II

Seneca, to the sorrow of his followers, follows Nero's orders and opens his veins in his bath. In other parts of Rome, Octavia's page boy and maidservant engage in amorous dalliance, and Nero and the poet Lucan drunkenly celebrate Seneca's death. Octavia convinces Otho that the only way to restore his honor is to assassinate Poppea. That almost happens: when Poppea has been lulled to sleep by the faithful Arnalta ("Oblivion soave"), Otho steals into her room dressed in Drusilla's cloak. But Cupid stays his hand.

ACT III

Nero banishes Otho and Drusilla for attempted murder, sends Octavia into exile, and crowns Poppea. [Cupid too is crowned king of the world by his adoring mother, Venus, and] Nero and Poppea surrender to sensuous love ("Pur ti miro").

♣

Poppea, written when Monteverdi was seventy-five, is generally thought his finest opera, and in recent years, as interest in baroque music has grown, it has all but established itself as the oldest opera in the standard repertory. But as all we have of it today are two manuscripts, divergent and in various hands, in which the vocal parts are accompanied by only three or four instrumental voices and a single bass line, the opera has had to be performed in various reconstructions, some of them decidedly overwrought, and musicologists have recently concluded that the original was a collaborative work, perhaps assembled under Monteverdi's supervision. The opening pages are certainly by his pupil Cavalli, whose own operas have, after a silence of three centuries, recently made their way back to the stage. Critical opinion would also deny Monteverdi authorship of "Pur ti miro," one of the score's finest pages. In any case, and under any reconstruction, *Poppea*, perhaps the first opera to deal with history instead of myth, is in many ways strikingly modern and in performance seems, like an ode of Horace, to have defied the flight of time.

Recording

Harnoncourt / Donath, Söderström, Esswood, Berberian, Lucciardi
(Teldec 1974)

L'Italiana in Algeri

(The Italian Girl in Algiers)
Music by Gioachino Rossini
Text by Angelo Anelli and Luigi Mosca
First performance: Venice, 22 May 1813

ACT I

An overture of dynamic contrasts and witty accelerating crescendos establishes the bubbly mood of the opera.

Mustafà, the Bey of Algiers, has tired of his wife, Elvira, and wants to pass her off on Lindoro, an enslaved Italian. As luck would have it, Lindoro's own beloved, Isabella, is washed up on the Algerian shore. She is just the spunky Italian type Mustafà has been waiting for, even though she has an unlikely suitor, the hapless Taddeo, following her. Isabella quickly demands that Lindoro be assigned to her as a personal slave. The five characters line up at the footlights, along with the Bey's captain and his wife's confidante, to proclaim in song that the situation is driving them crazy (Septet: "Sento un fremito").

ACT II

Isabella decides to show Elvira how to handle her man, and there follows a series of incidents in which the Bey is bamboozled, climaxing in his observing the bogus ritual of the "Pappataci," during which the Italians—including Taddeo—are able to sail away. Mustafà, suitably chastened, begs the pardon of his Elvira and swears off all Italian women henceforth.

♣

L'Italiana is a decidedly lightweight evening in the theater, but a thrilling one if a fiery mezzo coloratura is singing—and in recent decades we have had quite a few of those. With lyric cavatinas, patter songs, and the patriotic sentiments expressed in Isabella's arias (Italy was occupied by Napoleonic forces at the time), Rossini achieves something of that blending of *opera buffa* and *opera seria* that was the special achievement of Mozart, and the opera's success prompted Rossini to pen, a year later, a kind of "Italian Girl in Algiers" in reverse—"The Turkish Man in Italy," in some ways an even more Mozartian work. But the highlight of *L'Italiana*, the deliciously cock-a-hoop septet at the end of Act I, is the sort of thing only Rossini could compose.

Recording

Scimone / Battle, Horne, Palacio, Ramey, Trimarchi (Erato 1980)

Jenůfa

Music and text by Leoš Janáček
First performance: Brno, 21 January 1904

ACT I

As the mill wheel turns in a Moravian village, Jenůfa, a girl with a beautiful face, awaits the return of her cousin Števa, who has got her with child, while Števa's jealous and dispossessed half-brother Laca cuts a whip-handle with his knife. Števa arrives with a group of rowdies (the mayor has rigged it so that he will not be conscripted) and drinks himself into a stupor. Jenůfa's stepmother, the Kostelnička (sextoness), unaware of the girl's pregnancy, forbids her marriage to Števa until he proves he can stay sober for one year. The loveless Laca, left alone with Jenůfa, accidentally or on purpose slashes her face with his knife.

ACT II

In the midst of winter, Jenůfa has, unknown to the villagers, given birth to a son, and the Kostelnička, unable to persuade Števa to marry her stepdaughter (he cannot abide her disfigured face), appeals to Laca, assuring him that the baby died at birth. The rest of her plan is horrifying: she gives Jenůfa a heavy sleeping potion, and then takes the baby and rushes out to drown it in the river. When Jenůfa awakes, the Kostelnička tells the girl that she has lain in a fever for two days, during which time her baby has died. Jenůfa is comforted by the repentant Laca, who earnestly offers to marry her. The Kostelnička, almost maddened by what she has done, is terrified when the winter wind, like a presentiment of death, blows open the shutters.

ACT III

As winter ends, Jenůfa is about to marry Laca, and the Kostelnička is raising her hands to bless the couple, when the boy Jano rushes in to say that an infant's body has been found beneath the frozen mill stream. Everyone turns on Jenůfa, but the Kostelnička confesses that she is the guilty one, and allows herself to be led away to justice. Jenůfa, understanding why Števa, Laca, and her stepmother have acted as they have, forgives them all. Laca, left alone with Jenůfa, assures her that he will spend his life making up for what he has done to her, and Jenůfa, her forgiveness blossoming into love, is reborn.

♣

There is hardly a composer for the stage who has written such effective curtain scenes as has Janáček, and perhaps there is no scene anywhere in opera with so great a wash of human feeling as the ending of *Jenůfa*. Yet the work, like all of the composer's output, has been slow to find its way in the world. When Ernest Newman first saw it, splendidly cast, at the Metropolitan in 1924, he called the characters absurd and the music the work of a man only a cut above the amateur. And even today audiences, however moved they may be by the drama, can find the music spiky and idiosyncratic, the vocal lines supported by an orchestra that seems endlessly to repeat brief phrases that somehow refuse to stay in the memory. Actually, the music, both orchestral and vocal, is constructed from Czech speech rhythms, using the idiom of, but not actual quotations from, folk music, and all the works of Janáček (including the increasingly popular *Kátya Kabanová*, *The Cunning Little Vixen*, and *The Makropoulos Case*) come to life when sung in their own tongue. But perhaps what most needs to be said about the strikingly original work of Janáček is that, unlike other opera composers, who attempt to dramatize their characters' inner feelings, he seems, Godlike, to be lavishing pity on his characters from without. One of his oft-quoted sayings is "In every person there is a little spark of God." Nothing in opera is quite like his works, and *Jenůfa* is perhaps the best of them.

Early editions of *Jenůfa* were variously cut, adapted, and translated by friend and foe alike. Since the 1980s these have been superseded by the scholarly and influential editions of Charles Mackerras.

Recording

Mackerras / Söderström, Randová, Ochman, Dvorsky
(Decca/London 1982)

Lohengrin

Music and text by Richard Wagner
First performance: Weimar, 28 August 1850

ACT I

An ethereal orchestral prelude depicts, in Wagner's own description, the clear blue expanses of the sky (divided string choirs) from which the Holy Grail (imposing brass chords) descends and gives its benediction to a Christian knight consecrated to its service.

Henry the Fowler, the tenth-century king of the Germans, comes to Brabant with his herald and his army to gather additional forces for the defense of his states against the Hungarians, and finds the northern duchy torn by dissent. Gottfried, the boy heir to the throne, has disappeared, and Count Telramund has accused the child's older sister, Elsa, of murdering him. Elsa, called before the King, says that she will be vindicated by a knight in shining armor, who has appeared to her in a dream ("Einsam in trüben Tagen"). A summons is issued to the four winds, and the knight appears, sailing up the Scheldt in a little boat drawn by a white swan. He bids a tender farewell to the swan and declares to the King that he will champion Elsa's cause and marry her if she will never ask his name, or his calling, or where he comes from. She consents, and the shining knight defeats Telramund in combat but spares his life. The people rally in support of Elsa.

ACT II

Telramund's pagan wife, Ortrud, with her own ancestral claim to the throne, plans revenge: she will sow doubts in Elsa's mind about the strange promise she has made to the champion who will not reveal his name. Meanwhile, Telramund secures the support of four disaffected nobles. The two schemers interrupt Elsa's bridal procession, hurling their intimidating charges. The knight declares that he is answerable only to Elsa. Elsa has a fatal moment of doubt.

ACT III

A jubilant orchestral prelude celebrates Elsa's wedding to her knight, and the newlyweds are ceremoniously escorted ("Treulich geführt," the so-called "Wedding March") to their bedchamber. Left alone, they share an intimate love duet, but Elsa—with doubts crowding in on her, and driven by an almost hallucinatory vision of the swan reappearing to take her husband away—asks the forbidden question. At that very moment Telramund and his four silent followers enter with drawn swords. The knight quickly slays his enemy, and then tells Elsa he must now leave her forever.

Before the combined German-Brabantian forces, the knight announces that he cannot, as the King had hoped, lead them into battle; his name is Lohengrin, and now that his identity is known he must return to his father, Parsifal, and the Grail he serves ("In fernem Land"). The swan reappears on the river, and Ortrud in triumph recognizes, from the pendant around its neck, that the swan is the long-lost Gottfried, whom she had made disappear. Quickly Lohengrin kneels in prayer, and the swan sinks into the waves and rises again, now as young Gottfried, sent to lead the pan-German crusade in Lohengrin's stead. Ortrud cries out in defeat, and Elsa sees her knight fade from view, drawn away by the sacred dove that yearly renews the Grail's power. She dies in her young brother's arms.

♣

Lohengrin is the last opera Wagner wrote before the six-year silence from which the new musical world of the *Ring* would emerge. It is also the last and greatest romantic opera—if romantic means German, visionary, lyrical, and steeped in the folktales of the Middle Ages. Wagner was, at the time of the premiere, a political exile in Switzerland, and his still-active hopes for a united Germany are clearly part of the opera's texture. In many respects Lohengrin is, like Tannhäuser before him, a figure for the composer himself.

In *Lohengrin* Wagner's musical powers reach new heights, and he was never to surpass the orchestral coloring of the famous prelude, where soft divided strings in the traditionally "bright" key of A major softly suggest what Thomas Mann has called "a silvery-blue beauty." The score still features traditional arias, duets, choruses, and ensembles, but each act builds with a new and impressive architectonic sense, and increasingly the orchestra comments on the action with leitmotifs in the manner that would eventually pervade the *Ring*.

The mythic aspects of *Lohengrin* have not always been properly appreciated, and Elsa in particular has been maligned as a weak character, though Wagner, in the midst of composing the *Ring*, looked back on her and realized that she represented "the unconscious, the intuitive . . . the feminine, hitherto not understood by me, now understood at last." (He had composed his way to Brünnhilde, the questioning, intuitive, saving woman of his most massive work.) Elsa breaking an imposed taboo is one of a whole pattern of mythic heroines who give way to curiosity and bring immediate tragedy but also hope for the future, even the promise of a world savior. Brünnhilde's disobedience brings, eventually, Siegfried, as in other mythologies Pandora's disobedience brings Elpis, Semele's Dionysus, Psyche's Eros, and Eve's (as the Church sings in her liturgy) the redeeming Jesus. These taboo-breaking myths describe a great evolutionary moment in prehistory, when the human race passed from unconsciousness to the higher and much more problematic state of consciousness. Woman precipitates this, not because she is weaker than man, but because she is more intuitive. Elsa's questioning means the loss of Lohengrin but restores Gottfried, the Grail-sent hope for the future, preserved during a time of danger under a figure our interpreters of myth would call a transcendence symbol—the swan.

Lohengrin is an astonishing work for anyone with ears for the pre-Raphaelite beauty and brassy glory of its music, and with the insight to see deeply into its text. Baudelaire, astonished, wrote that *Lohengrin* held him suspended in an ecstasy of insight.

Recording
Kempe / Grümmer, Ludwig, Thomas, Fischer-Dieskau, Frick
(EMI/Angel 1962)

Lucia di Lammermoor

Music by Gaetano Donizetti
Text by Salvatore Cammarano (after Sir Walter Scott)
First performance: Naples, 26 September 1835

ACT I

On the moors in sixteenth-century Scotland, Lord Enrico Ashton is enraged to hear that his sister Lucia has been secretly meeting Edgardo, one of the hated Ravenswoods.

At a fountain on the moors, Lucia tells Alisa, her nurse, that she once saw emerging from the waters the ghost of an Ashton girl who was murdered by the Ravenswoods ("Regnava nel silenzio"), but that she nonetheless loves Edgardo ("Quando rapita in estasi"). He arrives to tell her that he must go on a diplomatic mission to France; they exchange rings and pledge fidelity (Duet: "Verranno a te sull'aure").

ACT II

Lucia's brother Enrico has intercepted all Edgardo's letters, and she thinks that he has forgotten her. Enrico, in desperate financial straits, demands that Lucia wed the wealthy Arturo Bucklaw. [The chaplain, Raimondo, reminds her of her duty to her family.]

In the great hall of the castle, Lucia has no sooner signed the wedding contract than Edgardo returns. He curses her for what he thinks is faithlessness (Sextet: "Chi mi frena"). Enrico, though repenting his duplicity, orders the hated Ravenswood out of his castle.

ACT III

[As a storm breaks over the Ravenswoods' ruined tower, Enrico challenges Edgardo to a duel.]

The guests are celebrating Lucia's wedding to Bucklaw when Raimondo appears with the shocking news that Lucia has gone mad and murdered her bridegroom. Lucia enters, stained with blood and imagining that she is being married to Edgardo ("The Mad Scene").

Among the Ravenswood tombs Edgardo awaits the duel with Enrico. Instead, Raimondo appears to tell him that Lucia has died. Edgardo fatally stabs himself to join her in heaven ("Tu che a Dio").

♣

Though the tenor in *Lucia* has the final curtain, Donizetti's melodious opera has, almost from its initial performances, been thought the soprano's property. Scenes not involving her, or not showing her to particular vocal advantage, were cut, and her arias transposed upward, with elaborate cadenzas added and high notes interpolated. The opera was, as a result, often dismissed, especially in Germany, as nothing more than a coloratura showpiece. But since Maria Callas proved the work's dramatic viability, and due attention was paid to the composer's original intentions, critics and audiences alike have responded to a truer bel canto opera of real dramatic stature. In the Donizetti revival of the 1950s and '60s, other operas among his tragic output (*Anna Bolena, Maria Stuarda, La Favorita*) were declared musically and dramatically superior to *Lucia*. But now that most of his long-neglected output has been restudied and freshly staged, popular taste has been vindicated: *Lucia* is, among Donizetti's tragic pieces, his masterpiece.

Recording
Karajan / Callas, di Stefano, Panerai (EMI/Angel 1955)

Lulu

Music and text by Alban Berg (after Frank Wedekind)
First performance: Zurich, 2 June 1937;
first complete performance, Paris, 24 February 1979

Act I

Prologue: An animal trainer exhibits the beasts in his care, which are the characters we shall see in the opera. Lulu is the snake, "created to make trouble."

In a German metropolis, the voluptuous Lulu is having her portrait painted, watched by the publisher Dr. Schön and his son, Alwa, a composer (who may represent Berg himself). When the two voyeurs leave, Lulu is caught *in flagrante* with the Painter by her husband, who promptly dies of a stroke.

Lulu is kept in style by Dr. Schön and visited by the asthmatic vagrant Schigolch (who may be her father). But it is the Painter she has married—and he cuts his throat when he discovers how sordid her past has been.

Lulu, in her theater dressing room, drinks with Alwa and encourages the attentions of an African prince. She pretends to faint onstage when she sees Dr. Schön in the audience with his fiancée, and forces him to break his engagement.

Act II

Lulu and Dr. Schön are now married, but she finds the Countess Geschwitz, a lesbian, more to her liking, and is variously pursued by the distraught Alwa, an arrogant Acrobat, and a delinquent Student. Schön, appalled, gives her a revolver and tells her to shoot herself; in the confusion she shoots him instead.

An orchestral interlude (Berg wanted it to accompany a silent film) depicts Lulu's arrest, trial, conviction, imprisonment, and escape disguised as the Countess.

All the characters conspire in different ways to get Lulu out of the country. The devoted Countess has even contracted cholera and infected Lulu, to enable her to escape from prison via the isolation hospital. But it is with Alwa that Lulu eventually flees, after making love with him on the very couch where his father bled to death.

Act III

In a Paris salon, Lulu, still wanted for murder, is blackmailed by a Marquis who traffics in white slaves and, separately, by the Acrobat. Schigolch and the Countess make arrangements to murder the latter, but all plans are foiled by the collapse of the railroad stock on which they were depending. Lulu, disguised as a bellhop, escapes with Alwa.

Living in London as a prostitute, Lulu is visited by the Countess, while sheltering Alwa and Schigolch—who is the only one of the four to survive: he is out drinking when Lulu's customers turn violent. The last of the three customers, from whom there is no escape and to whom Lulu surrenders as to a death wish, is Jack the Ripper.

♣

In plot summary, *Lulu* sounds farcical, and of course farce is one level along which it travels. But it is also a kind of intellectual exercise, like the two Wedekind plays, *Erdgeist* and *Die Büchse der Pandora*, on which it is based. George Martin observes that Lulu "passes through the plays like an atom of some unstable chemical element" whose "property is the ability to attract other atoms, oppositely charged, to fuse with her." (In Jack the Ripper she finally meets "an atom with the wrong chemical properties.")

More than that, *Lulu* is an opera charged, as was Berg's earlier *Wozzeck*, with immense sympathy for the pathetic creatures it depicts, caught this time not by social and economic forces they cannot understand, but by an irrational sexuality they cannot control. The opera is a kind of morality play, an atonal *Don Giovanni* about an intensely sexual creature, part earth-spirit and part Pandora's box, who without reflection destroys those she touches (all of whom see her according to their own desires and compel her to destroy them) until she is destroyed herself. The opera's only survivor, Schigolch, knows her for what she is and calls her Lulu (quite the equivalent of "rosebud" in *Citizen Kane*); the three husbands, who see in her only what they want in her, call her Nelly (petit-bourgeois), Eve (mother-temptress), and Mignon (child-actress).

Lulu is a good deal more musically complex than *Wozzeck*, built as it is on twelve-tone rows that define the various obsessed characters. Berg died before he could finish the opera, and his widow, probably because she detected coded messages in the music of Act III (nothing in Berg is without significance), kept the virtually complete but partially unscored last act from the public for more than forty years. Only after her death in 1976 was the opera given intact, with the third act completed—amazingly, to the general satisfaction of critics—by Friedrich Cerha. The opera was then rightly seen as musically and dramatically palindromatic, with the film interlude at the center. Lulu's three last-act customers thus became reembodiments of her three husbands, with Jack the Ripper a weirdly resurrected Dr. Schön.

Recording
Boulez / Stratas, Minton, Riegel, Tear, Mazura, Nienstedt
(Deutsche Grammophon 1979)

Macbeth

Music by Giuseppe Verdi
Text by Francesco Maria Piave and Andrea Maffei
(after Shakespeare)
First performance: Florence, 14 March 1847

Act I

On a blasted heath, a coven of witches tells the Scottish chieftain Macbeth that he will become king and that his companion Banquo will be the father of kings.

Lady Macbeth, reading of the prophecy in a letter from her husband, sees the opportunity of making it come true when the present king, Duncan, comes with Macbeth to the castle that night ("Vieni! t'affretta!"). She persuades the reluctant Macbeth to kill the King, and sees to the cover-up herself. Banquo and another chieftain, Macduff, discover the murdered body.

Act II

Macbeth, now crowned king, is convinced by his wife ("La luce langue") that Banquo too must die.

Banquo is felled by Macbeth's assassins but his son, Fleance, escapes to continue his line.

Banquo's ghost appears to a terrified Macbeth at a festive banquet. The guests fear for the sanity of their king, and Macduff decides to join the subjects who are already rising against him.

ACT III

Macbeth consults the witches and is warned by a vision of a severed head to beware of Macduff, told by a vision of a bloody child that no man born of woman can harm him, and assured by a vision of a crowned child carrying a bough that he can never be defeated unless Birnam Wood moves against him. But the ghost of Banquo also appears, holding up a mirror in which his royal line passes in succession before Macbeth's despairing eyes. The visions fade, and Lady Macbeth finds her husband alone on the heath. She advises him to direct his attention now toward killing Macduff.

ACT IV

Near Birnam Wood, Macduff hears that Macbeth has slaughtered his wife and children ("Ah! la paterna mano"). Duncan's son Malcolm arrives with an English army and an opportunity for revenge. The combined forces pluck boughs from the trees and advance against the king.

In her castle, Lady Macbeth, maddened by her guilt, confesses to the murders as she sleepwalks ("Una macchia").

Macbeth, strangely unmoved when told that his wife has died, gives way to remorse ("Pietà, rispetto"), calling life "a tale told by an idiot, full of sound and fury, signifying nothing." He is then slain by a man not born of woman: Macduff, with drawn sword, says "Macduff was from his mother's womb untimely ripp'd," and the guilty king curses the ambition that damned his soul.

♣

Macbeth, more than any other of Verdi's early operas, anticipates what was to come—the baritonal sonorities of Rigoletto and Boccanegra, the obsessed histrionics of Azucena and Amneris, and the Shakespearean ambience of his last two operas, still forty years in the future. Like many other Verdi pieces, *Macbeth* came into its own only after World War II, its advent prepared by prewar German renewal of interest in the composer's early works. The score is wildly uneven, but the role of Lady Macbeth, with its three demanding arias, has been both favored and feared by the world's sopranos. The opera is now generally performed in the Paris revision of 1865, for which the second of the arias, the stunning "La luce langue," was written.

Recording
Abbado / Verrett, Domingo, Cappuccilli, Ghiaurov
(Deutsche Grammophon 1976)

Madama Butterfly

Music by Giacomo Puccini
Text by Giuseppe Giacosa and Luigi Illica (after David Belasco)
First performance: Milan, 17 February 1904

ACT I

Benjamin Franklin Pinkerton, a U.S. naval lieutenant, arranges with a Japanese marriage broker, Goro, to rent a house on a hill overlooking Nagasaki harbor and, heedless of the warnings of the American consul, Sharpless, marries a fifteen-year-old geisha—Cio-Cio-San or, as he prefers to call her, Butterfly. Both arrangements are for 999 years, terminable within a month. The bride's uncle, a bonze, crashes the wedding party to denounce Butterfly for converting to Christianity, and all her relatives desert her. Her American husband comforts her (Duet: "Bimba, non piangere") and eagerly takes her into her new house.

ACT II

Three years have passed since Pinkerton's departure, but the faithful Butterfly assures her servant Suzuki that he will return one fine day ("Un bel dì"). Sharpless visits her with a letter from her husband, but she is too excited, and too busy putting off a wealthy suitor, to realize that Pinkerton has remarried. She proudly shows the consul her baby boy, Trouble. Sharpless, distressed, leaves without telling her that her husband's ship is due to return that day. Butterfly, hearing a cannon shot, sees the ship sailing into the harbor, and she and Suzuki fill the house with blossoms ("The Flower Duet"). Then they settle down with the child to await Pinkerton's arrival. Darkness falls as the city below goes to sleep ("The Humming Chorus").

ACT III

Morning finds the three still waiting. Butterfly puts the child to bed, singing a lullaby, and Suzuki sees Sharpless standing in the garden with Pinkerton's American wife and the lieutenant himself, now filled with shame and remorse ("Addio, fiorito asil"). Butterfly at last realizes what has happened, and agrees to give up her child if Pinkerton will return alone in a half-hour's time to fetch him. She gives Trouble a tiny American flag, blindfolds him, goes behind a screen and, just as Pinkerton comes rushing back up the hill calling her name, ritually kills herself with the dagger her father once used, at the emperor's command, for hara-kiri ("Con onor muori").

♣

Puccini was moved, though he knew no English, by David Belasco's one-act play when he saw it in London, and for operatic purposes he and his librettists developed its story further with details from John Luther Long's earlier novella on the subject. In the course of many revisions, a proposed act in the U.S. consulate was scrapped, and the roles of Pinkerton and Sharpless drastically reduced, only to be reenlarged in another overhaul after the opera failed catastrophically at its premiere. *Butterfly* now exists in several published versions, of which the first, the La Scala fiasco, still has its champions. But in every version Butterfly is the main character, perhaps the essential Puccini heroine in her uncomprehending and unfailingly melodious suffering, yet steelier than many interpreters give us to believe. (It is also a marathon role, much more demanding than is usually thought.)

The opera is, like *Tosca*, intricately woven out of leitmotifs and, like *Turandot*, bedecked with oriental melodies à la Italiana. But its great moments—the passionate first-act love duet in particular—are Puccini the lyric dramatist in high gear. Its popularity has been unstoppable, and its "ugly American" aspect can still touch a raw nerve. It was Puccini's favorite among all his works, perhaps because, like *Fidelio* with Beethoven, it was the one of his children that caused him the most—trouble.

Recording

Barbirolli / Scotto, di Stasio, Bergonzi, Panerai (EMI/Angel 1966)

Manon

Music by Jules Massenet
Text by Henri Meilhac and Philippe Gille (after the Abbé Prévost)
First performance: Paris, 19 January 1884

Act I

In the courtyard of an eighteenth-century coach-stop inn at Amiens, the ne'er-do-well Lescaut gives his adolescent convent-bound cousin Manon words of warning about the wide world—appropriately enough, as the lecherous Guillot and his associate de Brétigny have been eyeing her. For her part, Manon is soon taken with the fine young Chevalier des Grieux, and the two of them run off in Guillot's coach.

Manon and des Grieux are happy but poor in their Paris apartment when her cousin brings in de Brétigny and the offer of a courtesan's life of wealth and pleasure. When des Grieux, unaware of the temptation his new love is facing, goes off to post a letter to his father, Manon decides to leave him, and bids a childlike farewell to their little dining table ("Adieu, notre petite table"). He returns to sing of the idyllic life he hopes soon to have with her in the country ("Le Rêve"), but in another moment he is abducted by strong-arms sent by his own father.

ACT II

[On the Cours-la-Reine, a bejeweled Manon sings a Gavotte for de Brétigny and the crowd, and Guillot presents a divertissement by the corps de ballet from the Opéra. Manon is shocked to learn from des Grieux's father that the young chevalier is about to take holy orders.]

In the sacristy at Saint-Sulpice, des Grieux's father advises his son to reconsider taking such a consequential step. The son is still beset by thoughts of Manon ("Ah, fuyez, douce image"), and when Manon arrives to tempt him away, they run off together for the second time.

ACT III

In a gambling room at the infamous Hôtel Transylvanie, Manon sings a Fabliau (or her Act II Gavotte if the Cours-la-Reine scene has been cut), and des Grieux has a run of luck at the tables. The jealous Guillot accuses him of cheating and calls the police. The two lovers are arrested for illicit operations and taken away—des Grieux to prison (where he knows his father can get him released) and Manon (as she knows happens to women of her notoriety) to almost certain deportation.

On the road to Le Havre, des Grieux and Lescaut try unsuccessfully to save an exhausted Manon from deportation. She dies in her lover's arms.

♣

Manon, an essential French opera, made two notable contributions to the *opéra comique* tradition of mingling speech and song: mélodrame (intimate speaking over music) and what might be called the *phrase Massenétique* (a vocal line that expands and contracts according to the inflections of the language). The opera is also pervaded, to a degree unprecedented in France, with quasi-Wagnerian leitmotifs. Some thirty or more weave in and out of the score, many of them of an extraordinary pictorial evocativeness, all making dramatic points. Many singers have found the two leading roles grateful. Manon, like Violetta, may be said to be a role that requires a different kind of voice in each act, as well as a great deal of subtlety in the uses thereof. For the rest, Sir Thomas Beecham said he would happily give all the Brandenburg Concertos for *Manon* and think he had vastly profited by the exchange.

Massenet tells the famous story without overstatement, in six scenes set in six contrasting locales. Puccini, a few years later, was to tell it with all-stops-out passion, in just four settings, three of them different from Massenet's. See the next entry.

Recording

Monteux / de los Angeles, Legay, Dens, Borthayre
(EMI/Angel 1955)

Manon Lescaut

Music by Giacomo Puccini
Text by Luigi Illica, Giuseppe Giacosa, Giulio Ricordi, Marco
Praga, Domenico Oliva, and Ruggero Leoncavallo
(after the Abbé Prévost)
First performance: Turin, 1 February 1893

ACT I

In the courtyard of an eighteenth-century coach-stop inn at Amiens, the young Chevalier des Grieux, teased by a pack of students for never finding a sweetheart, sings a mocking serenade ("Tra voi belle"), and is very soon smitten when Manon arrives with her ne'er-do-well brother, Lescaut ("Donna non vidi mai"). Lescaut is interested in offering his convent-bound sister to the wealthy Geronte, but before that can happen des Grieux persuades her to run off with him to Paris—in Geronte's carriage.

ACT II

Manon has nonetheless ended up with Geronte, living in a luxury that astounds her brother ("In quelle trine morbide"), and learning the fashions in dancing and singing ("L'ora o Tirsi"). Des Grieux tracks her down and reproaches her ("Ah, Manon, mi tradisce"). Geronte discovers them alone together and calls the police. Manon lingers too long gathering up her jewels, and the two lovers are caught and arrested on charges of theft and immorality.

Act III

An orchestral intermezzo depicts des Grieux's sorrowful resolve to follow Manon to wherever she may be sentenced.

In the harbor at Le Havre, des Grieux and Lescaut are unsuccessful in rescuing Manon from deportation to America with other chained and convicted women. Des Grieux desperately appeals to the ship's captain to be taken aboard ("Guardate, pazzo son") and, given permission, races up the gangplank.

Act IV

Manon and des Grieux, having fled from New Orleans (where, she says, "My fatal beauty kindled still more hatred"), stumble thirsting across a barren landscape. She can go no further ("Sola, perduta, abbandonata") and dies in his arms, saying, "Time will obliterate my faults, but my love will never die."

❧

Massenet's Manon dies whispering, "It must be so, it must be so. That is the story of Manon Lescaut." But in fact it didn't have to be so, and the story, operatically speaking, was only half over. Within ten years, Puccini, who had a penchant for taking on subjects already contemplated or even completed by rival composers, produced a *Manon* every bit as popular as—and now perhaps even more popular than—Massenet's. "Massenet approached the story with powder and minuets," he said. "I shall approach it with desperate passion."

Though six names appeared on the published libretto, the dominant hand in shaping it was the composer's. Puccini was furious with the inept libretti written for his early *Le Villi* and *Edgar*. He was also determined this time to overwhelm his audience with melody; he borrowed from his youthful mass and minuets for the madrigal and dances in Act II, and from a string quartet for a doom-laden theme in Acts III and IV. But one wonders why he thought he had to do so, for in the rest of the score his melodic gift is in full flood for the first time. Much of the scoring is thicker in texture than anything that was to follow, and owes something to Wagner. But the fifty-odd melodies that push and jostle one another from moment to moment could only have been written by Puccini.

Recording

Mitropoulos / Albanese, Björling, Guarrera (Melodram 1956)

Mefistofele

Music and text by Arrigo Boito (after Goethe)
First performance: Milan, 5 March 1868

ACT I

A prologue in heaven shows Mefistofele, a fallen angel, taunting an unseen Lord because His creature man is such a poor thing, and wagering that he can lead even the most intelligent of men, Faust, to damnation.

At an Easter fair in sixteenth-century Frankfurt, Faust and his pupil Wagner notice a gray friar circling them, leaving footprints of flame.

Alone in his study, Faust, drawn by the beauty of nature ("Dai campi, dai prati") to meditate on the Bible, is visited by the friar, who shucks off his religious garb to reveal himself as Mefistofele, the whistling spirit of negation. Faust signs over his soul in exchange for what the demon promises will be a moment so beautiful that he will want to stay in it forever.

ACT II

Faust, restored to youth, woos the virginal Margherita in a garden, while Mefistofele distracts her neighbor Marta. Faust, eager to spend the night with the girl, gives her a sleeping potion for her mother, saying that it will not harm her.

At a witch's sabbath in the Harz Mountains, satanic creatures worship Mefistofele and ceremoniously present him with a symbol of the earth, which he disdainfully smashes to pieces. Amid the revels Faust sees in the sky a vision of Margherita in chains, with a bloody line encircling her neck, and is horrified to think what might have happened.

Margherita, maddened by Faust's desertion of her, is in prison awaiting execution for poisoning her mother and drowning her child ("L'altra notte"). Faust comes to her and begs her to flee with him (Duet: "Lontano, lontano"), but she, at last seeing Mefistofele for what he is, takes refuge in prayer and dies. A choir of angels pronounces her saved. Faust and Mefistofele escape as the headsman approaches.

Act III

At a classical sabbath in the Vale of Tempe, Faust, in his unending search for a moment of sheer beauty, woos Helen of Troy. Mefistofele, preferring Gothic witchery to Grecian romance, leaves him to his poetic pleasure.

An epilogue discloses Faust in his study, grown old again. He has not experienced his moment of beauty, but comes close to it as he dreams of founding among men a realm that would be heaven on earth. Mefistofele, fearing that he may lose his prey through good works, conjures up spirits to lure him again toward pleasure. But Faust hears the Celestial Host approaching, clasps his Bible, and experiences in that ecstatic moment the beauty he has always sought. As it was not Mefistofele who provided that moment, Faust does not lose his soul. The cherubim shower down roses that cause torment to the defiantly whistling demon but bring salvation to the ever-questing Faust.

♣

Boito was a literary man, and his version of the Faust myth is closer to Goethe than any of the others in the repertory. He was less gifted as a composer, but in *Mefistofele* he reaches Goethian heights in the prologue, with its blazing trumpet calls and startlingly unearthly choruses, and Goethian pathos in the prison scene, with its haunted aria and haunting duet. Much of the rest is patchwork. The opera was a disaster at its premiere but successful after Boito subjected it to two major revisions. Critics remain to this day divided in their opinions.

Boito wrote *Mefistofele* more than ten years before he became Verdi's librettist. In his youth he had deeply offended the Maestro by writing a foolish verse comparing the Italian art of his day to a stained brothel wall. And in the interim he had worked on Italian translations of Wagner (probably another sore point) and written librettos of dubious value, like the one he provided for Ponchielli's *La Gioconda*. His other opera, *Nerone*, an ongoing project, was never staged in his lifetime. The composer of *Mefistofele* will always be best remembered for having devoted twenty years of his life to Verdi, whose genius he reawakened from a long period of silence. Their working relationship became, after time and forgiveness had had their healing way, a lasting and very productive friendship. Boito was at the Maestro's bedside when he died. Perhaps at that moment he thought again of his Faust, finding peace after a long life of questing.

Recording
Rudel / Caballé, Domingo, Treigle (EMI/Angel 1973)

Die Meistersinger von Nürnberg

(The Mastersingers of Nuremberg)
Music and text by Richard Wagner
First performance: Munich, 21 June 1868

Act I

A joyous prelude gives us in succession (1) the confident theme of the mastersinger's guild, (2) a lyric strain from Walther's prize song, (3) the martial "Long Tune" Wagner fashioned from a piece by an actual mastersinger, (4) the soaring theme called "Art Brotherhood," and (5) the main melody of the prize song. The five themes are developed (the first is even parodied) along with subsidiary motifs, until, in a burst of counterpoint, numbers 1, 3, and 5 sound at once, soon to be swept along in triumph by number 4. It is very much a musical summary of the opera to come, but it makes no mention of the opera's main character, the shoemaker poet Hans Sachs, and perhaps that is why it leads directly into . . .

. . . a chorale sung in church on the eve of John the Baptist's day (Hans Sachs' name day) in sixteenth-century Nuremberg. Between verses, Walther, a young knight, exchanges romantic glances with Eva, the daughter of the goldsmith Pogner. When the service is done, he asks her if she is betrothed, and her nurse, Magdalene, tells him that she is to be given in marriage to the mastersinger who, in competition next morning, sings the best mastersong. Walther hasn't a notion of what a mastersong is, but he promptly decides to enter the contest and win his Eva. Magdalene asks *her* young man, Hans Sachs' apprentice David, to give Walther a crash course on the rules of songwriting. The worst of it, David says after a complicated run-through, is that there'll be an official "marker" at the audition, in a boxed enclosure, ready to chalk up every violation of the rules. "Seven mistakes, and you're out!"

Twelve good burghers who have advanced to master's standing enter the church for a business meeting. The wealthy Pogner announces that, as he wants to show the world that Nurembergers are more interested in art and its sacred traditions than in moneymaking, he will give in marriage his only child, Eva, together with all his possessions, to whoever wins the singing contest in the morning ("Das schöne Fest"). Hans Sachs, out of concern for Eva, is rightly wary of this proposal but is voted down, while the town clerk, Sixtus Beckmesser, a kind of poet and pedant overture in himself, is sure *he* can win the girl. Then, with Pogner's approval, Walther introduces himself ("Am stillen Herd") as a possible contender: he has learned the art of singing in the winter at his fireside, from an old book by the famous Walther von der Vogelweide (bird-meadow), and in the springtime from the meadow birds themselves. The masters, dubious of these qualifications, allow him a trial song ("Fanget an!"), but with Beckmesser noisily—and maliciously—marking every violation of the rules, a riot breaks out, and Walther loses his patience and fails his audition.

ACT II

As St. John's Eve turns to night, and Nuremberg puts up its shutters, Hans Sachs muses under his elder tree ("The Flieder Monologue") about a strain in Walther's trial song that he can't get out of his head. How is a mere man capable of anything so lovely? Because, Sachs concludes, a true poet, like a songbird, *has* to sing, and because he has to, he can.

Eva comes to Sachs to ask him to help her and Walther while there is still time. Sachs and Eva, despite the difference in their ages, have thought about marrying, but now he realizes that she has found a new love, and he resolves to find a way to make them one. He stays at his cobbler's bench past the ten o'clock watch to prevent them from eloping, singing a merry cobbler's song ("Jerum! Jerum!"), in which Walther is cast as Adam, Eva as Eve, Beckmesser as the devil, and Sachs himself as the angel guarding the exit from the Garden of Eden. Then, in a scene of comic cross-purposes, Sachs frustrates Beckmesser's attempt to serenade Eva, noisily acting as "marker" for Beckmesser's new song while he hammers away at Beckmesser's new shoes. The racket starts a riot, with all of Nuremberg going mad. The disturbance is quelled only when the night watchman reappears, announcing the eleventh hour. The moon rises on the empty cobbled street.

ACT III

A meditative prelude reveals what is transpiring in Sachs' heart: the orchestra states (1) the "Resignation" theme that sounded in the midst of his shoemaker's song in Act II, (2) an apotheosis of the song itself, and (3) the chorale that affirms Sachs as an artist in the final scene. The intimation is that Sachs' dedication to art will give him the strength to give up Eva, though he dearly loves her.

In the early morning on John the Baptist's Day, Sachs is in his workshop musing over his books ("The Wahn Monologue"): there is a mad streak (*Wahn*) in human nature that causes all our sufferings; we must recognize it and, if we can, direct it to constructive purposes. And that is what Sachs begins to do as the other characters come to him one by one for help with their problems: David hopes he can be freed from his long apprenticeship and marry his Magdalene; Walther has heard a beautiful melody in his dream and finds in Sachs a craftsman to help him shape his dream into a first and then a second draft of a master song; Beckmesser has despaired of *his* song, and Sachs, putting a little *Wahn* to work, lets him steal the words of the song he has written down with Walther; and Eva comes, radiant in a white wedding dress, pretending that she needs a shoe repaired but actually hoping to find a song for her knight to sing. And while Sachs is busy with the shoe, Walther appears in the doorway to sing the song—in a resplendent third version. Eva flings herself gratefully into Sachs' arms, and he gently places her in the waiting embrace of Walther. It is the moment of moments in the comedy; the "Resignation" theme sounds with almost tragic force, and Sachs nearly despairs.

A final caller comes to the door—Magdalene, hoping to wed her David. Sachs gives David the cuff on the ear that makes him a journeyman qualified to marry and, true to his namesake, asks the two couples to witness the christening of the new song. The five of them sing of the happiness that the song has brought them (Quintet: "Selig, wie die Sonne") . . .

. . . and the scene changes to the banks of the Pegnitz, to a parade of guilds, toymakers, trumpeters, and drummers. All Nuremberg rises to greet Hans Sachs with a "nightingale" chorale of his own composing ("Wach auf!"), but the "Resignation" theme sounds in the orchestra to color the final cadence. The contest begins as Beckmesser, limping in his new shoes, tries to fit Walther's song to his own melody, hopelessly garbles the words, and is laughed off the podium. He tells the crowd that the words were really written by their revered Hans Sachs, and Sachs, charged with artistic failure, claims that the song is actually beautiful when properly sung. He calls for a witness to the truth of this—and so Walther, though he has been officially disqualified, steps forward, not as a contestant but as a witness for the defense. His song ("Morgenlich leuchtend") deftly conflates the three earlier versions into one, and is so beautiful that in a moment the people are shouting "Give *him* the prize!"

Walther claims his Eva, then unexpectedly refuses to accept his master's title, so humiliated has he been by the official twelve. Sachs sings his last philosophical solo ("Verachtet mir die Meister nicht"), assuring Walther that he owes his success not to his ancestors, or coat of arms, or weapons, but to that fact that he is a poet, and for that he must thank the bourgeois masters, for they alone have kept poetry alive when the rest of Germany—warriors and knights included—have neglected it. Without its art, Sachs says, no nation can hope to survive. Walther accepts his mastership, and he and Eva contrive to crown Sachs, when he isn't looking, with the laurel he, more than any of them, deserves.

♣

Even in a summary as lengthy as the above (the opera itself clocks in at over five hours), one cannot begin to tell what is contained in Wagner's bounteous comedy, especially in the patterns of words and images that meet and mate in the text almost as the leitmotifs do in the music. The more one studies the text, the more one sees that the references to songbirds, shoes, and Biblical figures function metaphorically, grow in meaning as they accumulate, and finally constitute a whole aesthetic.

Perhaps the most important of the metaphors is baptism: the congregation singing the opening chorale asks John the Baptist to lift them up on the banks of the Jordan, and in the last scene Hans the Baptist, on the banks of the Pegnitz, is the answer to that prayer. Through the song that came to Walther in a dream, the *Wahn* that had beset all of Nuremberg on St. John's Eve is washed away on St. John's Day. (Schopenhauer himself had suggested a correlation between his concept of *Wille* (will), an irrational force in nature from which we must be redeemed, and the Christian doctrine of original sin, from which baptism redeems the believer.)

Structurally the opera is a marvel. Throughout its length we hear no less than seven attempts at a mastersong—five from Walther, one from Beckmesser, and one from David (the historical Hans Sachs wrote more than four thousand of them)—and gradually we school ourselves in the required structure: two *Stollen*, or stanzas, identical in length, with the same melody and with a rhyme at the end, must be followed by an *Abgesang*, or aftersong, equal in length to the two stanzas together, with a wholly new melody, effecting a kind of resolution. A little sleuthing will satisfy a listener that, if the overture is allowed to stand by itself, Acts I and II of *Die Meistersinger* have approximately the same length, share parallel incidents and bits of dialogue, and end, both of them, with a sort of rhyme—public rioting over what is judged bad singing. Then Act III, equal in length to the first two acts combined, introduces a new strain of seriousness (the Schopenhauerian "Wahn, Wahn") and a harmonious resolution. In short, the whole opera is a mastersong, gradually shaping itself before our very ears, Wagner's answer to the Beckmessers of his day who claimed he was incapable of such things as melody, counterpoint, and the poetic and dramatic sense needed to compose a proper opera.

Recent charges of racism in *Die Meistersinger* are unfounded but must—one hopes, only for a time—be addressed. In some of his prose writings Wagner propagated ideas that would now correctly be called anti-Semitic, even viciously so, though it has not by any means been proved that these made their way into *Die Meistersinger*. The Nazis, rallying in Nuremberg, found the opera's national spirit and pageantry ideally suited to their purposes, but they conveniently ignored the larger statements on goodness, truth, and beauty that did not suit, and indeed contradicted, those purposes. (Perhaps it should be mentioned that other great works of art, from the *Iliad* and the Bible onward, have been similarly misread and used to justify evil.) Further, Beckmesser is not a Jewish caricature; he *is* a caricature of Eduard Hanslick, Wagner's most influential critic, who was part Jewish, but he functions with equal importance as the alazon in comic ritual, the Miles Gloriosus in Plautine comedy, the devil in baptismal exorcism, and the mythic dragon from whom the knight in shining armor rescues the damsel in distress—all traditions on which *Die Meistersinger* deftly draws. Further still, Hans Sachs' final words are not an exhortation to master-race cruelty. They *were* written as a warning on the eve of war—the Franco-Prussian War—but their import is clearly that Germany will survive not by warring but by preserving old and creating new works of art.

Musically, *Die Meistersinger* is endlessly inventive, songful, and of a C-major richness and ripeness in deliberate contrast with the seething chromaticism of the opera written just before it, *Tristan und Isolde*. Wagner says as much when in Act III he has Hans Sachs quote the "Yearning" motif from *Tristan*, only to say that it is not for him—one of a thousand subtleties in this many-splendored work.

Recording

Kubelik / Janowitz, Konya, Stewart, Hemsley (Myto 1967)

Moses und Aron

(Moses and Aaron)
Music and text by Arnold Schoenberg
First performance: Zurich, 6 June 1957

ACT I

Moses is told by God, speaking through the Burning Bush, that he must free the Israelites from slavery in Egypt and lead them, with his brother Aron as spokesman, to the Promised Land. The people, less convinced by Moses' insistence that God must be found within than by Aron's outwardly impressive miracles, decide to follow the brothers through the desert to their God-promised goal.

ACT II

While Moses lingers on Mount Sinai, receiving the Law, Aron, to calm the people, gives them the Golden Calf as a visible god to worship. The celebration becomes an orgy of slaughter and sexual excess. Moses descends from the mountain, angrily scatters the people and, when reminded by Aron that even he needs images (witness the tables of Ten Commandments he has in his hand), smashes the Law to pieces. The people follow a Pillar of Fire onward, and Aron leaves Moses lamenting that God's word, when conceptualized, is not God.

☙

Schoenberg wrote a third-act text in which Moses' "God as idea" is proved more powerful than Aron's "God as image." But he never set it to music, and indeed the first two acts, short as they are, make a harrowing evening. Moses' final exclamation in Act II ("Oh Word, thou Word, that I lack!") is a devastating and powerful ending in itself.

The opera can be viewed as a personal statement of the composer's religious quandary (an unbeliever, he returned to his Jewish faith in solidarity with those who suffered and died under the Nazis) and of his defeats in the battle for acceptance of his twelve-tone music (he died without ever hearing his *Moses*, let alone seeing it performed). The forbidding work languished unstaged for a full quarter-century, subjected to scholarly analysis as if it were a patient etherized on a table, until productions, especially those in London and Hamburg, brought it to vivid life. Paradoxically, while the century-long tenure of twelve-tone music seems, with the new millennium, to have ended at last, *Moses und Aron* has only now found its public, which is ready to acknowledge it as among the most emblematic and important operas of the twentieth century.

Recording

Solti / Langridge, Mazura (Decca/London 1984)

Nabucco

(Nebuchadnezzar)
Music by Giuseppe Verdi
Text by Temistocle Solera
First performance: Milan, 9 March 1842

ACT I: JERUSALEM

Inside the Temple of Solomon, the Hebrews have taken refuge from the Assyrian king Nabucco's approaching armies. Among their number is Nabucco's captive daughter Fenena, in love with the young Hebrew warrior Ismaele. Nabucco's other daughter, the warlike Abigaille, also in love with Ismaele, arrives with her own forces in an unsuccessful attempt to claim his affection. When Nabucco himself reaches the temple with his army, the Hebrew high priest Zaccaria threatens to kill Fenena if he desecrates the sacred place. But Ismaele disarms the priest, and Nabucco orders that the temple be sacked and burned.

ACT II: THE BLASPHEMER

In the palace in Babylon, Abigaille discovers that she is not a legitimate daughter of Nabucco but the child of one of his concubines. Furiously she plots, in alliance with the high priest of Baal, to take the throne, circulating a rumor that Nabucco has died in battle and demanding that Fenena, who has been named regent in her father's absence and who has converted to Ismaele's faith, yield the crown to her. But Nabucco returns victorious, reclaims the crown, places it on his own head, and hubristically proclaims himself a god greater than Baal or Jehovah—whereupon a thunderbolt dashes the crown to earth and reduces the blasphemer to utter madness. Abigaille triumphantly snatches up the crown for herself.

ACT III: THE PROPHECY

In the Hanging Gardens, Abigaille and her priest order all the Hebrews to be killed. She even tricks the mad Nabucco into sealing the death warrant.

By the waters of Babylon, the enslaved Hebrews dream of their lost homeland ("Và, pensiero"), and Zaccaria promises them deliverance, predicting that Babylon will fall.

ACT IV: THE BROKEN IDOL

Nabucco in his chambers awakes from his madness with the sudden awareness that Jehovah is the one true God. He kneels to ask divine forgiveness and summons his armies to save the Hebrews.

In the Hanging Gardens, as Fenena is about to be executed, Nabucco arrives—and the statue of Baal crumbles of its own accord. [Abigaille meanwhile has taken poison. She begs the forgiveness of Fenena, urges her to marry Ismaele, and dies in hope that Jehovah will be merciful to her.]

♣

Nabucco was Verdi's first success, and exemplifies the raw passion and political commitment of his early style. Abigaille is perhaps his first three-dimensional character and a "killer role" for the prima donnas who brave its vaulting leaps and other terrors. In its day the opera was a rallying cry of Risorgimento sentiment. Its "Và, pensiero," the song of a whole people, has now become in effect the national anthem of Italy and is sung in remembrance of the Holocaust throughout the civilized world.

Recording
Muti / Scotto, Obraztsova, Luchetti, Manuguerra, Ghiaurov
(EMI/Angel 1977)

Norma

Music by Vincenzo Bellini
Text by Felice Romani
First performance: Milan, 26 December 1831

ACT I

An overture pits Roman force against Druid resistance.

In a sacred grove in Roman-occupied Gaul, the Druids assemble by night to watch their priestess, Norma, ritually cut the mistletoe, which will be a signal for them to rise against the Romans. Meanwhile Pollione, the Roman proconsul to whom Norma has secretly borne two children, confides to his centurion Flavio that he now loves a younger priestess, Adalgisa ("Meco all'altar di Venere"). As the moon rises, Norma enters in procession to perform the ritual ("Casta diva"). Still in love with Pollione, she tells her people that the time has not yet come to rise against their oppressors. Secretly, Pollione meets Adalgisa in the grove and persuades her to abandon her gods and follow him to Rome.

Adalgisa comes to Norma's dwelling to be released from her vows and is kindly treated. But when Pollione unexpectedly arrives, and both Norma and Adalgisa realize his perfidy, there is a three-way explosion of emotions (Trio: "Oh! di qual sei tu vittima").

ACT II

Norma, in despair, attempts to kill her two children, then decides to turn the dagger on herself. She summons Adalgisa and asks her to take the children with her to Rome. Adalgisa says that instead she will persuade Pollione to return to his first love (Duet: "Mira, o Norma").

The Druids hear from their high priest Oroveso, Norma's father, that an even harsher proconsul is to replace Pollione. Norma sounds a gong to call her people to rise up against the Romans. A sacrificial victim is required, and by a stroke of fate Pollione is captured in an attempt to carry Adalgisa off. He faces up stoically to Norma, saying she may kill him but must spare Adalgisa and his children. Norma ("In mia man al fin tu sei") says she will punish him by sentencing Adalgisa. But when she calls her Druids together and announces that she has found, as a victim for the sacrifice, a priestess who has been untrue to her vows, she names herself. Oroveso is persuaded to look after the children, and an awed Pollione walks side by side with Norma to the sacrificial flames.

♣

Norma is by common consent the finest of all bel canto operas, its every lyric element tensed inexorably toward dramatic effect. The title role, requiring complete command of lyric, dramatic, and coloratura styles, is often said to be the most demanding soprano role in opera. Only great singers with great stage presence—Pasta, Grisi, Malibran, Lind, Ponselle, Callas—have made their way unscathed from sustaining the long, Chopinesque line of "Casta diva" to wielding the wild histrionics of the vengeance scenes with Pollione. Lilli Lehmann said, famously, that one Norma was more difficult to sing than all three Brünnhildes, and ten times as exacting as Beethoven's Leonore. That may not be an exaggeration. Wagner and Beethoven had mighty orchestras to heighten and deepen the drama; in *Norma* the voices alone are called on to perform those fearsome duties.

Recording

Votto / Callas, Simionato, del Monaco, Zaccaria (Melodram 1955)

Le Nozze di Figaro
(The Marriage of Figaro)
Music by Wolfgang Amadeus Mozart
Text by Lorenzo da Ponte (after Beaumarchais)
First performance: Vienna, 1 May 1786

ACT I

An overture, swift as the wind, sets the whole orchestra laughing. (Beaumarchais' original was called "The Crazy Day.")

In a palace outside eighteenth-century Seville, the jack-of-all-trades Figaro is settling into the room that his employer, Count Almaviva, has given him and his bride-to-be, Susanna. She warily points out that the room is convenient to the Count's; the noble lord may, as an enlightened man, have renounced the feudal *droit du seigneur* that allows him to enjoy the bride of any of his subjects on her wedding night, but he is still randy and on the prowl. Figaro says that if the Count wants to dance ("Se vuol ballare") he himself will play the tune—that is to say, call the shots. Complications ensue with the appearances of old Dr. Bartolo, who wants to get even with Figaro for his scheming (see the prequel, *The Barber of Seville*); of old Marcellina, who has lent Figaro money on condition that he marry her; of young Cherubino, a pubescent page boy in love with every woman in the palace ("Non so più cosa son"); of Basilio, the Count's scheming chaplain and music master; and of the Count himself, entering the room to make advances to Susanna. Basilio is delighted when the Count's overtures are overheard by Cherubino, scampering from one hiding place to another. The furious Count sends Cherubino off to the army, and Figaro is relieved that at least this junior rival for his future wife's affections will be temporarily removed ("Non più andrai").

ACT II

The Countess, alone in her room, asks the god of love either to restore her husband's affection for her or to let her die ("Porgi amor"). She, Susanna, and Figaro draft Plan A to shame the Count into better behavior: they will arrange for him to meet Susanna in the garden that night—but "Susanna" will be a specially dressed Cherubino, who has been avoiding his military duty and hiding away in the palace. Complications ensue: Cherubino, full of amorous feeling ("Voi che sapete"), has to hide from the Count in the Countess' closet; the Count is sure that his wife has a lover in the closet and goes off to find a crowbar; Susanna, on the alert, takes Cherubino's place in the closet while Cherubino jumps out the window; Figaro, with a little prompting from the ladies, provides all necessary (though not altogether true) explanations. He even claims, when the gardener comes in with broken flower pots, that it was he who jumped out the window. But he is discomfited as the act ends: a fuming Marcellina enters with Bartolo and Basilio to advance the claim that Figaro is legally contracted to marry her.

ACT III

Plan A to humiliate the Count has had to be scrapped in favor of Plan B: now it will be not Cherubino but the Countess herself who will be in the garden disguised as Susanna. (Even Figaro isn't in on this plan.) Susanna assures the Count that she will be available to him if he meets her in the garden that night. The Count suspects that some plot is being hatched and is chagrined that the *droit du seigneur* is no longer his privilege ("Vedrò, metr'io suspiro"). Meanwhile, Marcellina brings her case to court and discovers that the Figaro she insists on marrying is actually the long-lost love child she had with Dr.

Bartolo. Figaro is overjoyed to be relieved of his difficulties with the two former enemies, but Susanna is not happy at first when she finds him embracing Marcellina (Sextet: "Riconosci in questo amplesso").

In her room the Countess wonders where her days of marital happiness have flown ("Dove sono"), and drafts with Susanna the letter inviting the Count to the garden ("The Letter Duet"). Cherubino is once again discovered hiding in the palace, but the Count can do nothing: Cherubino has an ally in the gardener's daughter Barbarina, and Barbarina knows more about the Count than the Count wants known.

In the throne room the nuptials of Figaro and Susanna are celebrated ("March" and "Fandango"). Figaro, still not in on Plan B, is amused to see the Count prick his finger as he pins together his written reply to the assignation in the garden.

Act IV

That night in the garden, Plan B is implemented but complications ensue: Barbarina loses the pin sent by the Count; Figaro finds it, is furious to discover what he thinks is a *real* assignation between Susanna and the Count, and inveighs against all women ("Aprite un po' quegl' occhi"); Susanna decides to teach him a lesson and sings the seductive "Deh vieni non tardar" to him, knowing that he, spying on her, will think she is singing it to the Count; Cherubino finds the-Countess-dressed-as-Susanna and makes advances; the Count appears, sends the boy packing, and is fooled into taking his own wife (the-Countess-dressed-as-Susanna) off to a pavilion, where he might have made love to her except that Figaro, thinking that the Countess *is* Susanna, scares him off. Then the furious Figaro is fooled into making advances to *his* own wife—for Susanna, still bent on punishing him, has disguised herself as the Countess. (They make up when he recognizes her voice.) The Count, returning to what he still thinks is an assignation with Susanna, is furious to find his "wife" embracing Figaro, and threatens to expose her publicly. The real Countess then appears in her own person to confound him. All the action comes to a halt as he kneels to ask her forgiveness ("Contessa, perdono!"), and she graciously grants it. The four couples (Count and Countess, Figaro and Susanna, Bartolo and Marcellina, Cherubino and Barbarina) are united, and everyone celebrates with fireworks.

And that's just *some* of the stuff that happened in a palace called Aguas Frescas on that long "crazy day."

♣

In France, Beaumarchais' play *La Folle Journée, ou Le Mariage de Figaro* was a none-too-subtle attack on the established order, and a grossly offended Louis XVI ordered that it never be performed. This condemnation stirred up such interest that, when the king finally gave his approval, the theater doors were broken down and the railings gave way as the most elegant people in Paris crowded in to see their follies reenacted in public view. Caron de Beaumarchais, who intended Figaro ("fils Caron") as a figure for himself, had fired what Napoleon later called "the first shot in the French Revolution."

In Vienna, Mozart, aged twenty-nine and desperate to write an opera on a contemporary subject, set *Figaro* to music in six weeks, while his librettist da Ponte convinced the emperor, Joseph II, that he had shorn the objectionable play of its excesses. Actually the opera goes much deeper than the play. Beaumarchais' *Figaro* gave voice to the era's emerging ideas of social justice, the rights of man, the freedom of the individual, and the supremacy of reason over hereditary privilege; Mozart's *Figaro* is only ostensibly about social justice and not at all about the supremacy of reason. Mozart was to sing of things which Beaumarchais' Age of Enlightenment actually suppressed: the demonic (in *Don Giovanni*), the irrational underside of reason (in *Così*), and the mythic and intuitive (in *The Magic Flute*). His *Figaro*, anticipating some of this, is an exploration of that most irrational of human experiences, love, and it seems already to know something of Freud. (There are even Freudian slips in the "si"/"no" exchanges between Susanna and the Count at the start of Act III.)

Mozart knows about adolescent love (Cherubino and Barbarina), happy marital love (Figaro and Susanna), betrayed love (the Countess), smoldering lust (the Count), loveless intrigue (Basilio), love's still-ardent vestiges (Marcellina), and its dead ashes (Bartolo). He knows about the shifting patterns of human relationships, about tenderness, trust, suspicion, misunderstanding, grief, resilience and, above all, forgiveness. The delicious complications of the play are compounded in the opera. When, in the last act, Susanna sings her idyllic "Deh vieni non tardar," Figaro is in the shadows listening, and she knows he is listening, but he doesn't know she knows he is listening. She is singing her chaste sentiments directly to him, fully aware that he will think she is singing unchaste sentiments to the Count, and so be properly punished for his doubts about her fidelity. This is far more ambivalent and perceptive than anything Beaumarchais ever thought of.

Later in the last act, the situation is reversed. Susanna appears to Figaro disguised as the Countess, and he doesn't know that it is she disguised as the Countess; then she makes a slip and he knows (but she doesn't know that he knows) that she is disguised as the Countess. And all the while the music modulates back and forth between the two keys associated with the two women, indicating what he knows, what she knows, and what he knows she knows.

In this marvelous work, Mozart combines the two familiar forms of opera of his day—the new, comic *opera buffa* and the older, fast-fading *opera seria*, enriching the former with the deeper feelings of the latter. What he accomplished in the course of this was to give the world the first opera to develop its characters so profoundly that we come to know them as we come to know the figures in a voluminous novel, and the first opera to expand the notion of comedy past the conventions of its period. *Figaro* is a great moment in the history of the theater. But in the last analysis it is no different from Mozart's other works—the symphonies, the sonatas, the quartets, and especially the quintets and piano concertos. All of them artfully blend the serious and the comic to give expression to complex human feelings. Alfred Brendel was thinking of the keyboard works when he described Mozart's music as "humor based on tragedy that understands, loves, and forgives," but he expressed what can be found even more abundantly in the perceptive, loving, understanding, and forgiving work that *Figaro* unquestionably is.

Recording
E. Kleiber / della Casa, Gueden, Danco, Siepi, Poell, Corena
(Decca/London 1955)

Orfeo
(Orpheus)
Music by Claudio Monteverdi
Text by Alessandro Striggio
First performance: Mantua, 24 February 1607

Act I

Prologue: After three fanfares that seem instantly to conjure up the Renaissance, Music appears to announce that she will present the story of Orpheus as an illustration of the power of her art.

In the fields of classic Thrace, nymphs and shepherds happily assemble for the wedding of Orpheus and Eurydice.

In a sylvan glade, Orpheus is making the trees respond to his song when he receives word that Eurydice, bitten by a poisonous serpent as she was gathering flowers, has died.

Orpheus, determined to bring Eurydice back to the world of the living, is led by Hope to the River Styx, and there, by the power of his music ("Possente spirto"), he gradually lulls Charon, the infernal boatman, to sleep. Orpheus boards the boat and drifts toward the land of the dead, sending his plea across the waters.

ACT II

At the underworld court of Pluto, Proserpina, who has heard the plea, asks her husband to return Eurydice to Orpheus. He agrees to do so, provided Orpheus not look upon his beloved until they reach the world above. But on the ascent, Orpheus, distracted by a Virgilian crashing from below, turns, looks on Eurydice, and loses her. The spirits wonder that a man can conquer hell but not his own emotions.

Orpheus wanders through a wild Thracian landscape, bewailing his loss. Suddenly his father, Apollo, appears, to take him to complete happiness— and to Eurydice—among the stars.

♣

Though Monteverdi's 1607 *Orfeo*, a paean to the power of music, is generally cited as the first opera, it had predecessors. More than a century earlier, possibly as early as 1472, the young Renaissance scholar Politian mounted in Mantua an *Orfeo* that was the first secular drama sung in a modern language. And in 1597 a group of Florentine humanists, in an attempt to produce something comparable to Greek tragedy, mounted a *Dafne* based on Ovid (almost all the music for this experiment has been lost), and followed that in 1600 with two rival treatments of the Orpheus myth, both titled *Euridice*, by Giacomo Peri and Giulio Caccini (for which the music survives). Whichever of these scattered pre-Monteverdi pieces can claim to be the first opera, it is clear that the myth of Orpheus, which requires song to dramatize every pivotal moment in its action, lies at the heart of opera. It is quite proper to speak of "the birth of opera from the spirit of Orpheus."

But with Monteverdi there appeared, in the words of Paul Henry Lang, "one of those extraordinary individuals who create and organize a new form of art, and whose advent into the domain of thought is analogous to the appearance of a superior species in nature, after a series of unfruitful attempts." Monteverdi, a madrigalist, blended for dramatic purposes the styles of a century of Renaissance music to tell, once again, the story of Orpheus. His extraordinary work actually looks far beyond the Renaissance: it contains in embryonic form the major traditions that still govern operatic composition—aria, recitative, duet, choral and dance interludes, musical characterization—even, with the reappearances of Music and her *ritornello* (refrain), something akin to continuity by leitmotif. And what other opera composer created a masterpiece the first time out?

Recording

Gardiner / Baird, Rolfe Johnson, White, Tomlinson
(Deutsche Grammophon 1985)

Orfeo ed Euridice

(Orpheus and Eurydice)
Music by Christoph Willibald von Gluck
Text by Ranieri de' Calzabigi
First performance: Vienna, 5 October 1762

Act I

At the tomb of his bride Eurydice, Orpheus, inconsolable at his loss, resolves to descend to the world of the dead and bring her back to life. Amor, god of love, appears to him and tells him that the gods below will be rendered harmless by the power of his song, and that the gods above, out of pity, will allow him to resurrect his Eurydice provided he not look upon her or speak to her till he has brought her to the world of light. Orpheus is sure of the all-conquering power of his music but not so sure he can fulfill the condition put on his love.

Act II

In the infernal darkness, Orpheus, singing to the accompaniment of his lyre, gradually moves the specters to tears, and they allow him to pass beyond their portals to the Elysian Fields ("Dance of the Furies").

The souls of the blessed are dancing ethereally in an idyllic landscape ("Dance of the Blessed Spirits"). Orpheus enters playing on his lyre, enchanted by sky, sun, rivers, and breezes such as he has never experienced

("Che puro ciel!"). Eurydice is brought to him, and he leads her away, carefully averting his eyes.

ACT III

On the upward journey, Eurydice cannot understand why Orpheus shows no affection and remains completely silent. She says that without his love she would rather die than live. He breaks his silence, eventually turns to look at her, and she falls lifeless. He sings then of an even deeper loss than before ("Che farò senza Euridice?"), and is about to slay himself when Amor appears again, restores Eurydice to life, and unites the couple, announcing that the gods have had sufficient proof of Orpheus' constancy.

[In the temple of Amor, the lovers and their shepherd companions celebrate the triumph of love.]

♣

Opera, born from the spirit of Orpheus (see the previous entry), was in need of reformation in 1762. Baroque opera had become cliché-ridden and undramatic, dominated by vain, posturing singers in love with their voices, and, most damning of all, in its excesses it claimed to represent the spirit of classical Greece. Gluck undertook to reform it, and chose as his subject the myth that brought opera to birth.

With his librettist Calzabigi he carefully mapped out his strategy: the drama must come first; music would be the means whereby the drama was realized; vocal ornament would be banished; truth to nature and to naturalness of expression would prevail. The result was a work that moved its audiences as no opera in memory had moved them.

Gluck gave his *Orfeo* an inadequate overture and made some unfortunate concessions to the tastes of his time, capitulating to rococo prettiness when Amor, not Hermes, comes as divine messenger, and again when, in an unconvincing *lieto fine*, Eurydice is restored a second time to life. But most of Gluck's *Orfeo* is true to the spirit of Johann Joachim Winckelmann's classic ideal, "noble simplicity and serene greatness." Orpheus' aria "Che farò" is the preeminent example of this, while the scene in the Elysian Fields, where one clear, calm, geometrically proportioned melody nobly follows another, is one of the wonders of music.

Gluck expanded the work for Paris in 1774, rewriting the part of Orpheus (originally alto castrato) for tenor and adding the incredibly beautiful flute solo in the Elysian Fields—perhaps the loveliest music ever inspired by Greek myth.

Recording

Solti / Horne, Lorengar, Donath (Decca/London 1969)

Otello

(Othello)
Music by Giuseppe Verdi
Text by Arrigo Boito (after Shakespeare)
First performance: Milan, 5 February 1887

ACT I

On the island of Cyprus, the fleet commanded by the Moorish general Otello battles its way safely through a storm after defeating the Turks, and the commander's shout of triumph ("Esultate!") stirs the crowd to celebration. But Iago, the Moor's jealous ensign, is set on destroying him. Enlisting the services of the cowardly Roderigo, he plies a superior officer, Cassio, with drink and starts a brawl for which Otello, suddenly appearing, blames Cassio. Otello dismisses Cassio and appoints Iago to take his place. The riot quelled, Otello and his chaste wife, Desdemona, recall how they fell in love when, years before in Venice, he told her of his many heroic adventures (Duet: "Già nella notte densa"). Stars appear over the calm sea. He kisses her three times.

ACT II

Within the seaport castle, Iago continues with his devious plan to destroy Otello. He slyly advises the dejected Cassio to ask Desdemona to intercede for him. Left alone, Iago boldly states his creed: the god he believes in is a cruel god who has created him in his own cruel image; man is intrinsically evil, the plaything of fate all his life; and the whole idea of life after death is a lie ("Credo"). He then suggests to Otello that Desdemona and Cassio may be lovers, and sends the impressionable Moor into a rage. Meanwhile, Iago wrests from the hand of his wife, Emilia, a delicately embroidered handkerchief that Otello had given to Desdemona as a token of their love. Otello is already close to despair ("Ora e per sempre addio") when Iago lies that he has heard Cassio speaking his passion for Desdemona in his sleep ("Era la notte") and seen him sporting her precious handkerchief when awake. Otello swears by heaven that he will be revenged, and Iago sanctimoniously kneels and joins him in his oath (Duet: "Si, pel ciel").

ACT III

Desdemona comes to Otello to plead for Cassio's reinstatement. Conditioned as he is by Iago's poisonous slanders, Otello misreads her intentions, and when she cannot produce the handkerchief, he accuses her of adultery and violently sends her away. He prays to an unanswering God ("Dio! mi potevi") that he could have borne military disgrace, poverty, and physical pain with resignation—but not this betrayal of his love. Iago then stage-manages a scene wherein Otello is duped into thinking Cassio is making merry over the handkerchief and Desdemona's lost virtue. This confirms the Moor's suspicions and, when the Venetian ambassador, Lodovico, ceremoniously arrives with a new appointment for him, he hurls Desdemona to the ground, orders everyone away, and falls into an epileptic faint. Iago alone remains—to plant his foot contemptuously on the prostrate hero.

ACT IV

Desdemona, attended by Emilia, prepares to retire ("The Willow Song"), prays for heaven's protection ("Ave Maria"), and falls asleep. Otello enters her bedroom silently, kisses her three times, wakes her to give her time to pray, and then violently strangles her. Emilia raises the alarm. Iago escapes when proof of his schemes is quickly pieced together. Otello, heartbroken as he realizes that his Desdemona was innocent, stabs himself and crawls dying to her bed to kiss her three times.

☙

The influential Shakespearian A. C. Bradley complained that *Othello* was the only one of the bard's great tragedies that didn't suggest "huge universal powers working in the world." That may be true of *Othello*, but it is certainly not true of *Otello*. Verdi's opera is about God as well as man, and asks whether God might be a force for evil in the world. The first chord, as unresolved as the famous first chord of Wagner's *Tristan*, flashes like lightning through the theater, a savage and destructive sound, elemental and full of fury. The chorus on shore sings that some terrible, blind, whirling spirit is ripping the heavens apart. Later, Otello and Iago, calling on their God to avenge them, swear by the lightning that is forked and the sea that exterminates. Otello, in the poignant "Dio! mi potevi," speaks of divine clemency covering its face with the mask of hell, while the opera's two main additions to Shakespeare, Iago's "Credo" and Desdemona's "Ave Maria," ring telling dramatic changes on liturgical prayers. Verdi clearly found in Shakespeare's play, as earlier in *La Forza del Destino* and the *Requiem*, a means of dramatizing his own agnosticism and his very ambivalent feelings about faith and providence. Only with his *Four Sacred Pieces*, composed a few years before his death, did Verdi—particularly in the "Te Deum"—offer some hope in these great matters.

Boito provided the composer with a skillful if somewhat preciously worded condensation of a much longer play, and Verdi, returning to the theater after more than twenty years' absence (during which time his archrival, Wagner, had died), produced what is perhaps the greatest—certainly the most overwhelming—of his scores. In recent decades, as the central role of the passionate Moor has been taken on by such heroic tenors as Jon Vickers and Placido Domingo, the opera has at last become one of Verdi's popular successes as well.

Recording

Levine / Scotto, Domingo, Milnes (RCA 1978)

Pagliacci

(Clowns)
Music and text by Ruggero Leoncavallo
First performance: Milan, 21 May 1892

Act I

In the midst of a carnival overture, a baritone (dressed as the clown Tonio) comes before the curtain to sing a prologue: the story you will see enacted is a true one, and will convince you that clowns are creatures of flesh and bone like anyone else.

On the feast of the Assumption in a Calabrian village, a troop of clowns announces an evening performance. Their leader, Canio, is furious when his wife, Nedda, is given undue attention by the misshapen Tonio, and he warns the local men to keep away from her ("Un tal gioco"). The villagers file off to vespers, and Nedda, left alone, envies the birds overhead their freedom ("The Ballatella"). She takes a whip to Tonio when he makes advances but agrees to meet Silvio, an ardent villager she has seen on previous visits, after the performance that night. Tonio overhears them and calls Canio. The passionate clown, unable either to catch Silvio or to force Nedda to reveal his name, is restrained by another performer, Beppe, and resigns himself to donning his costume and painting his face, even though his heart is breaking ("Vesti la giubba").

ACT II

After a poignant orchestral prelude, the evening's performance takes place, and the commedia dell'arte parallels the real situation so closely that Canio snaps ("No! Pagliaccio non son!") and knifes Nedda onstage and Silvio in the audience. Then he (or, in the original ending, Tonio) announces, "The comedy is over."

♣

Leoncavallo's all-out attempt to equal the success of Mascagni's *Cavalleria Rusticana* is actually more successful in some ways (with music of greater variety and subtlety, a pervasive sense of irony, and a set of play-within-a-play contradictions that impressed W. H. Auden), and at the Metropolitan Opera, thanks to Enrico Caruso's world-famous Canio, *Pagliacci* has chalked up thirty more performances than its rival and frequent companion. But the similarities between the two operas are legion: both are crime-of-passion pieces of verismo set in small Italian towns on church holidays; both have surefire before-the-curtain solos; both may be thought to be two-act pieces (*Cavalleria*'s action divided in two by its intermezzo) that are performed in one act (*Pagliacci*'s Act II prelude linking its two parts); both end with a single line of spoken dialogue; and both are far and away the most popular of their composer's works. Leoncavallo's piece is based on an actual criminal case that his father, a district judge, had presided over and at which the composer, as a small child, was present.

Recording

Serafin / Callas, di Stefano, Gobbi, Panerai (EMI/Angel 1954, paired with *Cavalleria Rusticana*)

Parsifal

Music and text by Richard Wagner
First performance: Bayreuth, 26 July 1882

Act I

An orchestral prelude begins with a hushed, long-spanned theme shaped by the words of Jesus at the Last Supper ("Take this my body, take this my blood"). This is followed by the gently rising "Dresden Amen," and by the "Faith" theme, intoned three times by the brass choir. Subsequently, a six-note "Suffering" motif assumes great importance.

In a forest clearing near the castle of Monsalvat, in the mountains of Spain, the four main figures of the drama make their appearances one by one: Gurnemanz, a kindly old knight of the Holy Grail; Amfortas, the Grail's king, wounded in his side; Kundry, the mysterious sleep-bound woman who brings him balsam for his wound; and finally young Parsifal, the "pure fool" the others are all, in their several ways, awaiting.

Bells toll, and Gurnemanz, after reprimanding Parsifal for slaying a sacred swan, takes him to the castle's inner shrine to witness the Grail ceremony: Amfortas uncovering the cup Jesus used at the Last Supper. The other knights, including Amfortas' aged father, Titurel, gain more-than-natural strength from the sight of the glowing cup, but Amfortas' wound, as always when he performs the ceremony, breaks out afresh. Parsifal, a young pagan brought up in the forest, understands nothing of what he sees, and Gurnemanz, with surprising brusqueness, orders him from the castle. Then a mysterious voice fills the empty room, proclaiming Parsifal the "pure fool" the knights had hoped would come.

Act II

In another castle, in Moorish lands beyond the mountains, a failed knight of the Grail, the eunuch magician Klingsor, summons Kundry from her sleep. She has been reincarnated by evil forces throughout the ages and has seduced many Grail knights for the renegade Klingsor. Now she is to entice Parsifal when he comes to the castle walls. She tries to resist but can only break out in a terrifying laugh; in centuries past, she laughed at the suffering Jesus.

Klingsor's garden of magic flowers rises, and Parsifal, having felled the unfaithful Grail knights who attacked him, wanders among the flowers, which are transformed into beautiful maidens. He is almost seduced by the fairest of them, the transformed Kundry. But at the moment when Kundry kisses him, he remembers Amfortas and the wound ("Amfortas! Die Wunde!") and realizes that his mission is to heal that wound by rescuing from Klingsor's castle the spear that pierced Jesus' side on the cross. (Amfortas had lost the sacred spear, one of the Grail knights' sacred possessions, years before, when Kundry seduced him and Klingsor drove the weapon into his side.) Parsifal, now in the same peril, grasps the spear when Klingsor hurls it at him, makes the sign of the cross with it, and thereby brings the garden and its castle crumbling to the ground. Standing on the ruined wall, he tells Kundry that she knows where they can meet again.

ACT III

A prelude depicts Parsifal's years of wandering with the spear, on the way back to heal Amfortas.

On a radiant Good Friday morning, Gurnemanz finds Kundry lying half-conscious in a meadow near the Grail castle, and Parsifal appears, now a mature man in black armor, bearing the Grail spear. He plants it in the earth and kneels in prayer. Gurnemanz tells him that Amfortas no longer performs the Grail ceremony and that the knights, without the strength it gives, no longer go forth on their deeds of mercy. Old Titurel, deprived of the sight of the Grail cup, has just died. With his hope renewed by the return of the "pure fool," Gurnemanz baptizes Parsifal and anoints him as the Grail's new king, while Kundry, a repentant Magdalen, washes his feet and dries them with her hair. Parsifal exclaims at the loveliness of the blossoms in the meadow, and Gurnemanz replies that, unlike the flowers poisoned by Klingsor's magic, these are made beautiful by the power of "Good Friday's Spell." Parsifal, carrying the spear, leads Gurnemanz and Kundry toward the Grail castle.

Bells toll, and the knights of the Grail assemble one last time, for the funeral of Titurel. They are at the point of forcing the wounded Amfortas to uncover the Grail cup and restore their failing powers when Parsifal appears, heals the wound of Amfortas with the spear's point, and uncovers the sacred cup himself. In the darkness both cup and spear, reunited after a long passage of years, begin to glow with the same radiant light. The dove that descends every year to empower the Grail wafts down to hover over Parsifal's head. Kundry falls lifeless, released at last from her cycle of rebirths, and Parsifal raises the glowing cup in blessing over the newly strengthened knights.

❧

As this plot summary may have indicated, Wagner, in telling the centuries-old tale of Parzifal (in the German tradition) or Perceval (in the French), has compressed an immense amount of mythic material—including some material from sources beyond medieval Christianity—into a compact structure almost symmetrical in shape.

Musically, the story is told with a new subtlety in the manipulation of leitmotifs: the expressive opening theme is in the course of the drama broken into three motivic parts—the first notes signifying the Grail cup, the last the Grail spear, and the intervening phrase the suffering brought to the world by the separation of cup and spear. Almost all of the music in Acts I and III is of a reverent slowness, and much of it is of an astonishing beauty: after the strings have played the prelude's long opening theme, it is repeated by a silvery trumpet, supported by three luminous woodwinds and shimmering string arpeggios. At that moment, anyone searching for the Grail may rightly claim that he has sighted it. Virginia Woolf remarked, sphinxlike, that in *Parsifal*, "music has reached a place not yet visited by sound." Debussy admired, synaesthetically, the stained-glass transparency of the work's musical textures, though he had no patience with the suffering characters in the text.

This, Wagner's last music drama, is the most controversial of them all. (Each successive work, it seems, has raised more controversy than the one preceding.) Nietzsche, in his famous falling-out with Wagner, first wrote that in *Parsifal* Wagner had forsaken his classic Greek ideals and sunk at the foot of the cross; but when he first heard the prelude, with its shining trumpet, he found in the music "a sublime and extraordinary feeling . . . an awful severity of judgment from on high that sees through the soul, piercing it as with knives." Finally, *Parsifal* was for him "a work of perfidy . . . a secret attempt to poison the suppositions of life . . . an assassination of basic human ethics."

In recent years we have been encouraged to view *Parsifal* as an anti-Semitic tract (Wagner wrote some viciously racist and remarkably stupid essays in the course of composing it and, we are to believe, patterned the figures of Kundry and Klingsor after prevailing Jewish stereotypes); as an act of self-adoration (Wagner's hero is, like any Wagner hero, to some degree a figure for Wagner himself); as the gospel of a new religion of art (Wagner dubbed the work a "stage-consecrating festival play," and his disciples have always insisted on an atmosphere of reverence for its performances); and generally as the receptacle of all that was rotten in nineteenth-century thought.

It should be remembered, in the face of all this, that Wagner depended on ideas—sometimes profound, sometimes deplorable—to power his creative engine. But that does not by any means mean that the ideas went into the text and music. And there are better, truer ways of explaining the work's complicated symbolism. *Parsifal* is clearly Wagner's final tribute to the concepts of his contemporary Arthur Schopenhauer, whom he read while composing all his works from *Die Walküre* onward. Wagner's "pure fool" embodies the pessimistic philosopher's central ethical concept, compassion (*Mitleid*): in the course of the drama Parsifal is, as the voice in the castle proclaimed he would be, "made wise through compassion" (*durch Mitleid wissend*). The other characters all cry out in the midst of their sufferings as if they longed for redemption from the terrible world-pervading force of what Schopenhauer called *Wille* (will). Other details in the text, from Kundry's repeated cycles of life to the emphasis on overcoming suffering by quelling desire, can be traced to Buddhist teaching, an influence on both Wagner and Schopenhauer.

Nor should the Christian symbols at work in the opera be denied their significances. Wagner's Grail knights may be thought to represent the Christian church of Wagner's century—out of touch, he thought, with the true Christian message. Wagner wrote, "When religion becomes artificial, art has a duty to rescue it, by showing that the mythic symbols which religion would have us believe literally true are actually figurative. Art can idealize these symbols and so reveal the profound truths they contain."

But above all Wagner's opera draws on myth, and Jungian patterns are a predictably helpful aid in sorting out much of its symbolism: Parsifal is the questing hero of a thousand cultures, encountering his shadow side (Amfortas), his ambivalent anima (Kundry), and his Wise Old Man (Gurnemanz), and integrating them all around a mandala-symbol of his Self (the Grail). Like the *Ring*, *Parsifal* may be taken as transpiring on the landscape of a soul in need of healing, where psychic forces that have been wrenched apart (the masculine spear and the feminine cup) must be brought together. When Wagner's Parsifal is first taken to the Grail castle, he asks, not "What is the Grail?", but "Who is the Grail?" Gurnemanz's line to Parsifal as they make their way to the Grail castle, "You see, my son, time becomes space here," was cited by Claude Lévi-Strauss, the founder of the modern structuralist approach to myth, as the most profound of all definitions of myth.

To skeptics who remain unconvinced, it might be said that Wagner's *Parsifal* is not unlike the legendary Grail itself: some knights drew sustenance from it and were sent by it to do great deeds in the world, some failed in the quest to find it, and some could not see it, even when in its presence.

Recording
Knappertsbusch / Dalis, Thomas, London, Hotter, Neidlinger
(Philips 1962)

The Pearl Fishers

(Les Pêcheurs de Perles)
Music by Georges Bizet
Text by Eugène Cormon and Michel Carré
First performance: Paris, 30 September 1863

ACT I

Zurga, newly chosen king of the pearl fishers of Ceylon, meets a friend of his youth, Nadir, on the shore, and together they remember falling in love with the same virgin priestess (Duet: "Au fond du temple saint"). Now each vows that, in deference to the other, he will never possess her. Then that very priestess, Léila, is sent, veiled, to keep vigil that year for the pearl fishers' safety. Consecrated to Brahma, she must remain inviolate. Nadir, still in love with her ("Je crois entendre encore"), recognizes her and, as she ascends a cliff overlooking the sea to begin her ritual watch, he follows her.

ACT II

The high priest Nourabad finds Nadir and Léila together in her temple. He alerts the pearl fishers, who advance against the lovers with drawn swords. Zurga, not knowing the identity of the priestess, is inclined to spare his friend —until the veil is removed from Léila's face. Deeply offended by this betrayal, he sentences the guilty pair to death.

ACT III

Léila pleads unsuccessfully with Zurga to spare Nadir. Led away to execution, she gives a young pearl fisher a golden chain, asking that it be sent to her mother as a remembrance.

As Léila and Nadir are about to be burned alive, Zurga sets fire to the pearl fishers' camp and allows the lovers to escape: he has recognized the golden chain as the one he had given years before to an unknown girl as a reward for saving his life. He then awaits his own fate at the hands of the high priest, as flames—the wrath of Brahma—consume the whole island.

♣

Some of *The Pearl Fishers* is second-rate, the work of a twenty-four-year-old protégé of Gounod still honing his skills. But the first-act tenor aria and world-conquering tenor-baritone duet are beautifully realized moments, unsurpassed even by the lyric outpourings of *Faust* and of the composer's own forthcoming *Carmen*, and the recent popularity of these excerpts has given the whole unlikely work a new and welcome lease on life.

Recording

Rosenthal / Micheau, Vanzo, Bacquier (Chant du Monde 1959)

Pelléas et Mélisande

(Pelléas and Mélisande)
Music by Claude Debussy
Text by Maurice Maeterlinck
First performance: Paris, 30 April 1902

ACT I

In a dark forest, Prince Golaud, whose wife has died, meets the elusive Mélisande, weeping beside a pool where she has lost her crown.

In the royal castle in Allemonde, Golaud's mother, Geneviève, reads a letter he has written to his half-brother Pelléas: he has married Mélisande and will return with her to the castle if their grandfather, King Arkel, will allow it. Arkel, almost blind, resigns himself to fate.

Mélisande, welcomed to Allemonde by Geneviève, meets Pelléas as night falls, and, by the beacon of a lighthouse shining through the mist, they watch the ship that brought her as it sails away. He says that he too will soon leave.

Pelléas speaks with Mélisande in the sunlight by a well whose waters once restored sight to the blind. Playfully she tosses her wedding ring in the air—and it plummets to the depths of the well. The hour strikes noon.

Golaud, thrown from his horse at the same stroke of noon, wonders why Mélisande is unhappy in the castle and notices that her wedding ring is not on her finger. She says that she lost it in a cave by the sea. He orders her to take Pelléas with her and search for it.

Pelléas and Mélisande look for the ring in the seaside cave, and a shaft of moonlight reveals three starving beggars sheltering there.

Act II

Mélisande is combing her long hair, which reaches from her tower window all the way to Pelléas, standing below. He winds its strands passionately about himself. Golaud sees the two and calls to Mélisande not to lean so far from the tower; she might fall.

Golaud then takes Pelléas to the frightening castle vaults and all but sends him falling to the depths.

The half-brothers emerge into the sunlight, and Golaud warns Pelléas to stay away from Mélisande, who is going to have a child.

Golaud holds his little son, Yniold, up to Mélisande's window, sure that Pelléas is with her. The innocent boy gives maddeningly elusive replies to his father's tormented questions about what he sees within.

Pelléas, now determined to leave Allemonde, arranges to see Mélisande one last time, at the well.

Golaud accuses Mélisande of unfaithfulness and, to King Arkel's horror, drags her by her long hair.

Yniold sees a flock of sheep being driven to the slaughter, doesn't understand why this must be, and runs to ask someone.

Pelléas and Mélisande meet at the well. Golaud surprises them there, kills his half-brother, and wounds his wife.

Act III

Mélisande, having given birth to a daughter, lies dying. Golaud, grief-stricken, desperately tries to find out if she and Pelléas were lovers. Her answers are as elusive as those he had from his little son. He despairs. Mélisande silently dies and, as the twilight from the sea comes through the castle windows and a distant bell tolls, King Arkel takes up the baby, whose turn it is now to suffer.

❧

Debussy, like the poets and painters of his day, was interested in representing, not the ordinary surfaces of human experience, but the sense impressions and the subliminal emotions human experience conveys. He devised a new palette of sounds for this purpose, blending Western medieval modes with Eastern pentatonic and whole-tone scales, and juxtaposing chords that were, by the academic standards of his time, unrelated. His piano works were a series of impressionistic images like those that recur in dreams. But he hoped to compose an opera, to find a dramatist who "saying things by halves, would allow me to graft my dream onto his . . . someone who would conceive characters not bound by time or place, someone who would leave me free to have more art than he, and to complete his work."

He found that dramatist in Maurice Maeterlinck, whose new symbolist play *Pelléas et Mélisande* was replete with the very images Debussy had already limned in his keyboard works—the forest, the castle, the sea, the ship, the moonlight, the girl with flaxen hair, as well as such dream images as the lighthouse, the peril, the fear of falling—all of them suggestive of the elusiveness of whatever it might be that lies beyond the senses.

The partnership was, however, far from friendly, and Maeterlinck eventually tried to sabotage the opera. Today, his fate-driven play survives only because Debussy, uninterested in fate, etched it in impressionistic colors and subtly reinterpreted it, cutting away what did not suit his purposes and adding orchestral interludes that, ultimately, turn the brutal Golaud into the most sympathetic figure in the opera: the composer found the elusiveness of truth that drives Golaud to his savage acts not unrelated to his own artistic conviction that, of the world in which we live (and Allemonde seems to be a Germanic-Gallic "all the world"), the only real knowledge we can have comes to us through impressions.

Recording

Désormière / Joachim, Jansen, Etcheverry, Cabanel
(EMI/Angel 1941)

Peter Grimes

Music by Benjamin Britten
Text by Montagu Slater (after George Crabbe)
First performance: London, 7 June 1945

ACT I

Prologue: At an inquest in a small town on a wild stretch of English coastline, the fisherman Peter Grimes, accused of causing the death of his young apprentice at sea, is acquitted but cautioned by Justice Swallow not to hire another boy. Ellen Orford, a schoolteacher who loves Grimes, assures him that they can build a life together.

An orchestral interlude depicts dawn on the sea and the lonely flight of a solitary gull. We then see, at their various exercises, the people of the Borough: the Methodist Bob Boles; the brothel-keeper, Auntie, and her two "nieces"; Mrs. Sedley, the town gossip, addicted to laudanum; the Reverend Horace Adams; Ned Keene, the apothecary; Hobson, the carter; and—the only one sympathetic to Grimes—the retired Captain Balstrode. The solitary Grimes hardly acknowledges the existence of the others and hopes only to make enough money to marry Ellen ("What harbor shelters peace?").

An orchestral interlude, built on Grimes' cry "What harbor shelters peace?", depicts a storm at sea. Grimes bursts half-mad into the village tavern while the storm is raging ("Now the Great Bear and Pleiades"), faces the fierceness of the villagers, and unwisely takes on another boy as his apprentice.

ACT II

An orchestral prelude depicts the sea-washed village on a sunny Sunday morning. Ellen sees with alarm that bruises are already visible on the new apprentice's neck. Grimes strikes her in anger and hustles the boy off to work. The townsfolk turn on the fisherman ("Grimes is at his exercise") and run to inspect his hut, leaving Ellen, Auntie, and the nieces to lament, from woman's perspective, the follies of men (Quartet: "From the gutter").

An orchestral passacaglia built on Grimes' phrase "God have mercy upon me" depicts the fisherman's torment over striking Ellen. In the hut, the new boy, weeping and hurried to his duties, exits from the cliffside door and falls to his death. Grimes rushes down after him. The crowd, when they enter, find only neatness and order. But Balstrode, opening the cliffside door, surmises what has happened.

ACT III

An orchestral prelude depicts moonlight on the sea. Grimes and the boy have been missing for days, though the boat has been found—and the boy's jacket, on which Ellen had embroidered an anchor ("Embroidery in childhood"). The villagers, spurred on by the vicious Mrs. Sedley, set off, torches in hand, on a manhunt.

An orchestral interlude depicts the fog floating in from the sea. On the shore Grimes emerges alone from the mist, maddened by the foghorn and the distant crowd shrieking his name ("Steady! Nearly home!"). Balstrode, despite Ellen's protests, advises Grimes to take his boat out to sea till he loses sight of land, and scuttle it.

The next morning the fog has lifted, and a report comes that a boat was sighted sinking out at sea. The unheeding Borough goes back to its daily tasks.

♣

Peter Grimes is among the few operas since the end of the Second World War to have permanently entered the international repertory. Its moody and powerful evocation of the sea is fully the equal of the seascapes in *Der Fliegende Holländer* and *Tristan*, its critique of a hypocritical society marshaled against a misunderstood loner is unmatched anywhere in opera, and critic London Green has rightly observed that "its alienated yet touching hero prefigured those of John Osborne, Harold Pinter, and even Samuel Beckett, and, to a greater extent than is sometimes realized, helped to form a major movement in postwar British theater."

Written for the special qualities of Peter Pears' tenor voice, the title role was reinterpreted (as the composer has ruefully regretted) by Jon Vickers in a performance of such overwhelming power and pathos that anyone who saw it is likely to say it was the experience of an operagoing lifetime. But even during the opera's first run, the literary critic Edmund Wilson wrote, "I do not remember ever to have seen, at any performance of an opera, an audience so steadily intent, so petrified and held in suspense, as the audience of *Peter Grimes.*"

Recording

Davis / Harper, Vickers, Summers (Philips 1978)

Porgy and Bess

Music by George Gershwin
Text by DuBose Heyward and Ira Gershwin
First performance: Boston, 30 September 1935

ACT I

The main characters in Catfish Row, a once elegant South Carolina square now populated by poor African-Americans, are Clara, a young mother ("Summertime"); Jake, her hardworking fisherman husband ("A woman is a sometime thing"); Porgy, crippled but brawny, and loved by everyone; Bess, a loose woman who is taken in by Porgy when the community rejects her; Sportin' Life, a dandy who wants Bess to come with him to New York; Crown, also crazy for Bess, a giant of a man who kills another in a crap game and flees; and Serena, the widow of the man killed ("My man's gone now").

Act II

Porgy ("I got plenty o' nuttin'") naively buys a "divorce" for Bess (Duet: "Bess, you is my woman now") [and is disturbed when he sees a buzzard overhead ("The Buzzard Song")].

At a community picnic on Kittiwah Island, Sportin' Life tells the pious believers that they oughtn't to take the Bible literally ("It ain't necessarily so"). Crown, who has been hiding on the island, induces Bess to stay there with him.

Bess, returned sick unto death after a week on the island, is prayed over by Serena and the people of Catfish Row ("Oh, doctor Jesus"), and her fever passes. Porgy knows that she has been with Crown and forgives her. She begs him to protect her if Crown ever returns ("I loves you, Porgy").

Sheltering from a hurricane, the community prays for Jake, who has not come back from fishing. Crown bursts through the door, boasting that not even God can harm him. When Clara, at the window, sees her husband's empty boat overturned in the waves, she runs out into the storm, leaving her baby with Bess. Crown rushes out to save her.

Act III

In the courtyard, the whole community sings a Requiem for Jake, Clara, and Crown, lost in the storm. But Crown suddenly appears, intent on carrying Bess away. Porgy, determined to defend her, lies in wait for Crown and quietly chokes him to death.

Porgy is taken away by the police for questioning, and Sportin' Life makes his play for Bess ("There's a boat dat's leavin' soon for New York"). Her resolve is weakened by the "happy dust" he gives her, and she follows him.

Porgy, released for lack of evidence, is heartbroken not to find Bess on his return ("Oh, Bess, oh where's my Bess?"). Told she has gone to New York, he starts out, knowing only that New York is somewhere north, to find her ("Oh Lawd, I'm on my way").

♣

Broadway show or opera (the irrelevant debate still rages), *Porgy* is riveting musical theater, as performances at La Scala, the Bolshoi, Glyndebourne, the Met, and dozens of German opera houses have amply demonstrated. The two most persistent and pernicious charges leveled against Gershwin's opera—that it deals in demeaning racial stereotypes and that its emotional peaks are little more than extended popular songs—were not addressed by the composer's comment, made to the *New York Times*, that *Porgy* was to be thought of as a "folk opera." He made a much more insightful remark, in the midst of composing, to the *Herald Tribune*—that *Porgy* would combine the drama of *Carmen* with the beauty of *Die Meistersinger*. His opera no more deals in demeaning racial stereotypes than does Bizet's work, and its sense of the community of human lives is expressed in superbly crafted songs and radiant choral outpourings, like those in Wagner's masterpiece. In the end, the only thing that matters is that Gershwin's black Americans are people with a depth of feeling that touches audiences deeply. That emotional communication is what opera is all about, and Gershwin knew it.

Recording

Rattle / Haymon, Clarey, Blackwell, Evans, White, Hubbard, Baker (EMI/Angel 1988)

I Puritani

(The Puritans)
Music by Vincenzo Bellini
Text by Carlo Pepoli
First performance: Paris, 24 January 1835

ACT I

On the embankment of a Puritan fortress near Plymouth, Riccardo, an officer in the war against the Stuarts, laments that his betrothed, Elvira, has fallen in love with one of the hated Royalists.

In her apartment, Elvira hears from Sir George Walton, her uncle, that he has persuaded her father to give his consent to the marriage.

In the fortress armory, Elvira's promised, Arturo, is welcomed by the Puritans ("A te, o cara"). But when he hears that his queen, widow of the exe-

159

cuted Charles I, has been arraigned there on a charge of spying, he vows to help her escape. Elvira arrives with her wedding veil ("Son vergin vezzosa"), and Arturo uses the veil to escort the queen undetected to safety. Elvira, thinking that Arturo has left her for another, loses her mind.

ACT II

Cromwell has ordered a search for Arturo, while Elvira madly imagines that he is still with her ("Qui la voce"). Sir George persuades the rejected Riccardo, in pity for the woman he still loves, to spare his rival should he be found (Duet: "Suoni la tromba").

ACT III

In a wood near the fortress, Arturo is fleeing his pursuers during a storm. He hears Elvira's voice, takes up the song, finds her, and gradually leads her out of her madness ("Vieni fra queste braccia"). She almost suffers a relapse when Arturo is captured and condemned to death. But a messenger arrives to announce that the civil war is over: the Stuarts have been defeated and Cromwell has issued a general pardon.

♣

Bellini wrote *I Puritani* for the four greatest bel canto singers of his day—Grisi and Rubini (the soprano and tenor who could provide lyric effusions of melting beauty and starburst explosions at stratospheric heights), and Tamburini and Lablache (the baritone and bass who could move easily from manly reserve to stentorian power). Unfortunately it was the first time Bellini did not have the skilled Felice Romani for his librettist, and nothing much could be done about the sorry text. One of Bellini's admonishments to the inept Pepoli is, however, a significant statement about his own art: "Engrave this on your heart in letters of adamant: opera must make people weep, shudder, and die through the singing." In a great performance of *I Puritani*, that almost happens.

Recording

Bonynge / Sutherland, Pavarotti, Cappuccilli, Ghiaurov
(Decca/London 1974)

The Queen of Spades

(Pique Dame)
Music by Peter Ilyich Tchaikovsky
Text by Modest Tchaikovsky and the composer
(after Alexander Pushkin)
First performance: St. Petersburg, 19 December 1890

ACT I

In the Summer Garden in St. Petersburg, Gherman, an officer of German extraction, addicted to gambling, sees a young lady among the parasols and confesses to Count Tomsky that he has for some time been in love with her without knowing who she is. Almost incidentally he discovers that she is Lisa, the fiancée of Prince Yeletsky. Cursing his luck, Gherman is startled to hear from Tomsky that the old Countess strolling with Lisa, her grandmother and once a great beauty, had learned from a lover the secret of three cards that, if played in succession, will always win. Known throughout Europe as the Queen of Spades, the Countess told the secret to two subsequent lovers but was then warned by an apparition that, if ever she told a third, she would die. As a thunderstorm breaks, Gherman resolves to learn the Countess' secret.

In her room in the Countess' palace, Lisa dismisses the friends who have tried to rid her of her melancholy. She regrets her engagement to Yeletsky for she has fallen in love, with equal obsession, with the obsessed soldier she saw staring at her in the Summer Garden. Suddenly, Gherman enters the room through the balcony and, intent on learning the secret of the three cards from Lisa's grandmother, seduces the girl.

ACT II

At a masked ball and pastorale in honor of Catherine the Great, Lisa, unable to respond to Prince Yeletsky's protestations of love, gives Gherman the key to her grandmother's bedroom, explaining that hers is the adjoining chamber.

At midnight, Gherman enters the old woman's room and tries without success to persuade her to reveal the secret of the three cards. Finally he threatens her with a pistol, and she dies of fright. Lisa, hearing noises, hurries in, realizes that she has been used, sees her grandmother dead, and, despite Gherman's insistence that he did not mean to kill the old woman, orders the "monster" away.

ACT III

The Countess' ghost appears to Gherman in his barracks and, so that he will make an honest woman out of Lisa, reveals to him the secret of the cards: he must play, in succession, the three, the seven, and the ace.

Lisa, still in love with Gherman, waits for him at the Winter Canal. He arrives half-mad, hopelessly obsessed with the secret of the cards. She, left in despair, throws herself into the icy waters of the Neva.

At the gambling table, Gherman wins handsomely with the first two cards, but when, challenging Prince Yeletsky, he stakes everything on the ace, he turns up the queen of spades. The ghost of the Countess appears, mocking him, and Gherman shoots himself, imploring the pardon of Yeletsky, who loved Lisa with a purer love than his.

♣

Like *Eugene Onegin*, *The Queen of Spades* changes the tone of its original. Gherman, in the pages of Pushkin a fairly typical cynic observed from without, becomes on Tchaikovsky's stage a self-destructive neurotic driven from within. And Lisa's character too is turned hysteric: her suicide is an addition made by the composer. The opera is really two stories: the descent of Gherman into madness (something admirably suited to the Tchaikovsky of the three last symphonies) and the emergence of Russia into international prominence under Catherine the Great (something admirably suited to the Tchaikovsky of the three great ballets). *The Queen of Spades* is perhaps the composer's finest opera, but it is extremely difficult to bring off: the hypnotic scenes, with their supernatural elements, must be held in dramatic balance with the scenes that celebrate a glittering society. Few productions have encompassed the whole of Tchaikovsky's vision, and until recently the opera was grossly underrated in the West.

Recording

Gergiev / Guleghina, Borodina, Arkhipova, Grigorian
(Philips 1992)

The Rake's Progress

Music by Igor Stravinsky
Text by W. H. Auden and Chester Kallman
First performance: Venice, 11 September 1951

ACT I

In an eighteenth-century English garden, Tom Rakewell, wooing Anne Truelove, rejects her father's offer of a position in business, sighing, "I wish I had money." The sinister Nick Shadow promptly materializes, telling Tom that his uncle has died and left him a fortune. With Nick offering his services for a year and a day, Tom goes off to London.

In Mother Goose's brothel, Nick sets the clock back while Tom, still cherishing his ideal of love, is schooled in vice and whores it up with a pack of Roaring Boys.

Anne in her garden resolves to find Tom in London and help him ("I go to him").

ACT II

Tom, utterly bored in his elegant London house, sighs, "I wish I were happy," and Nick suggests he become so by marrying a bearded lady, Baba the Turk: with that bold step he will prove his complete independence of both passion and reason.

Tom has married Baba and is bringing her home, veiled and curtained in a sedan chair, when he meets Anne in the street. He sends his true love away, saying he is now unworthy of her. Baba, emerging from her sedan chair, removes the veil from her face and basks in the applause of the crowd.

Baba has turned out to be a compulsive talker and a shrew, and Tom, profoundly unhappy, plumps his wig down over her head, silencing her in midsentence and rendering her immobile. Wondering if he might do some good in the world, Tom sighs, "I wish it were true," and Nick appears with a machine which he says is capable of turning stones into bread. Tom is overjoyed, thinking that if he mass-produces the machine and feeds the world's hungry he may again be worthy of Anne's love.

ACT III

Tom has been discredited as a fraud, and his goods are up for auction. Last of the lot is Baba, who, when the wig is removed, promptly resumes her interrupted sentence. Anne is there in tears, and Baba generously encourages her to search for Tom and save him.

A year and a day have passed, and it is time for Tom to pay up. In a churchyard, Nick tells Tom that he must consign his soul to him at midnight—but Nick is sporting enough to stop the clock with three strokes to go, and gives Tom a chance to save himself by guessing three cards. Tom thinks of Anne at the tenth stroke and correctly calls the first card: the queen of hearts. A graveyard spade clatters to the ground at the eleventh stroke, and Tom cries out, "The deuce!", correctly identifying the two of spades. Nick, not ready to lose a soul, reinserts the queen of hearts into the pack and cuts to it for the stroke of midnight. Tom, hearing in the distance the voice of Anne, the queen of his heart, calls the card rightly. He then says, wisely, "I wish for nothing else." Nick, a poor loser, dooms Tom to madness.

Confined in Bedlam, Tom thinks that he is Adonis and that Anne, when she comes to see him, is Venus. Surrounded by madmen, she quietly rocks Tom to sleep in her arms ("Gently, little boat") and then, summoned by her faithful father, takes her leave. Tom awakes and, finding her gone and his dream of springtime renewal lost, dies of grief.

Epilogue: Before the curtain, each of the characters finds his/her own moral in the tale, but all agree that "for idle hands and hearts and minds, the Devil finds a work to do."

♣

The longest work by the man thought in the mid-twentieth century to be the world's foremost composer, *The Rake's Progress* disappointed all but a few connoisseurs in 1951 ("tedious" was the watchword). But in the more than half-century since, the work has quietly developed, in performances in small houses, its own crisp, detached performance style, and the ears of the public, no longer expecting the opera to be a cross between Stravinsky's *Firebird* and Gounod's *Faust*, have gradually adjusted to its complex, often astringent musical subtleties. Now *The Rake* has progressed to critical respect and has almost achieved general popularity.

Stravinsky saw Hogarth's eight satirical engravings, "The Rake's Progress," when they were exhibited in 1947 in Chicago, and he rightly thought them perfectly suited to the acerbic neoclassic style he had made his own for three decades. Auden's sophisticated libretto turned Hogarth's disconnected pictures into a ritualized "Rake's Downfall" in which Tom, instructed in three progressively more insidious philosophies, denies Nature—and then finds it again when spring returns, and it is too late for him.

Stravinsky is uninterested in obvious crowd-pleasing: the seemingly sure-fire business of Baba resuming her long-interrupted sentence never gets so much as a titter in performance. Ironically, the composer's one concession to relatively straightforward sentiment, Anne's lullaby "Gently, little boat," uncannily suggests the lullaby in an opera by his rival and now chief claimant for the "foremost composer of the twentieth century" title—Richard Strauss, whose equally subtle but much more extroverted *Ariadne* has since 1951 gone from strength to strength.

Recording

Nagano / Upshaw, Bumbry, Hadley, Ramey (Erato 1996)

Rigoletto

Music by Giuseppe Verdi
Text by Francesco Maria Piave (after Victor Hugo)
First performance: Venice, 11 March 1851

ACT I

A brief prelude builds to a climax on the monotone theme of the curse laid on the hunchback Rigoletto.

At the dissolute court of Renaissance Mantua, the young Duke casts his eyes about for another conquest ("Questa o quella"), while his deformed jester, Rigoletto, advises him simply to get rid of any husband or father who might have objections. Rigoletto is hated by the underlings at court for his vicious tongue and, when they hear that he has a mistress, they plot revenge. Meanwhile, one of the nobles, Monterone, whose own daughter has been ravished by the Duke, publicly curses him and is put under arrest. Rigoletto taunts him mercilessly, and Monterone lays on him a father's curse. Rigoletto cringes in fear, for the supposed mistress is actually his daughter.

Returning to his home that night, Rigoletto, still smarting under the curse laid on him, is buttonholed by Sparafucile, a professional assassin offering his services whenever needed. The hunchback fearfully dismisses the man, reflecting ("Pari siamo") that they are both assassins, "I with the tongue, he with the knife." He is greeted at home by his beautiful daughter Gilda, whom he has jealously guarded through the months she has come to live with him.

(She cannot remember her mother, but he assures her that her mother was "an angel" who loved him in spite of his deformity.) The jester warns his daughter and her nurse not to let anyone into the house. But as he leaves, the very man he is most wary of, the Duke, slips in with the nurse's collusion, disguised as a student—and astonished to discover that the young girl he has been pursuing, ever since he first saw her in church, is actually his jester's daughter. Gilda is remorseful about deceiving her father, but charmed by the young man's seemingly innocent declaration of love ("È il sol dell' anima"). The Duke leaves hastily when he hears noises in the street, not knowing that the rowdies are his own courtiers, masked and come to abduct the girl they think is Rigoletto's mistress. Gilda retires with thoughts of her charming "student" ("Caro nome"). The courtiers find Rigoletto in the dark street, cruelly give him a mask that is actually a blindfold, and make him hold the ladder as they carry his daughter off. Suddenly suspicious, he rips off the mask and searches frantically but in vain through the house. "Ah!" he shouts in his grief, "It is the curse!"

Act II

The Duke has also searched the house in vain and, alone in his apartments, actually feels sorry for the "angel" that has been abducted ("Parmi veder le lagrime"). But his melancholy turns to lust when his courtiers tell him that Rigoletto's "mistress" is at his disposal in the next room—which he promptly enters. Rigoletto appears, pathetically looking for Gilda and taunted by the courtiers—until he tells them that the girl they abducted is his daughter ("Cortigiani, vil razza dannata"). Finally left alone with the ravished Gilda, he hears her remorseful confession of guilt ("Tutte le feste al tempio") and tenderly consoles her (Duet: "Piangi, fanciulla"). As Monterone is led through the palace to his execution, Rigoletto shouts to the old man that he will be revenged ("Sì! vendetta"). Gilda pleads with her father to spare the Duke, whom she still loves in spite of everything.

Act III

Rigoletto has availed himself of Sparafucile's services. The Duke has been lured by night to a dangerous inn on the river's edge. Maddalena, Sparafucile's sister, is the bait. The Duke, a paragon of faithlessness, brazenly sings that women are unfaithful ("La donna è mobile"), and makes advances to Maddalena while Rigoletto, standing outside, forces Gilda to see what her beloved is really like (Quartet: "Bella figlia dell' amore"). The hunchback then sends his daughter in male attire to safety in nearby Verona and leaves to await the stroke of midnight, when he is to collect the Duke's corpse. The Duke drops off to sleep in a room above, and Maddalena, charmed with her Adonis, pleads for his life. Sparafucile reluctantly agrees to kill, in the Duke's stead, anyone who comes to the door that night. Gilda, drawn back to the inn by feelings she cannot understand, overhears this dreadful bargain. As a storm vents its fury, she knocks at the door and receives the assassin's knife. Rigoletto returns at midnight to claim the Duke's corpse as stipulated—in a sack, and ready for the river. As he is dragging the sack to the water, he hears in the distance the Duke singing his arrogant song about woman's faithlessness. Terrified, he rips open the sack and finds his dying Gilda. She asks him to forgive her ("Lassù in ciel") and dies. "Ah!" he shouts in his grief, "It is the curse!"

♣

Rigoletto is famed for its wealth of melody, but it is doing an injustice to Verdi if those melodies are not seen as integral to the daring and incisive story. Verdi fought fiercely with the censors to keep every detail of that story—the hump, the curse, the rape, the murder, and the sack. He made the Duke a figure new to the tenor repertory, with florid music that is as handsome as he is, yet hopelessly corrupt and completely unanswerable for the consequences of his actions.

And Verdi thought the jester, when he found him in the pages of Victor Hugo, "worthy of Shakespeare"—a monstrous man who perverts and pimps for the Duke, pushing him further and further into vice and hating him all the while, yet preserving in his heart one love that keeps him, in spite of all, a human being—his love for his daughter. This character, Verdi knew, could draw great music from him. The ambivalent father, often fearful and yet loving to his children, was the figure that commanded his stage from his first opera, *Oberto*, to his recent triumph, *Luisa Miller*—and would continue to do so for another twenty years, through *La Traviata* (where the elder Germont comes to love the woman whose heart he must break more than the son for whose sake he intervenes) to *Simon Boccanegra, I Vespri Siciliani, Don Carlo,* and *Aida*.

Rigoletto, Il Trovatore, and *La Traviata*, three immensely popular operas written in white heat in the space of little more than two years, have often been thought, by critics and public alike, to constitute a sort of trilogy. This idea has been challenged in recent years, as the splendors of other middle-period Verdi operas have become increasingly well known. The fact remains, however, that these are the three operas in which Verdi, after laboring long through what he called his years in the galley, came at last into the fullness of his musical and dramatic powers. They are also three operas that extend uncommon sympathy to society's outcasts, to the sort of people we might go out of our way to avoid on the street—the ugly hunchback, hardened and corrupt, the old gypsy woman, demented and dangerous, and the fallen woman, rejected, impoverished, and fatally ill. Verdi speaks eloquently for these three unfortunates, and in one great arc of intense feeling. The "Verdi trilogy" is one of the miracles of musical drama.

Recording

Serafin / Callas, di Stefano, Gobbi (EMI/Angel 1955)

Der Ring des Nibelungen

(The Ring of the Nibelung)
Music and text by Richard Wagner
First performances: *Das Rheingold*, Munich, 22 September 1869;
Die Walküre, Munich, 26 June 1870;
Siegfried, Bayreuth, 16 August 1876;
Götterdämmerung, Bayreuth, 17 August 1876;
complete cycle, Bayreuth, 13, 14, 16, and 17 August 1876

Das Rheingold

(The Rhine Gold)

In the depths of the primeval Rhine, three alluring water nymphs—Woglinde, Wellgunde, and Flosshilde—guard a mass of gold, gleaming and pure in its natural state. The dwarf Alberich, one of the Nibelungs from the depths of the earth, pursues these Rhine maidens with amorous intent but without success. They tease and taunt him (water is not his element) and unwisely tell him that anyone who renounces love and fashions a ring from their gold will have power over the world. The dwarf promptly renounces love and steals the gold.

On an airy peak above the Rhine, the sky gods have had a castle built by two giants, Fafner and Fasolt. This Valhalla will house Wotan, the one-eyed father god; his wife, Fricka; the brothers Donner, god of thunder, and Froh, god of the rainbow; and their sister, Freia, the goddess of love. The giants expect to have the beautiful Freia as payment for their labors. But Wotan, wielding a great ashen spear that bears inscribed the treaties with nature that have given him his power, is loath to give up Freia, for her golden apples keep the gods eternally youthful. He has sent Loge, the crafty fire god, to search the world to find a way out of the dilemma. Loge, slyly late in arriving, suggests that Wotan offer the giants, as payment more attractive than Freia, the golden treasure that Alberich has stolen from the Rhine. The giants take Freia hostage till Wotan can secure the gold for them. The sky gods feel their youth and strength fading as Freia is taken away.

Wotan and Loge descend to the subterranean caverns where Alberich, empowered by the Ring he has fashioned from the gold, keeps his fellow Nibelungs enslaved, making additional wonders from the treasure. One of these wonders is the Tarnhelm, a cap that can grant its wearer invisibility, instant transportability, and the power of metamorphosis. Wotan and Loge learn of this marvel from Mime, Alberich's enslaved brother. The two gods humor Alberich into making a transformation or two and, when he temporarily assumes the form of a toad, take him captive easily and ascend with him to the upper world.

Alberich is forced to summon his minions to haul the whole of the golden treasure before the sky gods. Wotan wrests the most important part of the treasure, the Ring, from the dwarf's finger, puts it on his own, and tells Loge to let the dwarf go. Alberich, before he departs, puts a mighty curse on the Ring: death to all who wear it, envy to those who do not. The giants return with Freia and, even though one of them, Fasolt, has fallen in love with her, they accept the gold as alternative payment. They also claim the Tarnhelm and—when the wise earth goddess Erda rises from her slumber to persuade Wotan to relinquish it—the Ring itself. The curse on the Ring goes to work instantly, as Fafner kills Fasolt and packs off with the golden hoard. Wotan is shaken by Erda's prediction that the world he rules will soon end, but contents himself for the moment with his new sky castle. Donner thunders up a storm, and Froh creates a rainbow bridge across the Rhine and into Valhalla. Loge, as fire god not part of Wotan's airy family, is sure that the sky gods are walking to their doom. In the Rhine below, the nymphs lament the loss of their gold. The four elements of earth, air, fire, and water are thus at variance. A theme in the orchestra tells us that Wotan has conceived a plan to save the future—a sword.

Die Walküre

(The Valkyrie)

ACT I

Driven by a forest storm, Siegmund, Wotan's mortal son, unknowingly finds shelter in the house of Hunding, the very enemy from whom he has been fleeing. He is befriended by Hunding's young wife, the gentle Sieglinde, but he keeps his name from her. Hunding comes home from the chase and, observing primitive rites of hospitality, shelters the fugitive for the night, but will fight him in the morning. Siegmund, weaponless, calls out to his father, whom he knew only as a mortal named Wälse, for the sword he once promised to send in the hour of need. Sieglinde comes to him in the night, tells him she has given Hunding a sleeping potion, and points to a sword that a mysterious stranger had once thrust into the ash tree that supports the house. As Siegmund and Sieglinde fall in love ("Winterstürme" and "Du bist der Lenz"), they realize, from twinship of face and voice and from common parenthood under Wälse, that they are long-lost brother and sister. Sieglinde confers on Siegmund his rightful name. He pulls the foredestined sword from the ash tree, names it Nothung (need), claims his sister as his bride, and escapes with her.

ACT II

Wotan, who began his plan for the future by assuming human guise as Wälse and siring the mortal twins Siegmund and Sieglinde, has also sired in his own name nine immortal angel-warrioresses, the Valkyries. Their role is to defend heroes in battle, to greet them before their deaths, and to gather them from the battlefields after death and bear them through the air on horseback to Valhalla. There, in an afterlife, the heroes will defend the sky god from attack.

In a mountain gorge, Wotan tells his favorite Valkyrie daughter, Brünnhilde, whose mother is the intuitive Erda, that she must defend Siegmund in the coming encounter with Hunding. Brünnhilde is exultant ("Ho-yo-to-ho"), but Fricka storms in to remind Wotan that his power rests on the contracts he has made with nature: if he defies his own laws and defends an incestuous hero, he will lose everything.

Wotan, alone with Brünnhilde, explains to her that she must disregard his former command; she must now see to it that Siegmund dies at the hands of

Hunding. And, he predicts, when his own son is gone, a son of Alberich, just sired, will take possession of the Ring and the world.

Brünnhilde grieves that her father's mortal son, his hope for the future, must die, but she nonetheless obeys her father's command and appears to Siegmund ("The Todesverkündigung Scene") to announce his impending death. Then she is so touched by Siegmund's brave devotion to Sieglinde that she disobeys her father and attempts to defend Siegmund in the duel with Hunding. Wotan furiously intervenes with his spear, smashes the sword he had left for his son, allows Hunding to kill Siegmund, and then fells Hunding himself with a single word. Brünnhilde meanwhile has gathered up the pieces of the sword and rescued Sieglinde, who is carrying Siegmund's child.

ACT III

The Valkyries, en route to Valhalla with the bodies of slain heroes, land their horses on a mountaintop. Brünnhilde comes last to land, bringing Sieglinde, who, praising Brünnhilde's courage in a theme of striking beauty ("O hehrstes Wunder!"), hastens safely into the forest with the fragments of Siegmund's sword. Wotan appears in thunder, dismisses the eight other Valkyries, and sentences Brünnhilde, for her disobedience, to be reduced to mortal state and take as husband the first man who wakens her from sleep. She pleads that she has only done what she knew he wanted inwardly. He is moved, for what she says is true. He promises that her slumber will be surrounded by a wall of fire, so that only a great hero will waken her. They both know that that hero will be Siegmund's child. With great tenderness the father god kisses his daughter to sleep and summons Loge's flames to encircle her with a wall of magic fire.

Siegfried

ACT I

Young Siegfried, the son of Siegmund and Sieglinde, has been brought up after his mother's death by the dwarf Mime who, like his brother Alberich, has designs on the Ring. The giant Fafner still possesses the Ring and all the treasure, and he has used the Tarnhelm to turn himself into a dragon, the better to guard his hoard. Mime keeps the boy Siegfried in ignorance in the forest, far from any human contact, hoping that he will grow strong enough to slay the dragon, but also stay child enough to give him the Ring when the dragon is slain. Siegfried wonders who his parents were, and insists that Mime reforge the sword fragments his mother has left him. But this is something that Mime, for all his Nibelung skills, cannot do.

Wotan, who also has an interest in the prospective hero, visits Mime disguised once again as a mysterious stranger, "the Wanderer." He overawes Mime, challenges him to a game of wits with his life as forfeit, and defeats him. As he departs, Wotan tells the terrified Mime that only one who has never learned fear can forge the sword anew. He leaves the dwarf's life to be claimed by whoever that fearless one might be.

Mime immediately questions Siegfried and discovers that the boy has never learned fear, not even the fear of the forest's fire-breathing dragon. Mime knows then that young Siegfried will indeed be able to kill Fafner and get him the Ring—but that the boy might also be the one who will take his life. Siegfried, intrigued by the notion of fear and anxious to learn it, leaps to the anvil and joyously reforges his father's sword himself, while Mime lays his plans to slay the boy after the boy has slain the dragon.

ACT II

Deeper in the forest, Alberich and Wotan, in their first encounter since *Das Rheingold,* try to rouse the slumbering dragon-giant Fafner with warnings that he will soon lose the Ring. Fafner is unimpressed. Mime brings Siegfried to the place and leaves him there. While the forest murmurs, Siegfried wonders again about his mother, and imitates the song of a friendly forest bird, first on an improvised reed pipe and then on his faithful horn. The dragon wakes and attacks. Siegfried slays it in a mighty battle, and Fafner, dying, warns him that there is a curse on the gold he keeps in his cave. The boy, tasting the dragon's blood, is suddenly able to understand the three messages the bird has been singing: he must claim the golden treasure in the dragon's cave, beware of Mime who intends to kill him, and awaken the maiden who slumbers on a nearby mountain encircled by fire. Siegfried finds the Ring and Tarnhelm in the dragon's lair, slays Mime before Mime slays him, and joyously follows the forest bird toward Brünnhilde's mountain.

ACT III

At the foot of that mountain, Wotan summons Erda from the earth and questions her—in vain, for she has begun to lose her powers. The sky god admits to himself the truth of what she told him long ago: the world he has ruled will soon end. He predicts that Brünnhilde, when she is awakened, will make a better world. But when Siegfried reaches the ascent to the mountain, Wotan, in one last effort to stop what must happen, confronts him. Siegfried, angered and uncomprehending, smashes the god's great spear with the very sword the god had once given his father. Wotan vanishes on the instant, his power gone.

Siegfried scales the height, passes through the wall of fire, and finally learns what fear is when he sees the first woman he has ever seen—the slumbering Brünnhilde, still in her youthful beauty. He wakes her with a kiss. She greets the sunlight and then learns fear herself as the realization dawns that she is no longer a Valkyrie but a mortal woman who must give herself to a mortal man. Gradually the two fall in love over their reciprocal fears. They joyously welcome the thought that they will someday die, and laugh at the impending end of the old world.

Götterdämmerung

(Twilight of the Gods)

PROLOGUE

The three Norns, spinning the threads of past, present, and future atop Brünnhilde's mountain, tell how Wotan long ago gained control over the world when he drank at the stream of wisdom and broke off a branch of the world ash tree, making it his spear and inscribing on it his covenant with nature. Now the spear has been shattered, the stream has dried up, the ash tree has withered, and Wotan has ordered his slain heroes to cut it down and pile its timbers around Valhalla. Soon he will thrust the point of the spear into Loge's breast, and fire will issue forth to consume the world. Of what will happen after that the Norns can see nothing—only a dim vision of Alberich and his Ring. Their thread breaks in their hands, and they descend to their mother, Erda. The world's seers have lost their power.

Day dawns, and Siegfried and Brünnhilde, the hope for the future, declare their love as he sets out on further adventures. He gives her the golden Ring that he won as a youth, and she gives him Grane, the heroic steed that she rode as a young Valkyrie. He descends to the Rhine and journeys upstream.

Act I

In a castle on the Rhine, the villainous Hagen tells his cowardly half-brother Gunther, the Gibichung king, that he should take Brünnhilde to wife, and that his sister Gutrune would find a wealthy husband in Siegfried, possessor of a golden hoard. Hagen himself is mainly interested in getting Siegfried's Ring. The three of them give Siegfried, on his arrival at their castle, a potion that makes him forget Brünnhilde and fall in love with Gutrune. Gunther then asks Siegfried, after they have ceremoniously become blood brothers, to win Brünnhilde for him. Siegfried, as one last fleeting vision of the past dies in his memory, agrees to scale the mountain, pass through the fire, and subdue Brünnhilde—while disguised, through the Tarnhelm's magic, as Gunther. The duped hero and the cowardly suitor head downstream together, and Hagen, hoping eventually to lord it over them both, keeps watch on the Rhine.

On her mountaintop, Brünnhilde is visited by one of her Valkyrie sisters, Waltraute, who pleads with her to give up the Ring: their father Wotan sits in state surrounded by his warrior guardsmen, awaiting the end of his world. Only once has his grim visage softened—when he thought of Brünnhilde. The world will end unless the Ring is restored to its natural owners, the Rhine maidens. Brünnhilde refuses to part with the Ring; it is Siegfried's token of love. Waltraute rides off in despair. Then, in terrible irony, the very Siegfried who had given Brünnhilde the Ring suddenly appears, wrests the Ring from her finger, and claims her for Gunther. (She thinks that he, transformed by the Tarnhelm, really *is* Gunther.) For honor's sake, Siegfried places the sword Nothung between himself and Brünnhilde that night.

Act II

Back in the Gibichung castle, Hagen is visited in his sleep by his father, and we understand how he came to know so much about Siegfried and to have such a special interest in the Ring: his father is Alberich. Hagen is the one Wotan knew would come, the Nibelung's son sired for the sole purpose of recovering the Nibelung's Ring. Alberich reminds his son in the night that Siegfried, who now wears the Ring, must be destroyed.

At dawn Siegfried reappears at the castle, magically transported from Brünnhilde's mountain by the Tarnhelm, announcing that Gunther will follow soon (by ordinary conveyance) with his new bride. Hagen summons the Gibichung vassals, more loyal to him than to the king, as Gunther comes up the Rhine with the captive Brünnhilde. She is astonished to see Siegfried in this dastardly company, and suspects the worst when she sees the Ring on his finger. Hearing that he is to marry Gutrune, she swears an oath that he has lain with her. He, knowing nothing of their past together, swears that he has not, and leaves to prepare for his wedding. Hagen offers to right the wrong—that is to say, to kill Siegfried—and the humiliated Brünnhilde reveals that the hero's only vulnerable spot, unprotected by her magic spells, is his back. Gunther, thinking that Siegfried took advantage of his Tarnhelm disguise to lie with Brünnhilde, joins in the conspiracy.

ACT III

During a hunt on the wooded banks of the Rhine, the river's three nymphs invite Siegfried to amorous dalliance, but he remains faithful to the only wife he remembers, Gutrune. Then they tell him that the Ring he wears is cursed, and they almost persuade him to give it to them, but he keeps it to prove his defiance of the curse. They predict that he will die that day, and they swim away to find Brünnhilde, hoping that she will listen to them. The rest of the hunting party come to the riverside, and Hagen, thinking this an ideal spot for him to do away with Siegfried, maliciously gives the hero an antidote to the potion, so that before he is killed he will remember his past. Just when Siegfried has traced his way through memory to the moment when he awakened Brünnhilde, Hagen stabs him in the back. The others are horrified, and Wotan's ravens, who have watched for good tidings or ill, fly up to tell their god that the time has come at last for his world to end. Siegfried dies remembering Brünnhilde as she greeted him on her awakening.

Siegfried's body is borne in sorrow to the Gibichung castle ("Siegfried's Funeral March"). Gutrune in tears accuses Gunther of murder, but the exultant Hagen insists that the credit for the slaying is his: Siegfried is his spoil from the hunt. Hagen then kills Gunther in a quarrel over the Ring and reaches to take the cursed thing from Siegfried's finger, only to shrink back when the dead arm rises to threaten him. Everyone retreats as Brünnhilde arrives to take command of the hall ("The Immolation Scene"). She has learned the whole truth of the Gibichungs' treachery from the Rhine maidens, and now orders that a funeral pyre be raised for Siegfried's body. Solemnly she tells Wotan, awaiting the end in Valhalla, that he can fade away at last. Then she takes the Ring from Siegfried's finger, puts his body to the torch, and rides Grane into the flames to join her beloved in death.

The world is then purified through water (the Rhine floods the castle and the Rhine maidens recover the Ring) and fire (Valhalla too has been set ablaze and can be seen flaming in the sky). Hagen sinks to his death in the Rhine, drawn by the water nymphs to the depths where his father began the whole cycle. The music (especially the radiant theme with which Sieglinde long before had hymned Brünnhilde's courage) indicates that a new world is rising, a world that, if we read the *Ring* rightly, Wotan has finally willed into being through his wonderful daughter Brünnhilde.

♣

Wagner's fifteen-hour *Ring* cycle is the vastest piece of music ever conceived by the mind of man. And quite apart from its music, which is often overwhelming, it makes, more than a hundred years after its initial performance, a very contemporary statement about man's rapacious exploitation of nature and about the impending threat of the world's annihilation. It may even be said to be timeless in a mythic sense: it uses external nature to tell its audiences about their inner selves.

But Wagner, when he began it, intended it as a political allegory for his own century: the hero Siegfried would by his death effect a new ordering of human events, in which oppressive and outmoded governments would acknowledge, and give way to, the moral values found in great men and great deeds. In the early 1850s, Wagner, the composer of *Tannhäuser* and *Lohengrin*, was a failed revolutionary, driven into exile, rethinking his aims and methodology. And as the idea of the *Ring* grew in his mind, he wrote no music for six years.

Wagner thought initially of compressing the Siegfied myths into a single drama, *Siegfried's Death* (later, *Götterdämmerung*), but this involved so much exposition that he wrote an introductory *Young Siegfried* (later, *Siegfried*), which in turn was prefaced by *Die Walküre*, and that in turn by *Das Rheingold*. But it is not entirely correct to say that he "wrote the *Ring* backwards." Much of the "preliminary" material was presumed from the start. And all of the music, beginning with the memorable first page of *Das Rheingold*, in which the world seems to be evolving out of water, was composed in sequence.

In writing his text, the astonishingly well-read Wagner drew on several twelfth-century Norse and Germanic sources, each of them preserving earlier oral traditions. The prose and verse Eddas provided the raw stuff for *Rheingold*, the Volsunga Saga for *Walküre*, the Thidreks Saga for *Siegfried*, and the newly popular *Nibelungenlied* for *Götterdämmerung*. Wagner elaborated and unified this material with details, many more than is commonly realized, from Greek tragedy. Among these are the trilogy form (others may have called the *Ring* a tetralogy, but Wagner persisted in thinking of it as a trilogy with a "preliminary evening"); the system of recurrent leitmotifs, so close to the patterning of images in Aeschylus; the messenger speeches, the long duologues, and such narrative devices as the Nibelung's Promethean theft and the curse that, like the curse on the House of Atreus, operates through three generations. Finally, there is the solution provided by the sky god's daughter who, like Athena, combines her father's masculine wisdom with her own feminine intuition.

Above all, Wagner was fired by the Athenian ideal that the true purpose of theater was to dramatize for a people its ancestral myths and thereby show them themselves. He wanted to project the concerns of his Germany, his Europe, and his century into a mythic, elemental world. For this purpose, he built a theater at Bayreuth, Greek in concept and modern in execution, and reintroduced, more than twenty centuries after Aeschylus, the Greek idea of a dramatic festival with religious and political significances.

But the single most important influence on Wagner's thought, from the composition of the second act of *Die Walküre* onward, was Arthur Schopenhauer's *The World as Will and Representation*. The pessimistic philosopher saw the world as relentlessly driven by *Wille* (will), a force that drives us toward illusory goals and is in fact the cause of all our suffering. *Wille* was for Schopenhauer an evil to be recognized and to be renounced. Wagner read *The World as Will and Representation* four times while composing *Die Walküre*, and returned to it often while composing all of his subsequent works for the stage. He wrote that it was from reading Schopenhauer that he decided to make the central figure of his cycle not Siegfried but Wotan—a truly tragic figure, fatally compromised, realizing the futility of his plan for world power, renouncing it, and willing his own death. (Here and at other points in this and later works of Wagner the Nazis conveniently overlooked what did not suit their purposes.) Wagner changed the text of his final page five times, replacing a naive ending (in which Brünnhilde takes Siegfried to an afterlife in Valhalla) with increasingly pessimistic endings influenced by his reading in Ludwig Feuerbach and Schopenhauer, and opting finally for the ending we have, where the text is pared to a minimum and a single motif —the "hehrstes Wunder" that Sieglinde first sang in praise of Brünnhilde— promises a renewed world.

In the course of his rethinking, Wagner seems intuitively to have tapped into what Jung was to call the collective unconscious, and for the past half-century interpretations of the cycle (notably Robert Donington's *Wagner's "Ring" and Its Symbols*) have tended to view it as remarkably prophetic of the findings of Jungian and other psychologies, its various characters archetypes of the psyche, its story the story of a soul in crisis. Wagner's grandson

Wieland found effective ways of suggesting this on the postwar Bayreuth stage. More recent stagings, demythologizing and deconstructing the cycle in self-consciously "modern" approaches, miss much of this—and actually hark back to Bernard Shaw's dated (and not entirely serious) treatment of the work as a socialist allegory.

Musically, the *Ring* observes the principles outlined in the treatise Wagner wrote during his six-year silence, *Opera and Drama*: the text should share equally with the music in realizing the drama; the words should sound in alliterative clusters; the vocal line should spring directly out of the rise and fall of the words; the singers should not blend their voices but give the impression, while singing, of human speech; and the orchestra should reveal—in the recurrent musical themes Wagner called "motifs of memory"—what the characters onstage do not say and sometimes do not even know. But Wagner was not irretrievably bound to these principles. After he interrupted the composition of the *Ring*, at the end of the second act of *Siegfried*, to write the more practical (but inevitably massive) scores of *Tristan* and *Die Meistersinger*, he returned to the *Ring* less constrained by his earlier theories, and allowed himself to write duets, trios, and massed choruses with heightened powers of musical persuasion.

The *Ring* is remarkably consistent and unified for a project whose realization took some twenty-eight years, but each of its four parts has a quality of its own. *Das Rheingold* is almost a textbook on the skillful manipulation of musical motifs for narrative purposes. *Die Walküre*, the most popular evening of the four, has in Wotan's long second-act monologue the single most important scene in the cycle, and crowns its long series of impassioned duologues with an unforgettably moving final scene. Stretches of the first two acts of *Siegfried*, a kind of protracted scherzo movement, can seem perfunctory ("The Nibelungs are beginning to bore me," Wagner wrote), but its last act and virtually all of the final *Götterdämmerung* are a renewed Wagner operating at the height of his musical powers—luxuriantly manic, insistently gorgeous in sound, awesome in scope, and majestically ambivalent about all his meanings.

Recording

Solti / Nilsson, Sutherland, Flagstad, Crespin, Ludwig, King, Windgassen, Fischer-Dieskau, London, Hotter, Neidlinger, Frick
(Decca/London 1957–65)

Roméo et Juliette

(Romeo and Juliet)
Music by Charles Gounod
Text by Jules Barbier and Michel Carré (after Shakespeare)
First performance: Paris, 27 April 1867

ACT I

A chorus promises to tell the story of "a pair of star-cross'd lovers."

Juliet, attended by her nurse, Gertrude, is introduced into medieval Veronese society ("Je veux vivre") by her Capulet father. Romeo, from the hated Montagues, is encouraged by his friend Mercutio ("Mab, la Reine") to crash the party, and he and Juliet fall in love.

Romeo secretly comes to the Capulet garden ("Ah! lève-toi, soleil"). Juliet appears on the balcony above, and they agree to marry, come what may.

ACT II

In the quiet of his cell, Friar Laurence, a kindly master of "the powerful grace that lies in herbs," secretly marries the two.

In front of the Capulet palace, the Montague page Stephano taunts the family ("Que fais-tu"), and in the ensuing brawl Juliet's cousin Tybalt slays Mercutio, prompting Romeo to slay Tybalt. The Duke of Verona denounces both of the feuding families and banishes Romeo (Ensemble: "Ah! Jour de deuil!").

ACT III

Romeo spends his wedding night with Juliet and flees when the lark heralds the dawn. Juliet's father tells her she is to marry the wealthy count Paris that very day. Desperately she drinks a sleeping potion provided by the Friar [and, when ceremoniously led to her wedding, collapses as if dead].

In the Capulet crypt [Friar Laurence learns from Friar John that Romeo has not received his letter explaining the stratagem and] Romeo, thinking Juliet is dead, takes poison. She wakes too late to save him and, seizing a dagger, dies with him, imploring heaven's forgiveness.

♣

This plot summary does not list the five love duets sung by Gounod's Gallic Roméo and Juliette, because the whole opera has been rightly called "a love duet with occasional interruptions." While none of the duets reach the extraordinary sensuousness of the single, protracted love duet in *Faust*, they are fine examples of Gounod's intimate style and harbingers of more to come in Massenet. As with *Faust*, the score of *Roméo* underwent many revisions, is frequently cut in performance to its melodious moments, and has served as a star vehicle for a century and a half of famous singers.

Recording
Cooper / Sayão, Björling (Myto 1947)

Der Rosenkavalier
(The Cavalier of the Rose)
Music by Richard Strauss
Text by Hugo von Hofmannsthal
First performance: Dresden, 26 January 1911

Act I

In Vienna, during the reign of Maria Theresa, a field marshal's wife (Marschallin) named Marie Thérèse has consoled herself, in a loveless marriage, with an aristocratic young lover, Octavian. The two are interrupted in the early morning by the unexpected arrival of her cousin, the oxlike Baron Ochs, and Octavian has to disguise himself *pro tem* as a chambermaid. The Baron has come to ask the Marschallin to recommend a Rosenkavalier, a nobleman to bear a ceremonial silver rose to his fiancée, Sophie, who is from the parvenu family von Faninal. The Marschallin suggests for the purpose Octavian—even as the Baron is making lecherous passes at the "chambermaid." The gracious lady then holds her morning levée, in the midst of which the impoverished Baron thunders at her lawyer over the amount he expects to get from his marriage, interrupting the song of an auditioning Italian tenor ("Di rigori armato"). The Baron also acquires the professional services of Annina and Valzacchi, a pair of Italian gossipmongers. The Marschallin, left alone with the reclothed Octavian, reflects on the inevitable passage of time ("Die Zeit, die ist ein sonderbar Ding") and quietly ends their affair. He leaves uncomprehending, and she sends her Moorish servant boy Mahomet with the silver rose he has forgotten to take with him. Then she lifts a looking glass to her face.

ACT II

In the Faninal palace, Octavian ceremonially presents the silver rose to Sophie, and the two fall in love. When Ochs himself arrives, Sophie is appalled by his boorish behavior. Octavian comes to her defense and, found alone with her by the two Italians, fights a duel with the offended Baron and wounds him slightly. Sophie's nouveau-riche father is furious with her when she refuses to marry the Baron, and threatens to send her to a convent. Meanwhile, Octavian wins the two Italian schemers over to his side, and sends the Baron, bandaged and resting, a love note from the "chambermaid" he found so attractive. Ochs looks forward to the rendezvous ("The Rosenkavalier Waltz").

ACT III

In the *chambre separée* of a disreputable inn, Baron Ochs is humiliated by the outrageous tricks the two Italians play on him as he attempts to seduce the "chambermaid." Only the intervention of his tactful cousin, the Marschallin, saves him from a police investigation. Sophie is thus vindicated in the eyes of her father. The Marschallin, seeing that her Octavian is in love with Sophie, gives him to her with poignant feelings of regret and resignation (Trio: "Hab mir's gelobt"). The young lovers, left alone, wonder, "Is it a dream? Can it really be true?" When the stage is empty, little Mahomet rushes in to retrieve a handkerchief that Sophie has forgotten to take with her.

♣

Strauss and Hofmannsthal originally conceived *Der Rosenkavalier* as "thoroughly comic, as bright and obvious as a pantomime," a conflict between a "baritone buffo" and a "Cherubino" (Octavian, like Mozart's page boy, is sung by a young woman). But it wasn't long before another figure, the Marschallin, began to take over their imaginations and their pens, adding to the farcical situation that serious dimension that characterizes all great comedy. Under the Marschallin's benign influence, *Der Rosenkavalier*'s theme became nothing less than the differences effected in human lives by time, with its inexorable onward flow. And its music reached its greatest heights—supreme heights—in the Marschallin's Act I reflections and her Act III trio with Octavian and Sophie—both passages concerned with the inevitable flight of time.

There are undeniable longueurs in the opera, but never, when the Marschallin is onstage, is the music overwrought, or the dialogue spun too thin, or the drama anything less than three-dimensional. Marie Thérèse is supreme among the creations of the composer-librettist team, graciously accepting a transformation in her life as, later, Ariadne would, and Arabella, and the four characters in *Die Frau ohne Schatten*. She has also become, in the minds of operagoers, an emblem of Vienna itself, both the Vienna of Maria Theresa and Mozart's "Dove sono" and a later Vienna, with waltzes by other Strausses.

Recording

Solti / Crespin, Donath, Minton, Jungwirth, Pavarotti
(Decca/London 1969)

Salome

Music by Richard Strauss
Text by Oscar Wilde, translated by Hedwig Lachmann
and edited by the composer
First performance: Dresden, 9 December 1905

On the terrace of King Herod's palace, the page boy of Queen Herodias can't keep his eyes off the young soldier Narraboth, who is in turn infatuated with the Princess Salome, who is in turn obsessed with the imprisoned Jochanaan (John the Baptist), whose voice rises from a cistern beneath the terrace. Salome has Jochanaan brought up before her in chains, and lusts after his flesh, then his hair, and then his mouth. Narraboth, unnoticed by anyone except the page boy, kills himself in despair. Jochanaan curses Salome as he had cursed her incestuous mother, Herodias, and returns to his cistern. Herod and Herodias enter. He, sotted with wine and haunted by his guilty past, asks Salome to dance for him, promising to give her anything she wishes. Salome dances voluptuously ("The Dance of Seven Veils") and then asks the hapless Herod for the head of Jochanaan. The executioner descends into the cistern and returns with the severed head. Salome at last kisses the mouth she so coveted. Her mind gives way, and Herod in disgust shouts to his soldiers, "Kill that woman!"

♣

Strauss was known till 1905 mainly as composer of lush orchestral tone poems, but he made a breakthrough as an opera composer with *Salome*, his one-act shocker based on a deliriously decadent *fin-de-siècle* text by Oscar Wilde. Rather like a tone poem with sung parts, *Salome* drives its enormous orchestra to orgiastic heights and depths, and pushes its vocalists further than even Wagner had dared to do—albeit at much shorter length. The opera was at first thought depraved—denounced by the Kaiser, by the archbishop of Vienna, and by the New York boxholder Strauss called "a certain Mr. Morgan." The score is replete with musical imitations of Wilde's hundred or more Biblical images and similes—the Canticle of Canticles run riot. And the staging depends on a large, impassive moon overlooking all the action and reflecting the inner moods, the neurotic mental states, of each character in turn. Strauss, conducting it, said to his orchestra, "Gentlemen, there are no problems here. This is a scherzo with a fatal conclusion. Play it as if it were fairy music by Mendelssohn." Maybe he wasn't joking. Today the glittering *Salome*, while full of fascinating detail, has lost much of its power to shock.

Recording

Karajan / Behrens, Baltsa, Böhm, van Dam (EMI/Angel 1977)

Samson et Dalila

(Samson and Delilah)
Music by Camille Saint-Saëns
Text by Ferdinand Lemaire
First performance: Weimar, 2 December 1877

ACT I

Before the temple of Dagon in Gaza, the heroic Samson rouses his fellow Hebrews to revolt against their Philistine oppressors ("Israël! rompes ta chaîne") and, attacked by the satrap Abimélech, slays him. Dalila, a priestess of Dagon, congratulates Samson on his victory and invites him to come to her tent in the Valley of Sorek ("Printemps qui commence").

ACT II

A storm is threatening in the valley as Dalila anticipates her conquest ("Amour! Viens aider ma faiblesse") and is told by her priest that she must find the secret source of Samson's strength. She offers herself to the hero

("Mon coeur s'ouvre à ta voix") and lures him, weakened by desire, inside her tent. The storm breaks as she, having discovered that his strength lies in his hair, summons warriors to the tent to shear and blind him.

Act III

Samson, imprisoned and forced to turn a great millstone, calls on his God to take his life in atonement for his betrayal of his people.

In the temple of Dagon, amid a vast bacchanalian orgy, Dalila and her priest taunt the blinded Samson. He asks a small boy to direct him to the two great columns that support the structure and, praying to his God to restore his strength, brings the temple crashing down, destroying them all.

♣

It took Saint-Saëns fifteen years to get his French biblical opera on the stage, and even then the premiere was given, with Liszt's encouragement, in German Weimar. Almost thirty years passed before it reached the French stage, and it has often been treated condescendingly by critics, French and otherwise. And yet audiences have almost invariably responded to Samson's heroic utterances and Dalila's three luscious arias. Typical of its composer's general output, the opera is shrewdly eclectic, a facile blending of Handelian oratorio, Gluckian classicism, Gounodesque melodiousness, and Wagnerian bacchanality—and it works!

Recording

Prêtre / Gorr, Vickers (EMI/Angel 1962)

Semele

Music by George Frideric Handel
Text by William Congreve
First performance: London, 10 February 1744

Act I

In Grecian Thebes, the Princess Semele is about to be given in marriage by her father, Cadmus, to a mortal, Athamas, when Jupiter, who has already lain with her, disrupts the ceremony with a thunderbolt and sends his eagle to carry her to Olympus. The disappointed bridegroom is comforted by Semele's sister, Ino, who confesses her love for him, and soon Semele appears on a cloud to tell the amazed Thebans of the "endless pleasure, endless love" she enjoys above.

Act II

On a clouded skyway, an enraged Juno tells her messenger Iris that she is determined to destroy Semele, even though Jupiter has stationed two dragons to protect her: Iris must first persuade Somnus, the god of sleep, to seal the dragons' eyes ("Iris, hence away").

In her Olympian chamber, Semele awakes after a rapturous night ("O sleep, why dost thou leave me?") and asks Jupiter to bestow immortality on her. He distracts her from that request by transporting Ino to the chamber and conjuring up a magical Arcadian landscape for the two sisters to enjoy ("Where'er you walk").

Act III

In his cave Somnus is taking some sleep of his own ("Leave me, loathsome light") when Juno, continuing her plan, rouses him with the promise of his favorite nymph if he will lull Ino to sleep.

Juno then goes in Ino's form to the magical landscape, presents Semele with an image-enhancing looking glass, and asks her if Jupiter has kept his promise to make her immortal. Semele, struck by her own beauty ("Myself I shall adore"), begs Jupiter to come to her in all his godly thunder and lightning. Reluctantly, he does so and, as Juno gloats, Semele, only a mortal after all, is reduced to ashes.

Below in Thebes, Ino, restored to earth, is betrothed to a grateful Athamas, and cloud-borne Apollo appears to tell the assembled people that Semele's unborn child, the god Bacchus, will rise, a veritable phoenix, from the flames that have consumed his mother.

❧

Semele, the only oratorio featured in this book, is actually an opera in disguise. Congreve called his text (already set by another composer) "Semele, an Opera," but as the libretto was in English and Handel's treatment of it was to be performed during Lent, tradition demanded that the work be called an oratorio, despite its witty and decidedly secular subject. Staged performances of *Semele* are still regrettably few, but a single experience of it in a theater will reveal that it is unquestionably an opera, and a great one.

In *Semele* Handel, a German-born composer, sets the English language, in a libretto written by one of that language's best playwrights (with additions by Pope, Dryden, and others), with a clarity and dexterity unmatched by English composers of whatever century. And the score is that gifted composer operating at the top of his form, in an Act I quartet that anticipates Mozart's in *Idomeneo* by three decades, in arias as popular as any on the concert circuit (see the plot summary), in great lustful choruses ("Now Love, that everlasting boy"), and in the pastoral genre transcendent ("Bless the glad earth"). The second act in particular is a glorious succession of what those in the entertainment industry would call bell-ringers. In 1968 Beverly Sills gave the performance of her career in a concert performance of *Semele* with the Cleveland Orchestra under Robert Shaw, unfortunately not available commercially.

Recording

Nelson / Battle, Horne, McNair, Aler, Ramey
(Deutsche Grammophon 1993)

Simon Boccanegra

Music by Giuseppe Verdi
Text by Francesco Maria Piave and Arrigo Boito
(after García Gutiérrez)
First performance: Venice, 12 March 1857

PROLOGUE

At night in fourteenth-century Genoa, the plebeian Paolo Albiani is agitating to have the famous buccaneer Simon Boccanegra elected doge, while across the square the patrician Jacopo Fiesco comes heartbroken from his darkened palace: his daughter, Maria, has just died ("Il lacerato spirito"). He has kept her virtually imprisoned ever since she bore Boccanegra a child out of wedlock. Now Boccanegra, hoping for a reconciliation, sorrowfully tells Fiesco that the child, a daughter left in an old woman's care while he was fighting at sea for the Genoese cause, has disappeared without a trace. Fiesco, implacable, allows the repentant man to enter his palace, and waits outside to hear his cry of despair when he sees Maria's corpse. Boccanegra, candle in hand, finds the dead body and rushes grief-stricken into the square just as crowds of plebeians bring him the news that he has been proclaimed doge.

Act I

Twenty-five years later, Boccanegra's rule is still opposed by Fiesco, who under the assumed name Andrea Grimaldi lies in wait in his palazzo across the water from Genoa. There the beautiful Amelia Grimaldi awaits at dawn the arrival of the young patrician Gabriele Adorno ("Come in quest'ora bruna"). Old Andrea consents to their marriage—though he confides to Gabriele that Amelia is actually a foundling he adopted long ago to keep Boccanegra from confiscating his estate. The doge himself then arrives unexpectedly, to ask Amelia, in the interest of peace, to marry his longtime associate Paolo. But, as he questions her privately, they are both astonished to discover, in a tender recognition scene, that she is the daughter he lost years before (Duet: "Figlia! a tal nome"). Paolo, frustrated in his ambition to gain power by a lucrative patrician marriage, lays immediate plans to abduct the girl.

The riot resulting from the abduction erupts into Genoa's great council chamber: Andrea has roused the patricians, and Gabriele has killed the actual abductor, the plebeian Lorenzin—and tries now to kill the one he believes ultimately responsible, the doge himself. Amelia holds him back, and as the council breaks into opposing factions, Boccanegra appeals to their sense of common brotherhood ("Plebe! Patrizi!"). Sure that it is Paolo who lies behind the plot, Boccanegra orders him to pronounce a curse on whoever is guilty. Paolo shudders as he calls the curse down on himself.

Act II

That night, in the doge's chambers, Paolo secretly pours poison into Boccanegra's water goblet, then calls the arrested Andrea and Gabriele into his presence and invites them to join in his plot to murder Boccanegra. Andrea honorably refuses, but Gabriele, convinced by Paolo that the doge has lustful designs on Amelia, agrees. Boccanegra enters the empty room, wearily drinks from his goblet, and falls asleep. Gabriele steals up on him, and Amelia suddenly appears to prevent her beloved a second time from killing the man who—she reveals to him—is her father. When Paolo begins a rebellion against Boccanegra in the streets below, Gabriele, in a change of heart, offers to fight in defense of the doge.

Act III

The rebellion has been crushed, Paolo has been arrested, and all the lights of the city are to be extinguished in honor of the dead who have fallen on both sides. In a room in the doge's palace, with a balcony open to the sea, Paolo, led to execution, gloatingly tells Andrea that he has poisoned the doge. Andrea is horrified. Boccanegra enters, the effect of the poison already far advanced. He dies like a great ruler—recognizing at last that Andrea is the very Fiesco who has hated him all these years; forgiving him and asking his forgiveness; uniting the lovers; naming Gabriele his successor, and remembering his adventurous days on the sea—as in the distance the lights of his beloved Genoa go out one by one.

♣

Light plays a symbolic role in this darkest of Verdi's operas, and the sea is an ever-pervasive presence. The title role is one of Verdi's masterly character studies, a part much loved by baritones. Venice in 1857 found the work forbidding and its plot unintelligible, but this opera about fidelity and forgiveness, patriarchs and patriotism remained dear to Verdi's heart. More than two decades later, after *Aida*, he returned to it with Boito's assistance, clarifying situations, enriching the orchestral parts, and adding the council chamber scene, where Boccanegra's impassioned cry for reconciliation, and the stunning ensemble that follows it, forecast the greatness of *Otello*. All the same, the most touching moments—Fiesco's "Il lacerato spirito," the reunion of father and daughter, and the last-act mutual forgiveness of Boccanegra and Fiesco—were there from the start, and one wonders why audiences at Venice, another maritime city with a turbulent history, did not respond.

Recording

Abbado / Freni, Carreras, Cappuccilli, Ghiaurov, van Dam
(Deutsche Grammophon 1977)

Susannah

Music and text by Carlisle Floyd
First performance: Tallahassee, 24 February 1955

Act I

At a square dance in New Hope Valley, Tennessee, Susannah Polk attracts the attention of the new preacher, Olin Blitch, though the valley gossips tell him that she and her brother, Sam, are evil people.

At her farmhouse that evening ("Ain't it a pretty night?"), Susannah assures Little Bat, a retarded youth who all but worships her, that her brother won't hurt him. She and Sam sing the "Jay Bird" song their father taught them.

In the morning, four church elders see Susannah bathing nude, and decide that the whole valley must be told of this.

That evening, the four elders' wives tell Susannah that she is not welcome in the church.

At the farmhouse, Little Bat tells Susannah that his mother had made him say that Susannah had "loved him up." Shocked, Susannah sends him away, telling him never to come back. Sam comforts her but expects that "meantime, there'll be a lotta bad things."

Act II

Four days later, Sam urges his sister to attend the church meeting and show that she is not afraid. Then he leaves to look after his traps on the other side of the mountain.

In the church, Blitch preaches a hell-fire sermon and calls Susannah up the aisle to be saved. She is terrified by the lust on his face and flees.

An hour later, Blitch comes to Susannah's farm, and she, exhausted and defeated, yields to him.

In the church the next morning, the elders refuse to believe a repentant Blitch when he tells them they have misjudged an innocent girl. He asks Susannah to forgive him. She says she has forgotten what forgiveness means.

Sam returns that evening and, hearing what has happened, shoots Blitch dead and runs off. The elders and their wives demand that Susannah leave the valley. She takes a gun and orders them off the property, then invites Little Bat to "come an' love me up some." When he approaches her she slaps him viciously, laughs desperately, and steels herself for a future of loneliness.

♣

Susannah, the most often performed of American operas, has been seen in more than two hundred different productions in its first fifty years. Floyd wrote his version of the familiar story (from the apocryphal Book of Daniel) in his twenties, during the McCarthy hearings when, as he said, "accusation was all that was needed as proof of guilt."

The music, in a folk idiom without using actual folk tunes, owes something to nineteenth-century traditions, but, as the composer observes, his Susannah is "not the pathetic heroine we find in nineteenth-century opera, acted upon and destroyed. She stands down an entire community—and pays a tragic price."

Recording
Nagano / Studer, Hadley, Ramey (Virgin 1994)

Tannhäuser

Music and text by Richard Wagner
First performance: Dresden, 19 October 1845

ACT I

A famous orchestral prelude depicts an emotional struggle between pious Christian penitence and feverish pagan eroticism.

Tannhäuser, a German minnesinger, has deserted his chaste Elisabeth and the cliffed castle of the Wartburg and fled to the goddess of love and her subterranean realm in the nearby Venusberg. But when, amid the pagan revels, he hears a distant church bell, he tells Venus that he is weary of sensuality and longs to return to a life of striving, piety, and pain. The goddess' spell over him is broken when he invokes the Virgin Mary, and he suddenly finds himself kneeling before the Virgin's shrine in a springtime valley beneath the Wartburg, where he is found by Wolfram von Eschenbach ("War's Zauber?") and the other minstrel friends he had deserted. For Elisabeth's sake he agrees to return with them to the Wartburg.

ACT II

Elisabeth, overjoyed to hear of Tannhäuser's return, bursts open the doors of the Wartburg's famed Hall of Song ("Dich, teure Halle"). Tannhäuser finds her there, and she confesses to him that she once found in his songs emotional depths she had never known before, and that she has absented herself from the contests of song ever since he left her. The hall fills with guests as the Landgraf of Thuringia, Elisabeth's uncle, declares a singing contest in her honor, on the theme of love. The pious Wolfram sings the praises of courtly love, and Tannhäuser impetuously answers him with the song he sang in his erotic encounter with Venus. The assemblage is shocked to hear that he has dwelt in the Venusberg; the women flee and the men draw their swords. Elisabeth intervenes, and the Landgraf orders the repentant Tannhäuser to join the pilgrims passing through the valley below on their way to Rome, and beg pardon from the pope for his carnal sins.

ACT III

An orchestral prelude depicts Tannhäuser's tormented pilgrimage to Rome and the adamant refusal he meets there.

In the fall of the year, the pilgrims return through the Wartburg valley ("The Pilgrim's Chorus"). Tannhäuser is not among them. Elisabeth falls on her knees before the Virgin's shrine, offers her life in return for Tannhäuser's forgiveness, and then ascends to the castle to die. The faithful Wolfram sings to the evening star, which appears in the sky the moment Elisabeth dies ("O du, mein holder Abendstern"). In the dark valley, Tannhäuser appears, almost unrecognizable in his pilgrim's garb, and tells Wolfram ("Inbrunst im Herzen") that the pope has denied him absolution, thundering that the papal scepter will put forth green leaves before such a sinner as he will find redemption. The desperate man is about to return to Venus when Wolfram tells him that Elisabeth has died and is interceding for him in heaven. Shattered by the revelation, Tannhäuser falls lifeless in Wolfram's arms as new pilgrims arrive from Rome carrying the pope's scepter, which in a miracle of grace has blossomed in green leaves.

♣

Tannhäuser's complete title, *Tannhäuser and the Singing Contest at the Wartburg*, underlines the fact that Wagner blended two figures to make his hero—the legendary Tannhäuser, who sinned with Venus, and the quasi-historical Heinrich von Ofterdingen, who competed in song with Wolfram von Eschenbach and other minnesingers in the Wartburg. (When he is addressed in the opera, Tannhäuser is called Heinrich.)

The opera itself exists in two main versions, the earlier written for Dresden in 1845, the latter a revision, especially of the Venusberg scene, for the Paris Opéra in 1861. Its stormy reception there was perhaps the greatest musical scandal of the nineteenth century. The Paris version has passages of post-*Tristan* complexity, but in both versions *Tannhäuser* is a more or less traditional blend of arias, duets, ensembles, choruses, and even ballet. One remarkably prophetic passage, the hero's third-act "Rome Narrative," strikingly anticipates the powerful narratives of the music dramas to follow.

Tannhäuser has lost some of its once-immense popularity as Wagner's later scores have come to be better known, and is now often regarded as a melodious but simplistic conflict between good and evil. This verdict does the work a grave disservice. *Tannhäuser* is set in a historical era of some complexity, a time when a stable Christian society, confident of its political and spiritual values, was challenged by the new values of Renaissance paganism. The opera's hero is a man torn not between good and evil so much as between two opposing ideals, each important and essential to him, and he rises above his two experiences to achieve a synthesis of them. His redemption (to use Wagner's word) is won through what Goethe in *Faust* had called *das Ewig-Weibliche*, the power of woman intuitively to understand man and lead him upward. Wagner's final symbols are, as always, beautifully expressive. The evening star that marks Elisabeth's death is the planet Venus that in the morning becomes the "stella matutina," the Virgin Mary: Elisabeth has intuitively reconciled Tannhäuser's two worlds and will now light the way for him. The greening of the papal scepter is a sign that Tannhäuser has at last reconciled his Faustian "two souls." (The reconciliation is affirmed on the score's final page when, to quote the composer, "The music of the Venusberg sounds amid the hymn of God.") It is a sign too of what contemporary Jungians would call the healing of the psyche.

The opera may thus be seen as a kind of psychobiographical statement made by a young romantic composer defying the society he knows and seeking to change it, a neo-pagan unable to win a hearing for his music because of his unorthodoxy, an idealist soon to be driven into exile and forced to act out the scenario he had written. But ultimately the opera's hero is anyone who has had to relate a new world of intellectual, spiritual, or sensual awareness to the traditional values of the world in which he is placed. *Tannhäuser* represents that human struggle in mythic symbols and in music that, to listeners as varied as Hanslick and Baudelaire, came as a kind of self-revelation. "It seemed to me," the latter said, "that I already knew this music. It seemed to me that it was my *own* music."

Recording
Solti / Dernesch, Ludwig, Kollo, Braun, Sotin
(Decca/London 1970)

Tosca

Music by Giacomo Puccini
Text by Giuseppe Giacosa and Luigi Illica (after Victorien Sardou)
First performance: Rome, 14 January 1900

ACT I

In the church of Sant' Andrea della Valle in Rome, Angelotti, consul of the short-lived Roman republic, escaped from prison, takes refuge in the family chapel, where his sister has left him women's clothes to aid his flight. In the nave of the church, the politically liberal Mario Cavaradossi remarks that, in the picture of Mary Magdalen that he is painting, the face is a mysterious blend ("Recondita armonia") of the blonde, blue-eyed young woman who comes often to the church, and of his own dark-eyed, brown-haired mistress, the singer Floria Tosca. Then suddenly he finds himself shielding Angelotti, with whom he has been allied in liberal causes, from the prying eyes of a decidedly unliberal sacristan and from the jealous eyes of the politically naive Tosca. He assures his Tosca that, despite the face in the painting, he has not been meeting a woman in the church, and when she asks for a rendezvous with him that night, in the villa where they usually come together (Duet: "Non la sospiri la nostra cassetta"), he consents and bundles her off as quickly as he can. A cannon shot announces that Angelotti's escape from prison has been discovered, and Cavaradossi hastens away with the fugitive, to hide him, unwisely, in a well in the garden of the very villa where he and Tosca have their love nest. Angelotti in his haste drops a fan belonging to his sister and bearing the family crest. (His sister is, of course, the blue-eyed blonde so often seen in the church, where she has been planning his flight.)

The sacristan receives news that Napoleon and the liberal cause have been defeated at the battle of Marengo, and he is in the midst of merry prepara-

193

tions for a Te Deum when the chief of police, the rapacious Scarpia, comes commandingly up the main aisle. Hot on the trail of Angelotti, Scarpia questions the sacristan and quickly finds several clues in the church, most notably the face in the painting and the fan that the escapee left behind. He uses both to inflame the jealousy of Tosca when, still suspicious, she returns to the church searching for Cavaradossi. Shaken by Scarpia's insinuations, she hurries to the villa with the expectation of finding Cavaradossi and the blue-eyed lady *in flagrante* there. Scarpia orders his police to follow her, gloating that he is now in a position to send Cavaradossi to the gallows and force the beautiful Tosca to his will. Then, as the Te Deum begins, he sanctimoniously kneels and crosses himself.

Act II

That evening, in a room in the Palazzo Farnese, Scarpia, having a private dinner, is told by his henchman Spoletta that Angelotti could not be found at the villa but that Cavaradossi has been arrested. Scarpia orders Cavaradossi to be questioned under torture and sends for Tosca, who is in the royal apartments below, singing in a cantata in honor of the day's military victory. Tosca bravely stands up to Scarpia's intimidation but, unable to bear Cavaradossi's screams from the torture chamber, finally reveals Angelotti's hiding place. Cavaradossi, dragged into the room, is furious with her, then elated with the sudden announcement that Napoleon has actually won the battle of Marengo, that the struggle for freedom is still alive. Scarpia sends Spoletta after Angelotti and has Cavaradossi taken off to prison. Then, complaining that his poor dinner has been interrupted, he offers Tosca a choice—submit to his lust or see her Mario die. She wonders why God allows her to suffer so terribly when she has never harmed anyone ("Vissi d'arte"). Spoletta returns to say that Angelotti has killed himself. "Then have his corpse hanged on the gibbet" is Scarpia's reply. Terrified, Tosca agrees to give herself to Scarpia if Cavaradossi can be set free and they can be given safe passage together out of the city. Scarpia agrees but adds that, as appearances must be kept up, there must be a mock execution. Tosca suspects nothing when he instructs the knowing Spoletta, "As we did with Count Palmieri." He writes out the safe-conduct pass and, turning to embrace Tosca, receives what she calls "Tosca's kiss"—his own dinner knife in his chest. She taunts him as he dies: "Is your blood choking you? Die damned! Die! Die!" She shudders as she wrests the pass from his hand, places lit candles on either side of his corpse, drops a crucifix on his bleeding chest, and leaves.

ACT III

On the roof of the Castel Sant' Angelo, as the church bells of Rome sound at dawn, Cavaradossi awaits his execution, filled with memories of the starry nights he spent with Tosca ("E lucevan le stelle"). Suddenly she arrives with the safe-conduct pass and tells him that she has killed Scarpia. He is astonished that her gentle hands could have perpetrated a murder ("O dolci mani"). She explains to him that, by arrangement with Scarpia, he must undergo a mock execution—in which she is sure he will give a convincing performance. They eagerly anticipate their imminent freedom. The firing squad enters and Tosca, watching in suspense as they take aim and shoot, is fascinated by the realism with which her Mario falls to the ground. Then she discovers that (as in the case of Count Palmieri) the bullets were real. In a moment Spoletta charges at her, having made his own discovery—Scarpia too is dead. Before his men can catch her, Tosca rushes to the castle parapet and leaps to her own death, shouting to the dead Scarpia that they will meet before God.

❧

Often criticized for excessive brutality (the classic indictment is Joseph Kerman's "shabby little shocker"), *Tosca* is nonetheless composed with extraordinary skill, and for a full century it has not only held its place in the standard repertory but gained steadily in popularity, so that today it is one of the four or five most popular operas in the world, and criticism of it has become increasingly irrelevant. The opera is certainly tighter and more credible than the Sardou play on which it is based, and it offers three exceptionally rewarding and relatively undemanding roles to ever-grateful singers. (The role of Tosca is now coveted by, and for better or worse attempted by, sopranos of every description, in a way that Carmen was for a previous half-century.)

Some of the writing in the third act falls below the level of the rest (the publisher Ricordi thought that the duet "O dolci mani," which Puccini borrowed from his failed *Edgar*, reduced the characters to pygmies), but everywhere else in the score the drama is excitingly alive, subtly underlined by the composer's profuse use of motifs à la Wagner, and exploding at peak moments in chilling orchestral *tuttis*. And Puccini's gift for melody is very much in evidence.

Finally, the tense atmosphere of Rome in the melodramatic year 1800 is conveyed with remarkable swiftness and cogency. The Eternal City is as surely evoked here as is Genoa in *Simon Boccanegra*, Nuremberg in *Die Meis-*

tersinger, Vienna in *Der Rosenkavalier*, and for that matter Paris in Puccini's own *La Bohème*, and Florence in his *Gianni Schicchi*.

Recording
de Sabata / Callas, di Stefano, Gobbi (EMI/Angel 1953)

La Traviata

Music by Giuseppe Verdi
Text by Francesco Maria Piave (after Alexandre Dumas fils)
First performance: Venice, 6 March 1853

ACT I

A brief orchestral prelude begins quietly, forecasting the final illness of Violetta Valéry, a *traviata* (fallen woman). Then the prelude delineates her character: cellos sing the melody of her noble and impassioned cry, "Love me, Alfredo, love me as I love you," while skittish figures on the violins portray the life of pleasure from which she cannot escape.

Violetta, a successful Parisian courtesan already in the first stages of consumption, is giving a party at her salon. Introduced to Alfredo Germont, a serious young man from Provence, she asks him to lead the company in a brindisi, a toast to the pleasures of the demimonde ("Libiamo ne' lieti calici"). As her guests make their way to the next room, she suffers a fainting spell, and Alfredo, alone with her, expresses his concern and reveals that he has loved her from afar throughout the past year (Duet: "Un di felice, eterea"). When the guests have departed, Violetta realizes that she has felt something like real love for the first time ("Ah fors' è lui"), but that a life of pleasure is the only future she can realistically ever expect to have ("Sempre libera"). All the same, a voice sounds under her window, or perhaps only in her mind and heart: it is the earnest Alfredo, singing "Love is the pulsing of the universe, mysterious, ethereal . . ."

ACT II

Violetta and Alfredo have been living together in a villa outside Paris. He is blissfully happy ("De' miei bollenti spiriti"); she has been selling her personal belongings to pay the bills. When the maid Annina almost inadvertently reveals this to Alfredo, he rushes off to Paris in the hope of rectifying matters, just missing the arrival of his father—but it is Violetta the respectable man wants to see first. He demands that she give up his son: the boy's sister is about to be married (Duet: "Pura siccome un angelo"), and the family must avoid all scandal. She insists that her past is behind her. In due course he is touched by her dignity and devotion to his thoughtless son, and offers, instead of stern logic, paternal affection. She realizes that she must make the sacrifice he asks, and not just for a short time, but forever (Duet: "Dite alla giovine"). With a promise that he will eventually let his son know the sacrifice she has made, the father walks into the garden, and Violetta writes Alfredo a letter telling him she is returning to the demimonde. She is still at her writing table when Alfredo returns, too concerned about his own troubles to realize at first that her emotional greeting—"You do love me, Alfredo, isn't that true?"—is actually a farewell. She leaves the room, and he finds the letter. Suddenly his father is there, asking him quietly to come back to Provence ("Di provenza il mar, il suol"). But Alfredo also finds on the writing table an invitation to another scandalous Parisian party, and rushes off, intent on confronting Violetta there.

At the party, Alfredo, unlucky in love but lucky at cards, handily beats the Baron Douphol, who is keeping Violetta. She contrives to meet Alfredo alone and attempts an explanation, but, confronted with his blunt "Do you still love me?", says, in a noble lie, that she now loves the baron. He calls all the company in and, crying out that he is paying her for services rendered, flings his winnings in her face. As suddenly as before, his father is there. All are shocked by Alfredo's behavior, but Violetta forgives him ("Alfredo, Alfredo"). The baron, however, is intent on a duel.

ACT III

Another prelude depicts the *traviata*'s final illness.

Violetta is dying alone and impoverished in Paris. A doctor tells the faithful Annina that her mistress has only a few hours left to live. Violetta reads the letter Alfredo's father has written in repentance: the baron was wounded in the duel, but will recover; Alfredo is abroad, but now fully aware of the sacrifice she made for him; both father and son will come soon to ask her forgiveness; a happy future awaits her. "It's too late," she cries, asking for God's mercy ("Addio del passato"). Alfredo arrives and, with no idea that she is near death, promises to take her away from Paris ("Parigi, o cara"). She knows that her life is over ("O Dio! Morir si giovane"), and when Alfredo's father also arrives, she gives the boy a medallion for the good wife he will someday find ("Prendi, quest'è l'imaggine"). Suddenly she experiences a moment of euphoria, in which her health seems to be completely restored. Then she breathes her last.

♣

La Traviata has become in recent years the best loved and most often performed of all of Verdi's operas. Composed quickly in mid-career, and almost in tandem with the chaotic *Il Trovatore*, it is like that work a torrent of melody skillfully adapted from past bel canto traditions but is wholly unlike it in its intimate, almost psychological, probing of the main character. Thought morally objectionable at its first appearance, then subsequently viewed as an old-fashioned piece, it now seems a forerunner of realism on the operatic stage, as credible a drama as that other popular favorite with a consumptive heroine, Puccini's *La Bohème*, and far more credible, in its extraordinary sensitivity to human feeling and suffering, than full-fledged "realistic" works like *Cavalleria Rusticana* and *Pagliacci*.

The widespread story that *La Traviata* was a failure at its Venice premiere because it was staged in contemporary costumes is not true. Verdi wanted contemporary costumes, but the management of La Fenice insisted on setting the controversial subject safely in the past. Nor is it quite true that the singers were at fault. Verdi himself wrote, tersely, "A fiasco. My fault or the singers? Time will tell." There is no question that baritone Felice Varesi was not happy with his small role as the elder Germont (he had after all been Verdi's first Macbeth and first Rigoletto), and that the tenor had a throat ailment, and that the soprano, Fanny Salvini-Donatelli, as grandly proportioned as her name, was laughed at. But the opera was well applauded after the first act. The relevant fact is that Verdi himself, with little time left after writing, rehearsing, and directing *Il Trovatore*, wanted to withdraw *La Traviata* after its first performance and revise the second and third acts. He knew he could go much deeper, and he did. The additions he made to the scene between Violetta and Germont père and to Violetta's death scene are the finest things in the opera as we now have it.

Violetta grows so much in the course of the work that, it is often said, the role requires a different voice for each of the three acts—a coloratura for Violetta's abandonment to pleasure in Act I, a lyric soprano to show her rising to the sacrifice in Act II, and a lirico spinto to ride the tragic crest of Act III. Alexandre Dumas fils, who wrote the novel and play (*La Dame aux Camélias*) on which the opera is based, did not shrink from detailing the tawdriness of the life of the demimonde, nor does Verdi. But the central, poignant fact of the opera is that a woman despised by society gives up everything—friends, security, all her defenses, even though she is fatally ill—when she has been touched for the first time by the transfiguring power of real love.

Recording

Giulini / Callas, di Stefano, Bastianini (EMI/Angel 1955)

Tristan und Isolde

(Tristan and Isolde)
Music and text by Richard Wagner
First performance: Munich, 10 June 1865

ACT I

The four-note motif that begins the prelude overlaps with a second four-note motif, the "Yearning" theme, and at the point of intersection the two phrases form the so-called *Tristan* chord, perhaps the most famous chord in the whole history of music. (It has rightly been thought a harbinger of the atonal music of the twentieth century.) The prelude then builds, with many repetitions of the "Yearning" theme, into a kind of seascape: yearning for the infinite is what the opera will be about, and vistas of a vast sea will dominate its first and third acts.

On board the ship captained by Tristan, Isolde, an Irish princess, is stung to fury by what she thinks are the taunts of a young sailor singing from the masthead. When Tristan refuses to come to see her, and stays at the helm with his trusty aide Kurvenal, Isolde spills out the story of their past to her serving girl, Brangäne ("Isolde's Narrative and Curse"):

In a duel over the payment of tribute, Tristan, nephew and heir of King Marke of Cornwall, killed Isolde's betrothed, the Irish hero Morold, hacked off his head, and cruelly sent it back to Ireland in place of the tribute demanded. Isolde found in the head a splinter from the sword that had severed it, and she kept that splinter hidden, swearing vengeance on the hated Tristan. Meanwhile, the wound Tristan received in the duel would not heal, and his comrades, thinking he would die, sorrowfully put him adrift in a little boat without oars or sail. Fatally the boat drifted to Ireland, where Isolde, skilled in magic arts, tended the wounded man, not knowing who he was—till she saw a notch in his sword that matched the splinter she had found in Morold's head. She took the sword and raised it over Tristan as he lay helpless before her, but her hand was stayed when he looked piteously into her eyes. It was at that moment that they fell in love. Tristan swore his faith in "a thousand oaths" and sailed home. But when, a short time later, he returned to Ireland, he came to carry Isolde to Cornwall to marry her to his uncle, King Marke!

The spurned Isolde curses Tristan and, though she still loves him, vows to bring death to them both. She commands Brangäne to prepare, from the magic drafts her queenly mother gave her, a death potion. At that moment the crew sights land, and Tristan comes at last to face Isolde. He is still in love with her and too loyal to his king to explain to her how he was forced by jealous courtiers, by knightly honor and allegiances, to act as he has done. He is ready to let her kill him now. Ceremoniously he drinks from the cup she presents to him, and so does she. Then, strangely, they do not die. Instead, their passion for each other is terrifyingly intensified, for Brangäne, hoping to save her mistress, has poured a love potion, not a death potion, into the cup. Brangäne and Kurvenal hurry to separate the lovers, as King Marke approaches to claim his bride.

ACT II

King Marke and his retinue have left for a night's hunt, and Isolde, as a signal to Tristan, eagerly extinguishes the torch that lights the castle ramparts. The lovers meet in the garden below, breathless with excitement as they curse the hated light of day and bless the darkness that welcomes them (Duet: "O sink hernieder, Nacht der Liebe"). Brangäne, keeping watch from a tower, warns them that the night is passing, and the two lovers resolve to die together; life cannot fulfill the passion they feel, but death will merge their very identities ("So stürben wir"). But before Tristan can draw his sword to slay them both, night gives way to day, and Marke and his courtiers surprise them. The jealous Melot, who has set the trap, claims that he has saved the king's honor. But Marke wants only to know why the two people he loved most in the world have paid him in pain. Tristan can give him no answer ("O König"). He turns to Isolde and asks, "Will you follow Tristan to where he goes now, to the realm of darkness?" She quietly says that she will, and he kisses her. Melot rushes forward with his sword, and Tristan, all but impaling himself on that sword, falls back into the arms of the faithful Kurvenal.

ACT III

The wounded Tristan has been brought by Kurvenal to the lonely castle in Brittany where he was born. He has long lain unconscious. A shepherd is piping an "alte Weise," an old tune of inexpressible sadness. Kurvenal tells the shepherd to continue playing it until he sights Isolde's ship on the sea. Tristan awakes and lies musing on the "realm of darkness" he has seen in the depths of his unconscious. He tells Kurvenal that he has struggled upward from that land to find Isolde and bring her with him to the realm where she has promised to follow him. Feverishly he imagines he sees her ship arriving—only to hear the shepherd's sad tune float down again from the sea-wall. Then, with the past awakened by the sound of the "alte Weise," he remembers how the same mournful melody hung on the evening air when, as a boy, he first heard how his father died, and how it sounded again, in the early morning, when they told him that his mother had died giving him birth. The strain, he says, answers the question "Why was I born?" with the response "To yearn, and to die." As the "alte Weise" echoes through his memory, and the sun overhead burns into his brain, he comes to see what his life has been—an endless, painful torrent of yearning. Insatiate yearning, he now sees, is the human condition. He summons all his strength to renounce it, and curses the potion that he drank with Isolde, for it intensified beyond endurance the yearning that had tormented him from his birth. He sinks into unconsciousness (Kurvenal thinks for a moment he has died), and then wakes to a beatific vision of Isolde coming across the sea, walking on waves of flowers.

Suddenly the shepherd's tune changes, and Kurvenal sights Isolde's ship steering safely through the reefs, its flag flying. Tristan tears off his bandages and lets the blood stream from his wound, for Isolde has come to bleed and heal him. (He means, of course, to die with him.) "The torch is extinguished," he cries as he rushes to meet her. He breathes his last word, "Isolde," just as she arrives to take him in her arms. She doesn't understand at first, but then, as if from his dead lips, she hears a wisp of the melody he sang to her in Act II: "Let us die together." She follows him into unconsciousness. She doesn't react when a second ship arrives, and Kurvenal is killed slaying the hated Melot. She doesn't hear Brangäne calling to her, or King Marke saying he has been told everything and has come hoping to unite the lovers. As the wisp of melody from Tristan's lips expands into what we have called, since Franz

Lizst first gave it the name, the "Liebestod," Isolde surrenders to her lover's orchestral pleading as if she were walking on, engulfed by, and sinking into cosmic tides. And as she dies on his body, the restless "Yearning" theme, unfulfilled on the first page of the score and a hundred times thereafter, lifts at last to its resolution, washed away in peaceful major chords.

♣

Tristan und Isolde is much more than a love story, but Wagner, when he first planned it, wrote to Liszt to say that it would be "a monument to the true happiness of love, that most beautiful of all dreams." He conceived of it as a popular work for small houses, one that would quickly make him money and allow him to return to the composition of his mighty *Ring* cycle. But he was not far into *Tristan* when he wrote to Mathilde Wesendonck, his Muse at the time, "Child, this is turning into something terrifying! Only mediocre performances can save me. Good ones are bound to drive people mad!"

And they did. The Tristan of what was to have been the premiere, in Vienna (it was canceled after seventy-seven rehearsals), went mad. The Tristan of the first performances, in Munich in 1865, still in his twenties and a giant of a man, may rightly be said to have died of his exertions. The conductor of those performances, Hans von Bülow, wrote, "My intensive work on *Tristan*, that gigantic and devastating score, has literally finished me." He recorded that one of his assistants was driven mad during rehearsals. The number of other personal disasters that followed on exposure to the strange new music of *Tristan* is legion.

But the text too is new and strange. Wagner, like the Aeschylus who so often inspired him, reduced the action of a complicated story to a minimum and dramatized instead the character's inner lives and thoughts. He also invested one of the Western world's oldest stories of romantic love with Eastern, and specifically Buddhist, details. He had read extensively in Buddhist literature and knew all too well its first three truths, which sound like an exegesis of *Tristan*'s third act: all human existence is pain; pain is caused by desire; the highest wisdom lies in overcoming desire. Only when this is accomplished may the soul experience the state of nirvana. (Recall that only when Tristan has cursed desire is he rewarded with his nirvana vision of Isolde coming across the sea on waves of flowers.) The word "nirvana" means "blowing out," the extinguishing of the light of desire. (Recall Tristan's dying cry, "The torch is extinguished.") Chesterton once noted, contrasting the Buddhist afterlife with the Christian concept, "The Christian heaven is a heaven where they love one another; the Buddhist heaven is a heaven where they *are* one another." (Recall Tristan and Isolde resolving to die so they can merge their identities.) The word "buddha" means "awakened." (Recall how in Act III both lovers must fall into a sleep of unconsciousness before they can waken to their nirvana-visions of each other.)

Tristan's text owes much too to the philosophy of Arthur Schopenhauer (for details on this, see the entries in this book for the *Ring* and *Parsifal*), and seems in turn to have affected Oswald Spengler's classic study *The Decline of the West*. And no opera has had so great an influence on the subsequent art of the (perhaps declining) West. Bruckner, Mahler, Richard Strauss, Debussy, Puccini, Schoenberg, and Berg, to name only the best-known composers, were affected in their several ways by its relentless chromaticism. In literature, T. S. Eliot's *The Waste Land* uses *Tristan*'s offstage sailor in Act I to suggest the disorientation of twentieth-century experience and *Tristan*'s offstage shepherd in Act III to evoke a sense of twentieth-century emptiness and waste. Proust's *À la Recherche du Temps Perdu* derives much of its stream-of-consciousness technique from Tristan's third-act exploration of his conscious and unconscious memories; for Wagner's "alte Weise," Proust uses the famous madeleine dipped in tea. Thomas Mann, Gabriele D'Annunzio, D. H. Lawrence, and others wrote, early in their careers, feverish Freudian *Tristan* stories. "The world is poor," Nietzsche wrote, "for anyone who has not been sick enough for this voluptuousness of hell." One can subscribe to that statement and still think Joseph Kerman is right in saying of *Tristan* that "the nature of the experience is properly religious. . . . The extraordinary conception slowly and surely grips the audience: love is not merely an urgent force in life, but the compelling higher reality of our spiritual universe."

Recording

Furtwängler / Flagstad, Thebom, Suthaus, Fischer-Dieskau, Greindl (EMI/Angel 1952)

Il Trittico

(The Triptych)
Music by Giacomo Puccini
Text by Giacomo Puccini with Giuseppe Adami (*Il Tabarro*) and
Giovacchino Forzano (*Suor Angelica* and *Gianni Schicchi*)
First performance: New York, 14 December 1918

Il Tabarro

(The Cloak)

Michele, the owner of a barge moored in the Seine in a lower-class district of Paris, has lost the affections of his young wife, Giorgetta, to Luigi, a still younger longshoreman. Evening comes on, quitting time for the other workers—Tinca, who drinks heavily because his wife is unfaithful, and Talpa, whose rag-picking wife is more affectionate with her cat than with him. Michele reminds Giorgetta of the baby they have lost, and of how, when they were still in love, he used to shelter her and the child under his voluminous cloak on chilly evenings. She finds his tenderness impossible to bear and goes below. He, wondering which of the three men might be her lover, lights a match, which is the very signal Luigi and Giorgetta had agreed on. Michele surprises Luigi when he steals aboard, forces him to confess, strangles him, hides him under his cloak, and then has the sardonic pleasure of thrusting Giorgetta, when she comes to him in half-repentance, under the cloak, face-to-face with the corpse.

Suor Angelica

(Sister Angelica)

"The Penance": The monitress of a seventeenth-century Italian convent assigns small penances to the young novices and postulants.

"The Recreation": The other sisters wonder about Sister Angelica, who is rumored to be of royal blood and ostracized by her family.

"The Return from Alms Collecting": Two sisters bring provisions from town and report that a carriage has arrived outside the gate.

"The Principessa": Angelica is told by her elderly and imperious aunt that her younger sister is about to be married, and that, as she herself is in disgrace and now has no further need of money, she must sign away all her inheritance. Angelica does so and then asks about her illegitimate son. The aunt cruelly tells her that the baby died two years before, takes the signed document, and leaves.

"The Grace": Angelica, her maternal instincts quickened ("Senza Mamma"), mixes a lethal potion from the herbs she has tended at the convent, and drinks it. Then she realizes that the mortal sin of suicide will prevent her from seeing her little son in heaven. She prays to the Virgin to give her a sign of forgiveness.

"The Miracle": The room is suffused with light, and the Virgin appears to the ecstatic Angelica, gently urging her little child toward her.

Gianni Schicchi

In Dante's Florence, wealthy old Buoso Donati has just died, and his vulturous relatives are furious to discover that he, in expiation for his many sins, has left the whole estate to a monastery. Young Rinuccio hits on the idea of sending for Gianni Schicchi, the fix-it-all scoundrel who is one of the many wonders of Florence ("Firenze è come un albero fiorito"). In addition, Schicchi is prevailed upon by his daughter, Lauretta, who loves Rinuccio and cannot marry him without a dowry ("O mio babbino caro"). Since no one else knows that old Buoso has died, Schicchi has the corpse removed from the bed, gets in it himself, has a notary summoned, and dictates a new will, leaving the relatives with insultingly small pittances and bequeathing the bulk of the estate to "my devoted friend Gianni Schicchi"! The relatives can do nothing, for Florentine law decrees that whoever falsifies a will must lose a hand and suffer banishment. (During the dictation Schicchi reminds them of this by waving a hand from under the covers and singing "Addio, Firenze.") The young lovers are united, and Schicchi chases the relatives out of the house that is now his, begging the forgiveness of Dante, who put him in the Inferno for "this bizarre little incident," and the approval of the audience—"If you have enjoyed yourselves."

♣

Each of Puccini's three one-act operas is effective in its own way, but together they seem mismatched and make a long evening. They are far less often performed in tandem than are the separately composed *Cavalleria Rusticana* and *Pagliacci*, or for that matter the four parts of Wagner's *Ring*. Puccini first thought of a triptych to illustrate the three parts of Dante's *Divine Comedy* (Inferno, Purgatorio, and Paradiso) but settled instead for a typical evening at the Grand Guignol (a horror story, a tearjerker, and a farce).

Atmosphere more than theatrics impresses in *Il Tabarro*, in which the Seine, impassive and omniscient, painted in Debussyesque tones, is as much the chief character as the Mississippi was to be in Jerome Kern's *Show Boat*. (Luigi's lament "Bow your head and bend your back" anticipates Kern and Hammerstein by seven years, and in the first draft of the opera Michele actually had a solo to the "eternal river" that witnesses the miseries of human lives.) The vignettes of life along the river's edge, the song-peddler quoting from *La Bohème*, the quizzical ditty Talpa's wife sings about her cat—all contrast effectively with the main story, which can seem pointlessly brutal.

A surfeit of atmosphere, convent atmosphere, has made *Suor Angelica* seem the weakest of the three, but strong performances in the roles of the Principessa (a forerunner of the icy Turandot) and her hapless niece (sister under the skin to the hapless Liù) have often redeemed the piece from persistent charges of sentimentality.

Just the right touch of Florentine atmosphere pervades the popular *Gianni Schicchi*, a delicious ensemble piece, a kind of miniature *Falstaff*, crafted with great skill and proof positive that Puccini ought not to have neglected his very real comic gifts in favor of a succession of prepatented successes on melodramatic subjects.

Recording

Maazel / Scotto, Cotrubas, Horne, Domingo, Wixell, Gobbi
(CBS/Sony 1976)

Il Trovatore

(The Troubadour)
Music by Giuseppe Verdi
Text by Salvatore Cammarano and L. E. Bardare
(after García Gutiérrez)
First performance: Rome, 19 January 1853

ACT I: THE DUEL

During the civil wars in fifteenth-century Spain, Ferrando, the captain of the royalist di Luna forces, gathers his soldiers around a fire and tells them the horrendous story of the di Luna family's past:

> Some fifteen years ago, a gypsy hag was found bending over the cradle of the family's newborn boy, Garcia ("Abietta zingara"). The baby's health soon began to fail, and the family, fearing that the gypsy had cast a spell on him, hunted her down and burned her at the stake. Then the gypsy's daughter avenged her mother by stealing little Garcia from his cradle. The di Lunas made a frantic search and found a half-charred infant skeleton on the spot where they had burned the old woman. The baby's father refused to believe that his infant son was dead. He died of grief, but not before he had made his surviving son swear that he would never stop searching for his brother.

That son has grown up to be the Count di Luna, enamored of the lady Leonora, and keeping watch every night in her garden—for, as Leonora confesses to Ines, her lady-in-waiting, she has fallen in love with a mysterious black knight who, in a recent tourney, has vanquished all opponents and since then has come in the quiet of the night to sing troubadour songs beneath her window ("Tacea la notte placida"). In a moment the jealous Count accosts the troubadour, who lifts his visor to reveal himself in the moonlight as Manrico, a political enemy of the di Lunas, fighting in the rebel cause. The two men cross swords as the curtain falls.

ACT II: THE GYPSY

In the mountains of Biscay, a shelter for gypsies ("The Anvil Chorus"), Manrico has been nursed back to health by his mother, the gypsy woman Azucena. He has defeated the Count in their duel, but in the subsequent battle of Pelilla his forces were overcome and he was left for dead. We now hear, before another fire, more of the terrible events of a generation past ("Stride la vampa"). Azucena tells Manrico that *she* was the gypsy daughter who had stolen the di Luna baby. Haunted by her mother's dying scream, "Avenge me!", she had taken it, with her own infant at her breast, to the spot where they had burned her mother ("Condotta ell'era in ceppi"). There, in crazed confusion, she had thrown her *own* baby into the fire. (Who can hear Verdi's shattering climax at "Il figlio mio! Il figlio mio!" unmoved?) The horrified Manrico wonders then about his own identity. Azucena, still filled with hatred of the di Lunas, asks him why he spared the Count in the duel. He replies ("Mal reggendo") that some instinct, like a voice from heaven, had told him not to strike the fatal blow. News comes to him that Leonora, thinking him dead, is about to become a nun, and he hurries off to stop her.

The Count has surrounded the convent with his forces, also intent on carrying Leonora off before she takes her vows ("Il balen del suo sorriso"). Suddenly Manrico appears, as if risen from the dead, with his rebel forces. The two enemies clash again as the curtain falls.

Act III: The Gypsy's Son

The Count is about to storm the cliffed castle of Castellor, where Manrico has taken Leonora, when his soldiers find Azucena, half-crazed and wandering in search of her son. The Count's man Ferrando recognizes her as the gypsy daughter who had stolen little Garcia. The di Luna forces prepare to burn the daughter as, a generation back, they had burned the mother.

Manrico, above in the castle, is about to wed Leonora ("Ah! sì, ben mio") when he sees below the pyre being readied for his mother. He arms himself ("Di quella pira") and rushes out to defend her.

Act IV: The Punishment

Manrico has arrived in time to save his mother, but in the ensuing battle has been defeated and imprisoned in a tower of the di Luna fortress; at dawn he will be led to the block and his mother to the stake. Leonora comes secretly to keep watch beneath his window ("D'amor sull'ali rosee"). In terror she hears the di Luna monks praying for his soul ("Miserere") while Manrico sings a troubadour lament from the tower, longing for death. Leonora in desperation offers herself to the Count in return for Manrico's life. The Count, not knowing that she has taken poison, assents.

Within the tower, Manrico comforts the raving Azucena with a song about returning home (Duet: "Ai nostri monti"). Leonora is admitted to the cell and tells Manrico he can now go free. At first, his honor is offended at the thought of the price she may have paid; then she dies before his eyes. The Count, furious at being deceived, orders Manrico's immediate execution and drags Azucena to the prison window to watch. When the axe falls, she shrieks at the Count what we have feared even to suspect—that he has killed the brother he had sought for all his life. Azucena falls lifeless with the cry, "Mother, you are avenged."

⚜

The plot of *Il Trovatore*, often unjustly maligned, is partly based on actual events, vividly represents Verdi's pessimistic view of the world, and even reflects to a degree some of his own experience. When he himself was a baby, during the Napoleonic Wars, his mother fled with him in her arms to the parish belfry to escape the sabers of a vindictive Russian regiment. In his twenties he saw his two children die of illness within the span of a few months, followed in time by their young mother. The year before he wrote *Il Trovatore* his own mother died. His librettist died in the midst of writing it. When the opera appeared, Verdi wrote, "People say that it is too sad, that there are too many deaths in it. But death is all there is to life. What else is there?"

Il Trovatore's chaotic text is, on close inspection, full of subtleties, ironies, and patterns of imagery (windows, flames, streaks of light, staring eyes). Manrico is associated in Leonora's first aria with the moon, and the moon emerges from the clouds to reveal his face as he lifts his visor—though no one present, not even he, knows that his real name is Garcia di Luna (Garcia of the Moon), and he goes to his eventual death without knowing who he was. The four main characters, caught in fixed attitudes, are emotionally charged symbols of life's ironies—Manrico of the inability of any man to know himself, the Count of the destructiveness of uncontrolled passion, Leonora of the utter futility of self-sacrifice, and Azucena of the relentless and confused operation of instinct in a universe that is overwhelmingly cruel to its creatures. Azucena is crazed by the thought that she would die as her mother had died—at the stake. Instead, she is killed, as Verdi insisted she must be, by a sudden confluence of the two great passions of her life—her compulsion to avenge her mother and her love for the baby who had become a son to her. At any moment she might have saved that son by telling the Count that he was his brother. When she is dragged to the window to watch Manrico's execution she shouts, "Oh, wait! Listen to me!" But the opera's terrible events had by then hurried to their terrible end.

Il Trovatore was for several decades the most popular opera in the world, for its instantly recognizable (and often parodied) Anvil Chorus; for "Di quella pira," that most heroic of all cabalettas; and for the "Miserere" and "Ai nostri monti" that issued nostalgically from barrel organs in the Little Italys of big cities the world over. More than that, Manrico's "Ah! sì, ben mio" and Leonora's "D'amor sull'ali rosee," which draw on past bel canto traditions, are perhaps the most beautiful arias Verdi ever wrote, while the Count's "Il balen" illustrates the composer's new and demanding way of writing for high baritone, and all of his music for Azucena looks forward to the dramatic intensity of his later work. But the source of *Il Trovatore*'s strength lies in more than its famous melodies. Francis Toye has rightly said of it, "Something emerges and hits you, as it were, between the eyes, something elemental, furious, wholly true."

Recording

Cellini / Milanov, Barbieri, Björling, Warren (RCA 1952)

Les Troyens

(The Trojans)
Music and text by Hector Berlioz (after Virgil)
First performance of Part II: Paris, 4 November 1863;
first complete performance, Karlsruhe, 6 and 7 December 1890

PART I: LA PRISE DE TROIE
(The Capture of Troy)

Act I

In the tenth year of the Trojan War, the Greeks appear at last to have sailed away, and the Trojans rush jubilantly out of their walled city and down to the shore, to see there the huge wooden horse that the Greeks have left behind, supposedly as a votive offering for their safe return home. The prophetic princess Cassandra, who has seen the ghost of Troy's mightiest hero, Hector, stalking the ramparts and gazing out across the strait, knows that the city, its king, and its people are still in danger ("Malheureux roi"). But the

Trojans have never heeded her warnings, thinking her mad. Even her loving fiancé, Coroebus, refuses to flee the city when she predicts his death (Duet: "Reviens à toi, vierge adorée").

At the citadel, King Priam and Queen Hecuba burn incense and thank the gods for victory. Andromache, Hector's young widow, approaches an altar dedicated to his memory and kneels there in silence with Astyanax, their little son. Suddenly Aeneas, Hector's cousin and now Troy's best defense, rushes in to announce that the priest Laocoön, who hurled his spear into the side of the wooden horse and urged that it be burned, has been attacked by two massive sea serpents and eaten alive. Aeneas interprets this terrible death as a divine punishment for an act of impiety, and encourages the Trojans to bring the votive offering into the city. As the people haul through the gates the instrument of their own destruction ("The Trojan March"), the clash of arms is clearly audible within it. Cassandra cries out her warning, but the mad procession cannot be halted and passes by. She enters the city alone, to die in the conflagration to come.

Act II

That night, Hector appears to Aeneas in a dream to tell him that Greek warriors have issued from the wooden horse and opened the gates of Troy to the invading enemy; he must escape with what people he can save, and found a new city in Italy. But Aeneas, learning from Ascanius, his young son, that the city is already on fire, forms a small band of warriors, Coroebus included, and rushes out to fight, with the repeated Virgilian cry, "The only hope for survival now is to hope for no survival!"

In Priam's beleaguered palace, Cassandra tells the women of the royal family that her Coroebus has been killed, but that Aeneas has escaped with a remnant of their people. Many of the women die rather than submit to the victorious Greeks—stabbing themselves and leaping from the parapet, crying out to Aeneas to lead their sons safely to Italy.

PART II: LES TROYENS À CARTHAGE

(The Trojans at Carthage)

Act III

Aeneas and the survivors of the Trojan War, shipwrecked off the coast of Carthage, are received with hospitality at the prosperous court of Queen Dido. Though she has sworn fidelity to her dead husband Sychaeus, Dido falls in love with Aeneas when, after a tender farewell to Ascanius, he successfully defends her city against the threatening Numidians.

ACT IV

A storm interrupts the royal hunt of Dido and Aeneas and drives them into a cave, where they consummate their love amid violent manifestations of the spirits of earth, air, fire, and water ("Royal Hunt and Storm").

On a terrace overlooking the sea, Anna, Dido's sister, is overjoyed at the turn of events, but the royal minister Narbal is apprehensive, knowing that Aeneas must someday leave for Italy. The minstrel Iopas sings sweetly of the arts of harvesting and peace, and Aeneas impresses Dido with accounts of the dangers he has passed. Left alone in an enchanted night, the two declare their love in subtle mythic exchanges ("Nuit d'ivresse"). But when they retire, a ray of moonlight reveals the figure of Mercury, striking Aeneas' abandoned shield, pointing to the sea and crying "Italy!"

ACT V

That night the Trojan fleet is at anchor in the harbor, and two sentries hear a young sailor singing from the masthead, rocked by the swaying of the ship and remembering the home he will never see again. When morning dawns, Aeneas is determined to sail ("Inutiles regrets"), urged on by the pale ghosts of Priam, Hector, Coroebus, and Cassandra. Dido hurries in to stop him from setting sail. He swears that he still loves her but must be faithful to his mission. She calls him a "monster of piety." The ships are quickly readied for departure.

In her palace with Anna and Narbal, Dido considers pursuing the Trojan fleet with her own ships and setting it on fire. Then she realizes that death is the only honorable course left to her ("Adieu, fière cité").

On the terrace overlooking the sea, Dido orders a great fire to be built; she will ritually burn every reminder of Aeneas. But in the course of the ceremony, she mounts the pyre, falls on his sword, and immolates herself amid the flames, predicting that from her ashes an avenger, Hannibal, shall rise. Then she despairs as she sees a vision of the imperial Rome that will eventually be the fulfillment of Aeneas' mission and the destruction of her Carthage. As their queen dies in flames, the Carthaginians swear eternal war against Rome, but their cries are drowned in the surging music of the Trojan March, as in the sky we see the vision Dido saw—the Roman Capitol, its legions, and Augustus surrounded by his poets and artists, and among them, surely, Virgil.

❧

Virgil was a main source of inspiration for Hector Berlioz, who, named for the noblest Trojan of them all, was moved to tears when, as a boy, he first construed the *Aeneid* in Latin with the help of his father. In *Les Troyens*, he limits himself mainly to the first four books of Virgil's twelve-book epic, but the song of the young sailor in the masthead, written by Berlioz with his own sailor son in mind, is derived from the famous Palinurus episode in Book V; Aeneas' touching lines to Ascanius ("Others, my son, will teach you to be happy") come from Book XII; and there are echoes of Virgil's earlier *Eclogues* and *Georgics* in the song of the minstrel Iopas, the figure in the opera who may be thought to represent Virgil himself. Virgilians will also detect the sound of the dactylic hexameter, "the stateliest measure ever molded by the lips of man," in such passages as the chorus of Trojans processing into Priam's palace in Act I, and in the whispering orchestral nocturne that accompanies the Act IV love duet of Dido and Aeneas, where mythological references are knowingly exchanged in the manner of the amoebean (responsive) verses in Virgil's *Eclogues*. Another main influence, Shakespeare, enters at that moment: the amoebean verses are cast in the language Jessica and Lorenzo use in the moonlit night in *The Merchant of Venice* ("In such a night as this . . .").

On many pages of the score, Berlioz shows his extraordinary sensitivity to the suggestive qualities of various instruments, and his feeling for voices in combination is manifest throughout, from massed choruses to vocal quintet, septet, and octet. His long-lined melodies remain, after more than a century, absolutely unique. Because the epic work is cast in the style of *tragédie lyrique*, the occasional declamatory passage may seem curiously cold and chiseled—classicism in the wrong sense. But most of *Les Troyens* is quick and alive with feeling, as a real classic must be. Berlioz in the course of his epic drama subsumes the nobility of Gluck, the historical sweep of Handel, the spectacle of Spontini and Meyerbeer, the romanticism of Hugo and Delacroix. He may even be thought to have anticipated the ambivalent confluence of music, text, and scenic effect that marks the concluding scenes in Wagner: when, on the last page of *Les Troyens*, Dido dies in flames, and the chorus forecasts the Carthaginian victories of the Punic Wars while the orchestra and visuals affirm the eventual triumph of Aenean Rome, one feels something, not just of the sweep of history, but of the awesome power of the last page of Wagner's *Ring*.

Les Troyens was regarded as eccentric and unperformable in Berlioz' day, and the composer never saw his five-hour masterpiece staged complete. Its rejection was a source of immense sorrow to him, and Gounod remarked that, like his namesake, Hector Berlioz died beneath the walls of Troy. The groundbreaking Covent Garden performances under Rafael Kubelik in 1957, the first publication of the complete score in 1969, and the subsequent complete recording, with Covent Garden forces under Colin Davis, are among the most important musicological events of the twentieth century. *Les Troyens* is now rightly thought to be *the* classic of French opera.

Recording

Davis / Lindholm, Veasey, Vickers, Glossop, Soyer (Philips 1969)

Turandot

Music by Giacomo Puccini
Text by Giuseppe Adami and Renato Simoni (after Carlo Gozzi)
First performance: Milan, 25 April 1926

Act I

In imperial Peking, the Prince of Persia is beheaded at moonrise. He is the most recent of many suitors to have lost his life for failing to answer the three riddles asked by the misandric Princess Turandot. In the excited crowd, Calaf, an unknown Prince, rescues an old man, Timur, from being trampled on, and recognizes him as his long-lost father, driven out of his kingdom. Timur has been accompanied in his wanderings by Liù, a slave girl who has loved Calaf ever since, on a day long before their exile began, he smiled at her. But Calaf is smitten with desire for the Princess Turandot when he catches a glimpse of her beneath the moon. Despite the warnings of her three ministers Ping, Pang, and Pong, and the pleas of Liù ("Signore, ascolta!"), Calaf tells the slave girl to look after his father ("Non piangere, Liù") and sounds a gong signaling his intention to face Turandot's three riddles.

Act II

Ping, Pang, and Pong, weary of Turandot's cruel riddles and longing to return to their peaceful homes, are summoned with all Peking into the Emperor's presence for Calaf's testing.

Princess Turandot publicly declares that she is cruel to men because, in the imperial palace long ago, a man raped and killed her ancestor, the Princess Lou-ling ("In questa reggia"). Calaf, undeterred, rises to the challenge of her three riddles and correctly answers them all. Then he heroically allows the humiliated Princess the rest of the night to find out his name. If she succeeds in that, she will not have to marry him, and he will willingly bow to the axe.

Act III

On a terrace overlooking the city, Calaf hears a herald announce that, under penalty of death, no one is to sleep that night in Peking until the name of the unknown Prince is discovered, and he eagerly looks forward to possessing the Princess ("Nessun dorma"). Timur and Liù are captured and tortured but refuse to reveal Calaf's name. Liù, predicting that the icy Princess will some day love the Prince ("Tu, che di gel sei cinta"), seizes a dagger and kills herself. Moved by this sacrifice, Calaf takes Turandot in his arms and reveals his name, thereby offering his life as well. Turandot triumphantly calls for all the people to be assembled again.

In the presence of the Emperor and all the people, Turandot announces that she knows the Prince's name. But instead of sentencing him to death, she surrenders to him. His name, she says, is Love.

❖

Now that "Nessun dorma" has topped the pop charts, it is almost impossible to believe that *Turandot*, after the excitement of its first performances, lay neglected by most opera houses for almost three decades. It was the clarion voice of Birgit Nilsson in the title role that renewed the world's interest. Since then, the work, with its exotic orchestration, its massed and masterly choruses, its opportunities for spectacle, and its "Nessun dorma," has firmly established itself in the active repertory.

Puccini died before he could complete the last act, and Franco Alfano, at the request of Arturo Toscanini, composed everything from the death of Liù onward, using sketches the composer had left behind but not attempting the "great orchestral peroration" à la Wagner that Puccini had hoped would convince listeners that they should care about the two callous principals. As Puccini made thirty unsuccessful attempts over the course of two years to complete that last scene, it seems churlish of commentators—and of Toscanini—to have faulted Alfano for not solving the ultimate *Turandot* riddle.

The most affecting music in the score is, predictably, that written for the quietly suffering Liù, the last in a long line of Puccini heroines designed to wring tears. But *morbidezza* is not all that there is to admire in *Turandot*: Puccini had learned much from the Debussys and Schoenbergs of his time, and he braved the atonal climate of 1926 to give his public a score, perhaps the last great score, that drew its main strength from the traditions of Italian song. In light of this, the eminent Verdian Julian Budden has called *Turandot* "the summit of Puccini's achievement."

Recording

Leinsdorf / Nilsson, Tebaldi, Björling, Tozzi (RCA 1959)

The Turn of the Screw

Music by Benjamin Britten
Text by Myfanwy Piper (after Henry James)
First performance: Venice, 14 September 1954

ACT I

"The Journey": A Governess, half in love with the man who has employed her, speeds in her coach to Bly, where she will tutor his two orphaned charges. She has been told not to bother her employer if any troubles arise.

"The Welcome": The housekeeper, Mrs. Grose, and the children, Flora and Miles, greet the Governess excitedly.

"The Letter": A shocking report arrives from Miles' school: he has been expelled.

"The Tower": The Governess, enchanted with the beauty of Bly, is startled to see a strange man standing on a tower.

"The Window": The Governess now sees the man staring in a window. Mrs. Grose identifies him from the Governess' description as Peter Quint, a former employee, a scoundrel who had had his way with the former governess and taught the children evil things. Both former employees, the Governess hears with a shock, are now dead.

"The Lesson": The Governess, now resolved to protect the children from evil, tutors Miles in his Latin. He sings the mnemonic rhyme "Malo malo malo malo" ("I would rather be in an apple tree than a naughty boy in adversity").

"The Lake": The Governess sees her dead predecessor, Miss Jessel, across a lake—and realizes that Flora sees her too.

"At Night": Quint calls in the darkness to Miles, and Miss Jessel calls to Flora. Miles says, when questioned, "You see, I am bad."

ACT II

"Colloquy and Soliloquy": Quint and Miss Jessel sing, "The ceremony of innocence is drowned"; the Governess sings of the evil that is hovering over the children.

"The Bells": The children are playing in a churchyard, and the Governess fears they are with "the others." Miles asks, "Do you like the bells? I do." The Governess now feels that she must flee from Bly.

"Miss Jessel": The Governess finds Miss Jessel at the desk in the schoolroom and defies her. Miss Jessel vanishes, and the Governess finds the courage to stay and fight for the children.

"The Bedroom": Miles, ready for bed, sings his "Malo, malo." The Governess tells him she has written a letter to his guardian. Quint's voice is heard, and the candle goes out. "'Twas I who blew it," Miles says.

"Quint": Quint induces Miles to steal the letter.

"The Piano": Miles plays the piano furiously while Flora slips away from the Governess and Mrs. Grose.

"Flora": The two women find Flora by the lake with Miss Jessel. Flora claims she sees no one there and shouts abuse at the Governess, who realizes that evil has claimed the child.

"Miles": Mrs. Grose, after a night with the now hysterical Flora, takes her away from Bly, and the Governess is left alone with Miles. Quint's voice from the tower tells the boy not to betray their secrets. Miles admits that he took the letter, and when asked to name the one who made him take it, he cries out, "Peter Quint, you devil!" and falls dead in the Governess' arms: she may have saved his soul but at the cost of his life. She lays him out on the floor, repeating the word "malo," which now seems to mean, unambiguously, "evil."

⚘

Each of the sixteen scenes, scored for chamber orchestra, is prefaced by a variation on a theme stated at the opera's beginning: each is a new tightening of the screw as the suspense mounts. This ingenuity is not apparent to most listeners on first hearing, let alone to most operagoers at a staged performance, but the opera rewards study and is slowly winning its public. As with the Henry James original, nothing is specific. The ghosts may actually exist as harmful influences on the children or may be only figments of the imagination of a sexually repressed governess. Britten had the stage sense to allow the ghosts to appear, and the musical skill to keep them, as it were, disembodied. Critics have traced the opera's themes of sexual ambivalence and threatened innocence throughout much of the composer's work.

Recording
Britten / Vyvan, Cross, Dyer, Hemmings, Pears (Decca 1955)

Werther

Music by Jules Massenet
Text by Édouard Blau, Paul Milliet, and Georges Hartmann
(after Goethe)
First performance: Vienna, 16 February 1892

"The Bailiff's House": In the outskirts of Wetzlar, a small eighteenth-century German town, an elderly bailiff, lovingly cared for by his daughters Charlotte and Sophie, is teaching a Christmas carol to his six younger children. (His cronies Johann and Schmidt can only wonder why he is doing so in July.) Werther, a dreamy young romantic, is entranced by the scene and especially by Charlotte, whom he accompanies to a party that night. When they return arm-in-arm in the moonlight, Charlotte tells Werther that she has promised her dying mother to marry her fiancé, Albert. Werther despairs.

"The Lime Trees": Charlotte and Albert, now married, go to church together. Werther waits outside, sadly reflecting that such happiness can never be his. Charlotte afterward tells him he must leave; perhaps they can meet again at Christmas. Albert suddenly realizes that the two are in love.

"Charlotte and Werther": On Christmas Eve, Charlotte weeps over Werther's letters, all of which she has saved. Werther returns as promised, and Charlotte almost yields to him but finally bids him farewell for the last time. Werther leaves, resolved to kill himself, and in a moment sends his servant with a letter requesting of Albert the loan of his pistols, for he is going on a long journey. Albert makes Charlotte hand over the pistols and goes coldly to his room. She rushes out in a snowstorm to find Werther, hoping she is not too late.

"Christmas Eve": The moon rises over the rooftops of snowswept Wetzlar. The lights in the houses go on one by one.

"The Death of Werther": Charlotte finds Werther in his apartment, mortally wounded. They kiss for the first time. Werther dies as, outside the window, the children sing the Christmas carol they have learned.

☘

Massenet's series of "five tableaux," variously divided into two, three, or four acts, is skillfully evocative of life in a provincial German town of two centuries past, and the score is so beautifully melancholic, almost Tchaikovskian in its sadness, that the optimistic chirping of sister Sophie, like the similar pipings of cousin Ännchen in *Der Freischütz*, are jarringly unwelcome. But at least those mood-shattering interruptions may prevent young males in the audience from turning to suicide, as did the youth of Europe when Goethe's romance first appeared in print. For lovers of Massenet, it is impossible even to think of the poignant arias of Charlotte ("Les larmes qu'on ne pleure pas") and of Werther ("Pourquoi me réveiller") without weeping.

Recording

Plasson / Troyanos, Krauss, Manuguerra (EMI/Angel 1979)

Wozzeck

Music and text by Alban Berg (after Georg Büchner)
First performance: Berlin, 14 December 1925

Act I: Five Character Pieces

"Suite": Wozzeck, a penniless German soldier, shaves his Captain, who chides him for having a child out of wedlock. Wozzeck humbly answers that "wir arme Leut" ("we poor people") cannot afford to have morals.

"Rhapsody": Wozzeck, cutting sticks in a field with Andres, another soldier, sees mad visions at sunset.

"Military March and Lullaby": Marie, Wozzeck's common-law wife, is attracted by a Drum Major strutting past her window. Taunted by her neighbor Margret, and alarmed at Wozzeck's state of mind, she desperately sings their little son to sleep.

"Passacaglia": Wozzeck, subjected to a sadistic Doctor's dietary experiments, confesses his anxieties; the Doctor, pleased that Wozzeck seems to be going mad, looks forward to the fame he is sure will result from his research.

"Andante affettuoso": Marie's admiring remarks to the Drum Major about his fine figure arouse his interest, and she takes him to bed.

ACT II: SYMPHONY IN FIVE MOVEMENTS

"Sonata": Wozzeck, wondering where Marie got her new earrings, dutifully gives her his soldier's pay and his pittance from the Captain and the Doctor. Her conscience plagues her.

"Fantasia and Fugue": The Captain and the Doctor tease Wozzeck about his poor state of health and the faithlessness of his woman.

"Largo": Wozzeck confronts Marie with the charges. She defies him, and he becomes obsessed with her words, "Better a knife in me . . ."

"Scherzo 1 and 2": At an inn, Wozzeck finds Marie dancing with the Drum Major. A drunken worker attempts a sermon on the nature of man, Andres sings a lewd song, and Wozzeck is driven into a panic by an idiot's talk of blood.

"Rondo marziale": Wozzeck, in a barracks full of snoring soldiers, starts out of his sleep with demented visions of couples dancing and the flashing of a knife blade, and is brutally beaten by the drunken Drum Major.

ACT III: SIX INVENTIONS

"Invention on a theme": Marie reads the Gospel account of the woman taken in adultery and penitently tells her child a story about a deserted orphan boy.

"Invention on a note": As the moon rises red over a pool, Wozzeck kisses Marie and then cuts her throat.

"Invention on a rhythm": Wozzeck dances madly with Margret in a tavern, but rushes out when she sees blood on his hands.

"Invention on a six-note chord": Wozzeck returns to the pool to retrieve his knife, wades in too far, and is drowned. The Captain and the Doctor, passing by, hear the sound of someone drowning but ignore it.

"Invention on a key": The orchestra eloquently pleads for understanding of the world's "arme Leut."

"Invention on a continuous quaver rhythm": Children tell Wozzeck's little son that his mother is dead, and run off to see the corpse. Uncomprehending, the boy follows them, hop-hopping on his hobbyhorse.

♣

The titles for the three acts of *Wozzeck*, and the musical designations for its scenes, were useful to Berg in composing, but he asked his first audiences to experience the work viscerally, without recourse to formal analysis. And *Wozzeck* is indeed a visceral work, a wrenching example of expressionism in music: the truth about the human condition is conveyed not through "realism" but through violent distortions of reality, expressive of internal anguish.

Using a self-imposed maze of formal structures and a partially atonal musical language that challenges singers, instrumentalists, and audience in about equal degrees, Berg brings Georg Büchner's disturbing play to life with new power and overwhelming compassion. Critic John Simon called the nineteenth-century play "the first true tragedy of the common man"; Berg's opera has been thought to represent, as no other musical work does, victimized twentieth-century man—rootless, faceless, unredeemed, driven to acts of violence by external and internal forces he cannot comprehend and from which he cannot escape.

Recording

Dohnányi / Silja, Wächter (Decca/London 1979)

Die Zauberflöte

(The Magic Flute)
Music by Wolfgang Amadeus Mozart
Text by Emanuel Schikaneder
First performance: Vienna, 30 September 1791

ACT I

An overture in E-flat, the key of three flats, begins with three solemn, shivering chords. (Three is a number with Masonic significances, and Mozart's symbolic fairy-tale opera will present three ladies, three boys, three temples, three trials—and much more music in three flats.) A quasi-religious adagio follows, and then the overture settles into a fugue on a happy theme, interrupted for another startling minute by the three solemn chords: this is to be an entertainment both serious and comic.

In a mountainous landscape overgrown with exotic flowers, a Japanese Prince rushes on with a dragon in pursuit and falls exhausted into a faint. The dragon is promptly dispatched by three ladies with silver spears, who exclaim aloud at the Prince's handsomeness and go off to call their sovereign, the Queen of the Night. The Prince revives, and Papageno, a birdcatcher who almost seems to be part-bird himself, introduces himself with whistles on his panpipes ("Der Vogelfänger bin ich ja"), and claims to have killed the dragon with his bare hands. The three ladies return, give Papageno a stone and water instead of bread and wine, and place a padlock on his mouth to punish him for lying. For the Prince they have another gift—a miniature portrait of the Queen's daughter, Pamina. The Prince, to a tune in three flats ("Dies Bildnis ist bezaubernd schön"), falls in love with Pamina. How could he not? His own name is Tamino.

Then, as thunder sounds, the mountains part to disclose the Queen of the Night, riding a crescent moon. She tells Tamino that Pamina has been carried off by an evil sorcerer named Sarastro, and that, if he rescues her, he can claim her as his wife ("O zittre nicht"). Then she vanishes. The three ladies give Tamino a magic flute and Papageno, released from his punishment, a set of magic bells, and they send the unusual twosome off, promising that they will be escorted on their adventure by three angelic boys (Quintet: "Drei Knäbchen").

In the castle-fortress of Sarastro, Papageno frightens away the Moor Monostatos, who is guarding Pamina, and tells the Princess about the Prince who has fallen in love with her. Overjoyed, she hopes that Papageno too will find someone to love (Duet: "Bei Männern").

Tamino has been led by the three boys, flying ahead of him, to three Egyptianesque temples in Sarastro's realm. Mysterious voices tell him not to approach the side temples of Nature and Reason, and he turns to the central temple of Wisdom. An old priest issues from it to tell him, surprisingly, that Sarastro is not evil, but good. Left alone, Tamino wonders, "O everlasting night, when will you end?", and the voices respond, "Soon, soon, young man, or never." He asks, "Is Pamina still alive?", and they answer, "Pamina —Pamina still lives!" ("These measures," said Ingmar Bergman, "are to me the center of all of Mozart and also of the whole history of civilization.")

Heartened, Tamino raises his magic flute to his lips and, as with Orpheus, animals of every description appear and dance to his music. Meanwhile Papageno has escaped from Sarastro's castle with Pamina. For a moment the two fugitives are threatened by Monostatos and his Moors, but Papageno plays a nursery rhyme on his magic bells and sets the pursuers dancing. Sarastro appears, in a chariot drawn by lions. He rightly orders that Monostatos be punished, but also separates the two lovers just as they have seen each other for the first time, and decrees that Tamino and Papageno must surrender their magic musical instruments. (We might well wonder why Sarastro's people end the act extolling his virtue and justice.)

ACT II

In a grove of silver palm trees with golden leaves, Sarastro nominates Tamino for admission into his priesthood. The Prince must undergo a series of tests. Papageno will be tested with him, and Pamina will help him. Sarastro and his priests pray to Isis and Osiris for the successful outcome of these trials.

In a dark and thundering part of the castle, the Prince and the Birdcatcher pass their first test (silence in the presence of non-initiates), even though the three ladies appear out of nowhere to dissuade them.

In a moonlit garden, Monostatos attempts to ravish the sleeping Pamina, but is sent scurrying by the sudden appearance of the Queen, who gives her overawed daughter a dagger and tells her she must kill Sarastro with it ("Der Hölle Rache"). Then she vanishes as quickly as she came, and Sarastro appears to tell Pamina that forgiveness, not vengeance, rules in his masonry ("In diesen heil'gen Hallen").

In a dim-lit hall of the castle, the Prince and the Birdcatcher face their second test (silence in the presence of the women who are to be their life companions). Papageno, of whom less is expected, almost fails his test by chatting with an amorous old crone; Tamino passes his, remaining silent when Pamina appears. But she cannot understand why he does so, and is heartbroken ("Ach, ich fühl's"). Meanwhile, the three boys restore to Tamino his magic flute and to Papageno his magic bells. These will help them in their third trial (facing death).

In a pyramidal vault, as his priests invoke Isis and Osiris, Sarastro has Pamina and Tamino—his new Isis and Osiris—brought before him: they must say farewell before Tamino meets his third and greatest test (Trio: "Soll ich dich, Teurer").

In another part of the castle, Papageno, bored with all the testing, asks for a glass of wine, gets it magically, and then, playing on the magic bells, asks for a wife ("Ein Mädchen oder Weibchen"). What he gets is the old crone again —and just for a moment she turns into the Papagena of his dreams. But in another moment, she is gone.

In the moonlit garden, Pamina has taken up the dagger her mother gave her: since Tamino seems not to love her any more, she will kill herself. The three boys appear to assure her that Tamino really does love her but must first prove himself a hero. They can take her to him. Is she strong enough to help him?

In a mountainous landscape where two men in armor guard a pyramid, Pamina and Tamino meet and, at last, speak—in matching musical phrases, complementing each other like Isis and Osiris. Together they pass through the pyramid's potentially lethal fire and water, he playing all the while on the magic flute that, she tells him, her father once carved from a primeval oak tree. They emerge from this third test unscathed.

Papageno, forlorn under a palm tree, is about to hang himself, half-hoping the audience will tell him to stop. Suddenly the three boys are there to remind him that he has the magic bells to help him. He plays them and lo! his Papagena appears, no longer a vintage virago but a helpmate as fully feathered as himself. They sing a barnyard duet about all the little Papagenos and Papagenas they will have (and there isn't a more joyous piece of music in existence).

Finally, at the very bottom of Sarastro's castle, the Queen of the Night, her three ladies, and Monostatos (who has gone over to their side) are overwhelmed in darkness. There is a burst of light, and Sarastro, the three boys, the Prince and Princess, and Papageno and Papagena all appear ranged about the sun, proclaiming the victory of light.

♣

The summary offered here is unusually detailed because the received wisdom among many operagoers is that, while *The Magic Flute* contains a lot of charming and often sublime music, it is saddled with a completely nonsensical libretto. That is hardly the opinion entertained in German-speaking lands, where the opera was an instant success and has been perhaps the most popular work in the repertory for more than two centuries, where its characters' names have become household words, where both philosophers and those humble people the poet calls the "best philosophers"—children—still watch it with equal amounts of levity and gravity, and where that greatest of intellectuals, Goethe, was so taken with it he began work on a sequel.

The Magic Flute is, on one level, a Masonic allegory depicting, with details culled from largely Masonic sources, the conflict between the Enlightenment and the Counter-Reformation. Attempts have been made to identify the Queen as Empress Maria Theresa, Tamino as Crown Prince Joseph, Monostatos as the black-robed clergy, and so forth. But these explanations tend to make a mere allegory, only partly true, out of what is, in the end, a universal and profoundly true mythic statement.

Mozart's opera may be more profitably seen as a symbolic depiction of mankind's progression from nature to culture. Our first deities, so far as we can tell, were not father-gods but mother-goddesses. The first social groups were familial and tribal. Taboos, spells, and magic were important to them. Only when, inevitably, there was contact and conflict with outsiders was there a slow, painful movement toward larger communities. Magic was succeeded by ritual, taboo gave way to morality, the family circle recognized the rights of a wider civilization, and the mother-goddess yielded to a father. This may be thought to be one of the great evolutionary moments in the prehistory of the race, and if we scale it down to a fantasy level, we have a surprisingly workable analysis of Mozart's opera. It is not at all inconceivable that Mozart and even Schikaneder could have planned their opera along these lines. They could easily have discussed them with Ignaz von Born, a fellow Freemason versed in Greek and Egyptian lore.

It is also possible to think less anthropologically and more mythically: Tamino is the Jungian hero "with a thousand faces"—that is to say, from every culture—questing for his Self, encountering en route his shadow (Papageno), his anima (the Queen), and his Wise Old Man (Sarastro).

Or we can think in terms of mother and father principles: Pamina moves from the mother, whose love is protective and lavished unconditionally, to the father, whose love is won through obedience to commandments. Psychologically, a child reaches maturity when she (or he) achieves a synthesis of maternal intuition and paternal reason in herself (or himself).

Seen in these ways, the Queen of the Night is not a personification of evil. She is a personification of the dark unconscious, where intuition reigns and reason is unknown; of nature, which nurtures and also destroys; of the closed family or tribal circle, which guards its own traditions in the face of change; of motherhood, which wants to but cannot (however much the child might wish it) be indulgent forever. The ambivalent Queen is served by three ambivalent ladies who bestow magical, intuitive gifts. Together they represent a never-never land which children are delighted and contented with, but must outgrow.

On the other hand, Sarastro is not a personification of good. He is that bright consciousness which is the beginning of reason, which builds cities and civilizations and is associated archetypally with the father. He too is ambivalent, abducting those he would purify, subjecting them to cruel ordeals, yet behind the frightening exterior benevolent and ultimately just. He is served by a villain who, like those shadow-figures Caliban in *The Tempest* and Mephistopheles in *Faust*, is not so much evil as the unwitting instrument of good. And he preserves in his new world the best of the Queen's old world: flute and bells, three boys, beautiful princess—that is to say, intuition, incipient wisdom, natural beauty.

We now know, two centuries later, that what the Queen represents was in fact not destroyed, that the irrational reemerged, after the eighteenth century's attempt to suppress it, in nineteenth-century romanticism. Goethe wanted to show this in his sequel to *The Magic Flute*: the Queen reappears to claim Pamina's infant son—the new century—and Sarastro leaves his masonry to journey across the earth, a nameless wanderer. Goethe was anticipating the great musical myth of the new age, Wagner's *Ring*, and the eventual triumph there of the intuitive, the irrational, and the feminine *over* father Wotan, his city-building schemes, and his misguided hopes for world power. In the nineteenth-century *Ring*, everything we see in the eighteenth-century *Flute* comes full circle: the father's masonry falls, the mother returns to her eternal dreams, the hero and heroine die, the three maidens regain their intuitive heritage. The Enlightenment is over. Only nature and the feminine unconscious are left to guide the world.

Is Mozart's opera then incomplete, lacking in vision, naive in its optimism? No, for the movement toward reason, civilization, and father-archetype will always begin again. Creation balances destruction, classic answers romantic. Perhaps that is why opera lovers like to hear a little Mozart between their long sessions with Wagner. The balance is important. With Wagner we are plunged into a subconscious world that affirms the reality and exalts the power of unreason. With Mozart we regard the progress toward reason and order with an emotion that is conscious and clearly objectified, and we do not miss the thunder of Wagner.

Those who love *The Magic Flute*—and their number grows yearly—see it as supremely civilized music, blending as it does classicism and romanticism, reason and unreason, culture and nature, masculine and feminine, Osiris and Isis, Apollo and Dionysus, the sophisticated and the unsophisticated, as no other music does. There is a wonderful completeness about it, and a marvelous lightness. Almost any other composer, confronted with the issues in this opera, would have weighted it with Significant Music. With Mozart, even the most sublime moments are luminous and light.

Recording
Klemperer / Janowitz, Popp, Gedda, Berry, Frick
(EMI/Angel 1963)

A SHORT GLOSSARY OF TERMS

bel canto
(It.). Literally, "beautiful song." Specifically, the art of florid singing developed in Italy in the late eighteenth and early nineteenth centuries, especially in the operas of Rossini, Bellini, and Donizetti.

cabaletta
(It., possibly derived from *cavallo*, "horse"). The excited homestretch of an extended aria or duet. A famous example is "Sempre libera" from Verdi's *La Traviata*. See **cavatina**.

castrati
(It., pl.; sing. **castrato**). Adult male sopranos and altos whose trumpetlike voices were the result of their having been castrated before puberty. Many became the superstar singers of the seventeenth and early eighteenth centuries, in operas by Monteverdi, Handel, Gluck, and even Mozart—by whose time the vile practice of castration for commercial gain, always illegal but long tolerated, was fast becoming obsolete.

cavatina
(It.). A short song, usually in a slow tempo. In bel canto operas and in early- and middle-period Verdi, a cavatina may be followed, after a quick plot development, by a rapid **cabaletta** (see the entry above); in *La Traviata*, the cavatina "Ah fors' è lui" is followed by "Sempre libera."

da capo
(It.). Literally, "from the beginning." A direction at the end of an aria that the singer is to go back to the beginning and repeat the music as far as the designation *fine*. The singer was, however, expected to ornament the repeated section freely. Long *da capo* arias were the rule with Handel and other baroque composers. Gluck's reforming *Orfeo ed Euridice* was probably the first opera to dispense with them, and by Mozart's time their days were numbered.

A Short Glossary of Terms

grand opera
Once in common use as a generic term to refer to opera as opposed to operetta, "grand opera" now designates almost exclusively the elaborately produced five-act opera on historical subjects favored in the nineteenth century at the Paris Opéra. See the entry on Meyerbeer's *Les Huguenots*.

leitmotif
(Ger.). Literally, "leading theme." Specifically, a short, recurrent musical motif, usually associated with an operatic character. Though recurrent phrases are used as a dramatic device by virtually every major opera composer, the term leitmotif is most properly applied to Wagner's work, where scores of such phrases may recur hundreds of times, gathering additional meanings and resonances as they group together in different combinations.

morbidezza
(It.). Literally, "softness." Specifically, the languid melodic style characteristic of Puccini, and the school of singing developed for its purposes.

opera buffa
(It.). Literally, "comic opera." Specifically, the style developed in eighteenth-century Italy in opposition to *opera seria* (see the entry below). Mozart fused the two genres in *Le Nozze di Figaro*, *Don Giovanni*, and *Così Fan Tutte*. Rossini and Donizetti continued to write their comic operas in unmixed *buffa* style.

opéra comique
(Fr.). Not "comic opera," but small-scaled French opera with spoken dialogue, especially as written for the Opéra-Comique in Paris. Opposed to grand opera as performed at the larger Paris Opéra. Examples are *La Fille du Régiment* and the original version of *Carmen*.

opera seria
(It.). Literally, "serious opera." Specifically, the long, elaborate, courtly operas on the myths and history of classical Greece and Rome that flourished in Handel's lifetime. Mozart wrote the last two *opere serie* to hold the stage, *Idomeneo* and *La Clemenza di Tito*. In his greatest operas he fused elements of *opera seria* with **_opera buffa_** (see the entry above).

recitative
The rapidly sung dialogue that, in some operas, continues the action between

arias and ensemble pieces. Closer to speech than to song, it is often accompanied by a single keyboard instrument.

Singspiel
(Ger.). Literally, "song-play." Specifically, the light opera with spoken dialogue that flourished in German-speaking lands in the eighteenth and early nineteenth centuries. Mozart combined elements of *Singspiel* with *opera seria* in *The Magic Flute*.

twelve-tone
The twentieth-century system of musical composition (also known as serialism) in which all twelve tones of the scale are treated as of equal importance and used in a predetermined sequence. Arnold Schoenberg and his disciples hoped thereby to develop a new music free of tonality. Critics were more impressed than the public, however, and after more than a half-century of tonal experimentation the system has largely gone out of favor.

verismo
(It.). Literally, "realism." The violently naturalistic style of late-nineteenth-century Italian opera (exemplified in *Cavalleria Rusticana* and *Pagliacci*) that was taken up by composers of other countries during the first decades of the twentieth century.

A LIST OF TITLES IN ENGLISH

The Abduction from the Seraglio. See *Die Entführung aus dem Serail*
The Barber of Seville. See *Il Barbiere di Siviglia*
Cinderella. See *La Cenerentola*
The Coronation of Poppea. See *L'Incoronazione di Poppea*
The Daughter of the Regiment. See *La Fille du Régiment*
The Elixir of Love. See *L'Elisir d'Amore*
The Flying Dutchman. See *Der Fliegende Holländer*
The Girl of the Golden West. See *La Fanciulla del West*
The Golden Cockerel. See *Le Coq d'Or*
The Italian Girl in Algiers. See *L'Italiana in Algeri*
Julius Caesar. See *Giulio Cesare*
The Magic Flute. See *Die Zauberflöte*
The Marriage of Figaro. See *Le Nozze di Figaro*
A Masked Ball. See *Un Ballo in Maschera*
The Tales of Hoffmann. See *Les Contes d'Hoffmann*
The Trojans. See *Les Troyens*
The Woman Without a Shadow. See *Die Frau ohne Schatten*
Women Are Like That. See *Così Fan Tutte*

A LIST OF COMPOSERS
WITH THEIR OPERAS

Bartók, Béla (1881–1945)
  Bluebeard's Castle (1918)

Beethoven, Ludwig van
  (1770–1827)
  Fidelio (1805)

Bellini, Vincenzo (1801–1835)
  Norma (1831)
  I Puritani (1835)

Berg, Alban (1885–1935)
  Wozzeck (1925)
  Lulu (1937)

Berlioz, Hector (1803–1869)
  Les Troyens (1863)

Bizet, Georges (1838–1875)
  The Pearl Fishers (1863)
  Carmen (1875)

Boito, Arrigo (1842–1918)
  Mefistofele (1868)

Britten, Benjamin (1913–1976)
  Peter Grimes (1945)
  Billy Budd (1951)
  The Turn of the Screw (1954)

Debussy, Claude (1862–1918)
  Pelléas et Mélisande (1902)

Donizetti, Gaetano (1797–1848)
  L'Elisir d'Amore (1832)
  Lucia di Lammermoor (1835)
  La Fille du Régiment (1840)
  Don Pasquale (1843)

Floyd, Carlisle (b. 1926)
  Susannah (1955)

Gershwin, George (1898–1937)
  Porgy and Bess (1935)

Giordano, Umberto (1867–1948)
  Andrea Chénier (1896)

Gluck, Christoph Willibald von
  (1714–1787)
  Orfeo ed Euridice (1762)
  Alceste (1767)

Gounod, Charles (1818–1893)
  Faust (1859)
  Roméo et Juliette (1867)

Handel, George Frideric
  (1685–1759)
  Giulio Cesare (1724)

A List of Composers With Their Operas

[Handel, George Frideric]
Semele (1744)

Humperdinck, Engelbert
(1854–1921)
Hansel and Gretel (1893)

Janáček, Leoš (1845–1928)
Jenůfa (1904)
The Cunning Little Vixen
(1924)

Leoncavallo, Ruggero
(1858–1919)
Pagliacci (1892)

Mascagni, Pietro (1863–1945)
Cavalleria Rusticana (1890)

Massenet, Jules (1842–1912)
Manon (1884)
Werther (1894)

Meyerbeer, Giacomo (1791–1864)
Les Huguenots (1836)

Monteverdi, Claudio (1567–1643)
Orfeo (1607)
L'Incoronazione di Poppea
(1642)

Mozart, Wolfgang Amadeus
(1756–1791)
Idomeneo (1781)
Die Entführung aus dem Serail
(1782)
Le Nozze di Figaro (1786)
Don Giovanni (1787)
Così Fan Tutte (1790)

La Clemenza di Tito (1791)
Die Zauberflöte (1791)

Mussorgsky, Modest (1835–1881)
Boris Godunov (1874)

Offenbach, Jacques (1819–1880)
Les Contes d'Hoffmann (1881)

Ponchielli, Amilcare (1834–1886)
La Gioconda (1876)

Poulenc, Francis (1899–1963)
Dialogues of the Carmelites
(1957)

Puccini, Giacomo (1858–1924)
Manon Lescaut (1893)
La Bohème (1896)
Tosca (1900)
Madama Butterfly (1904)
La Fanciulla del West (1910)
Il Trittico (1918)
Il Tabarro
Suor Angelica
Gianni Schicchi
Turandot (1926)

Purcell, Henry (1659–1695)
Dido and Aeneas (1689)

Rimsky-Korsakov, Nikolai
(1844–1908)
Le Coq d'Or (1909)

Rossini, Gioachino (1792–1868)
L'Italiana in Algeri (1813)
Il Barbiere di Siviglia (1816)
La Cenerentola (1817)

A List of Composers With Their Operas

Saint-Saëns, Camille (1835–1921)
Samson et Dalila (1877)

Schoenberg, Arnold (1874–1951)
Moses und Aron (1957)

Smetana, Bedřich (1824–1884)
The Bartered Bride (1866)

Strauss, Johann (1825–1899)
Die Fledermaus (1874)

Strauss, Richard (1864–1949)
Salome (1905)
Elektra (1909)
Der Rosenkavalier (1911)
Ariadne auf Naxos (1912)
Die Frau ohne Schatten (1919)
Arabella (1933)
Capriccio (1942)

Stravinsky, Igor (1882–1971)
The Rake's Progress (1951)

Tchaikovsky, Peter Ilyich
(1840–1893)
Eugene Onegin (1879)
The Queen of Spades (1890)

Thomson, Virgil (1896–1989)
Four Saints in Three Acts (1934)

Verdi, Giuseppe (1813–1901)
Nabucco (1842)
Macbeth (1847)
Rigoletto (1851)
Il Trovatore (1853)
La Traviata (1853)
Simon Boccanegra (1857)
Un Ballo in Maschera (1859)
La Forza del Destino (1862)
Don Carlo (1867)
Aida (1871)
Otello (1887)
Falstaff (1893)

Wagner, Richard (1813–1883)
Der Fliegende Holländer (1843)
Tannhäuser (1845)
Lohengrin (1850)
Tristan und Isolde (1865)
Die Meistersinger (1868)
Der Ring des Nibelungen (1876)
Das Rheingold (1869)
Die Walküre (1870)
Siegfried (1876)
Götterdämmerung (1876)
Parsifal (1882)

Weber, Carl Maria von
(1786–1826)
Der Freischütz (1821)